"Everyone wants to grow. The problem is we often get stuck because we don't know how. In *You Can Really Grow*, John Hindley shows us, by helping us look at the obvious in refreshing new ways. John doesn't offer us a quick fix—he points us to real, lasting, exciting growth."

TIM LANE, author of *How People Change*; President of the Institute for Pastoral Care

"This is a gem of a book—wonderfully readable, deeply heart-warming, and beautifully Jesus-centred. Growing as a Christian is no longer a burden, but a joy. You won't find techniques and strategies here, but a thrilling and inspiring picture of what it is to live as a child of a loving heavenly Father. Grounded in the reality of everyday life, this book will help you love Jesus more and delight in becoming more like him."

ANNABELLE COOMBS, St Paul's, Banbury, Oxfordshire

"Honest and oh-so-encouraging, this book is pure fertiliser for every Christian to grow. It should be on every church bookstall and in every Christian's hands."

MIKE REEVES, Director of Union; author of *Enjoy your Prayer Life*

"I loved this book. It's a really practical look at growing as a Christian—but it may surprise you. It's not a list of things to do, but an invitation to a relationship. I encourage you to read it. But even more, I encourage you to read it with someone else—for, as John Hindley reminds us, we grow together as a community."

TIM CHESTER, Director of the Porterbrook Seminary; author of *You Can Change*

"This is pure gold—few books have driven me back to the Bible and to the Jesus of the Bible more than this one. It humbles and exalts, and makes sense of th⸺ ⸺ ⸺ ⸺ the battles we face. It will help to take a shrir⸺ renewed desire for Jesus."

SIMON AUSTEN, Rector of St

"With biblical insight, honest self-appraisal and wise counsel that comes from years of faithfully following Jesus Christ, John Hindley helps us navigate the challenging and sometimes frustrating pursuit of spiritual growth. You Can Really Grow is packed with gospel-motivated, practical, real-life instruction that really will help you to grow."

JASON ROBERTS, Pastor of Crosscurrent Church, Virginia Beach, Virginia

"I couldn't put this book down. If you've ever been urged to grow as a Christian but haven't known how, or if you have a nagging feeling that your relationship with God has gone stale, then you are going to love this."

MARCUS HONEYSETT, Director of Living Leadership

JOHN HINDLEY
YOU CAN REALLY GROW

How to thrive in your
Christian life

To my three curly girls
and their amazing mother

You can really grow: *How to thrive in the Christian life*
© John Hindley/The Good Book Company, 2015.

Published by
The Good Book Company
Tel (UK): 0333 123 0880
International: +44 (0) 208 942 0880
Email: info@thegoodbook.co.uk

Websites:
UK: www.thegoodbook.co.uk
North America: www.thegoodbook.com
Australia: www.thegoodbook.com.au
New Zealand: www.thegoodbook.co.nz

ISBN: 9781910307373

Design by André Parker

Printed and bound by CPI Group (UK) Ltd, Croydon, CR0 4YY

Contents

1. I know I ought to grow...

I'm amazed they come each week.

Every Tuesday, the older boys from our church meet up with me to look at the Bible together. To be honest, meeting with me is not a huge draw. I am very uncool (so uncool I don't even know if "cool" is still used!); I know little about sports, and even less about music. My grasp on films is at primary-school level.

I am amazed they turn up week by week; and I am even more amazed that they want to get to grips with the Bible. They answer questions, not caring if they have got it right—they just want to learn. They feel awkward reading out loud, but they all volunteer. They feel awkward praying out loud, but they have a go at it. They speak honestly about their sins and struggles, and they smile when they talk about the ways they have shared Jesus with their friends.

I love "Boys Bible Study" (I haven't even managed to come up with a cool name for it). I love it because the boys show me what I want to be. They want to follow Jesus more closely. They are eager to share the gospel with their friends. They love to tease each other, but they also love to show patience, gentleness and love. They want to overcome their struggles in the Christian life. They are so keen to grow as Christians.

And I am not.

I am eager to get my work done well. I am eager to spend enough time (with enough emotional energy) with my girls. I am eager to keep space to have an evening or two with my wife. I am eager to go on holiday. I am hoping to just cope without going under.

I am not that eager to grow as a Christian.

What about you? If a friend asked you how you had grown as a Christian over the last year, what would you say? Would the answer come easily, or would you have to think up something to say that was just about honest enough not to be a lie and just about impressive enough not to be humiliating?

Ought to, used to, told to...

If you are a Christian, you will know deep down that you ought to be growing. Sometimes you get an unwelcome reminder of this. Maybe a sermon tweaks your conscience. Or you hear of a friend from youth group who has gone to be a missionary and you wonder why you are glad it is her who is going, not you. Perhaps you hear of another friend who was baptised with you who has fallen away, having stagnated in faith—and you wonder if you will be next.

You know you ought to be growing, and you know that you used to grow. For many of us, when we first started following Jesus, there were so many moments when we realised that life needed to be different, and changing things seemed so easy. Perhaps it wasn't even easy, it was actually effortless. Perhaps your family said they had noticed a change in you—you had become more generous, or more cheerful. They simply remarked on a positive change, and you took the opportunity to remind them that the change had come about since you started following Jesus. Maybe you even saw a relative begin to investigate the gospel seriously because of what they saw in your life.

That used to happen. But it's a long time since anyone in your family noticed any change in you at all.

I started following Jesus wholeheartedly at university, and I can remember growing as a Christian. I remember reading the Bible earnestly, praying for change, learning that Jesus had power to stop my habitual cursing and swearing. But that feels like a long time ago now.

We ought to grow. We used to grow. And we are told to grow. Peter was Jesus' closest friend and a leader of the church, and his parting command to the church in his final letter is:

> But grow in the grace and knowledge of our Lord and
> Saviour Jesus Christ. To him be glory both now and for
> ever! Amen. (2 Peter 3 v 18)

We are told to grow. We are commanded to grow in the grace and knowledge of Jesus—to grow in our trust of his love and our knowledge of him.

Maybe you are even someone who calls others to grow. Perhaps you teach a group in your church, a Sunday-school class, maybe even the whole church. Perhaps you have an uncomfortable nagging worry that you are calling others to grow in Christ when you're not really sure you know what you mean. If so, then you're not alone. The idea for this book came from me realising that I was calling the church I serve to grow, when I didn't really know what I meant for myself or them.

And that's a large part of the problem. Though we know we ought to grow, we don't know what we mean by "grow". When we think about it, it often seems like a list of do's, which we should do more, and don'ts, which we should do less. So growing as a Christian becomes a case of carrying out a to-do list. And most of us have enough to-do lists at work and home. We don't want another one, and so Christian growth isn't something that we really want to do. I ought to clear my bedroom cupboard out, but I never get round to it. I ought to read that report on my desk at work, but I never get round to it. And I ought to do something about growing as a Christian...

Why standing still is not standing still

The truth is that most of us are quite content with how things are. That God has saved us, that he loves us, and that he'll come back and live with us—and that's great. We're happy with that. That's enough for us. We're standing still, and that works for us.

But God wants more for us than this. He wants us not just to keep going, but to keep growing—not merely to survive as a Christian, but to thrive as a Christian. He wants more for us than we do!

And God warns us that, in fact, standing still is not an option. Peter's full conclusion to his letter reads like this:

> Therefore, dear friends, since you have been forewarned, be on your guard so that you may not be carried away by the error of the lawless and fall from your secure position. But grow in the grace and knowledge of our Lord and Saviour Jesus Christ. To him be glory both now and for ever! Amen. (2 Peter 3 v 17-18)

The alternative to growth is not simply staying at the same height—it is shrinking. Peter here says that you can "fall" or you can "grow". The options are falling or growing. A lack of growth in a Christian is serious. If a child fails to grow, their parents don't simply ignore it; they take their child to the doctor. It is a cause for concern and a spur to action.

You cannot stand still in the Christian life. The challenging truth is that if you are not growing, you are shrinking. So growth is not just something we ought to do and are told to do... it is something we need to do.

So how can we grow? How can we want to grow? How can we become more like the boys in my group on Tuesdays—and how can they make sure they're still like that in 2,000 Tuesdays' time?

The first step is to see what Christian growth actually is. And, as we do that, we'll begin to realise why Christian growth is wonderful.

2. I don't really want to grow...

Chances are that you're trying to grow at the moment in one way or another.

Maybe you're reading a book to help you be a better parent; maybe you've enrolled on a course at work to grow your knowledge and skills; perhaps you are going to classes to learn how to garden, or watching clips on the internet to pick up a new skill. Growing, realising our potential, developing. These are ideas we are familiar with.

Growing is part of life. But growing as a Christian isn't always part of this growth. It might be because you don't really know how to grow as a Christian (and we'll come to that); but for me, that isn't the biggest barrier to my Christian growth. My problem is very simple: often, I don't really want to grow as a Christian.

Most of the time, this doesn't bother me too much. Life is often really busy. I feel as if I am not spending enough time on my marriage or caring for my children. Work is busy and there is a lot I leave undone. I try to keep up with friends; I struggle to keep involved in the local community; I want to prioritise my church family more than I do. And it is ages since I rang my mum! You probably feel the same—that there is a lot going on in your life.

Life is busy, and I am trying to grow in lots of these areas. I am trying to learn what it means to be a good husband, father, church member, pastor, friend and neighbour. At the same time, I am trying to learn how to put up shelving straight. I read books, go to conferences and talk with people to get advice. Why? Because I want to get better, to develop, to grow.

I don't really have time for growing as a Christian as well. I guess I think about it sporadically, and try to do something about it even more sporadically. I think that's where a lot of us are: Christian growth is just one more thing to try to fit into a life that already feels a bit too full.

We won't grow unless we want to grow. And we will only want to grow if and as we begin to appreciate what Christian growth actually is. Then it will stop being a duty, and become something delightful; something we're desperate to do; something that comes naturally. It really will.

Growing up in the family

When we become followers of Jesus, we are given a whole new set of relationships. The most profound of these is the change in our relationship with God. Before Jesus rescued us, we were "alienated from God" (Colossians 1 v 21). We had spurned God's love, refused to trust his kindness, broken his rules and rejected his authority.

And then we discovered the glorious truth that the King of the universe was offering to forgive us. We grasped the wonderful truth that we could be counted as his friends, that we could be reconciled (v 22).

That is awesome. But the truth gets far more awesome than that:

> ... those who are led by the Spirit of God are the children
> of God. The Spirit you received does not make you
> slaves, so that you live in fear again; rather, the Spirit you

received brought about your adoption to sonship. And by him we cry, "*Abba*, Father." The Spirit himself testifies with our spirit that we are God's children. Now if we are children, then we are heirs—heirs of God and co-heirs with Christ, if indeed we share in his sufferings in order that we may also share in his glory.   (Romans 8 v 14-17)

We are children of God. When we call our God "Father", we are not simply using a nice form of speech. God has adopted us as his actual children.

And God is a perfect Father. If the man you call, or called, "dad" here on earth was great, then every good aspect of that relationship is a glimpse of the kind of perfect Father the Creator is. He is the perfect Father you were being pointed to. And if the man you know as "dad" was flawed or worse in his dealings with you, then you need to know that all that is bad is totally absent from God's fatherhood. He is the perfect Father you need.

And that means that when we are called "heirs of God and co-heirs with Christ" (v 17), Paul means children equal with Jesus. The astonishing reality is that there is no difference between how God treats his eternal Son and how he treats his adoptive sons and daughters. We inherit from God in the same way Jesus does. On Christ's return or your death, you will enjoy the same closeness of love with the Father that Jesus has. Every day until then and beyond then, you will be treated by God as Jesus deserves. Right now you have that relationship, just not the physical closeness. You have the Father's love; you just don't see his smile yet.

We are children of God. And children grow. So the first thing you need to understand about Christian growth is that it is the growth of a child in a family. God is not your Boss, asking you to grow in your professional abilities so that you are of more use to him. He is your Father, enabling you to grow up in his family as he delights in you, so that you and he will grow even closer.

We will grow up as children of God, just as children in a natural family grow up. This is Christian growth. It is not about knowing your Bible better, taking on some new ministry in church, getting better at sharing the gospel or spending more time praying. It may involve those things, but that is not what it is.

To grow up means that we will grow closer to Jesus. We are growing up as his brothers and sisters. We are called to share in his sufferings, to stand with him in a world that hates him. This has profound challenges, but also a deep promise. We get to be with Jesus. To grow as a brother or sister of Christ is to grow in our love and knowledge of him and it is to grow in our closeness to him.

And that is good. Jesus is a Friend who gave his life for his friends; he is a Husband who did not abandon his bride (us, the church) when we abandoned him. He is faithful, generous, good and kind. Whether you are clutching a rifle on the way to battle, a tool-bag on the way to work, or a cake on the way to a party, Jesus is the Brother you want with you. As Hebrews 2 v 11 says: "Both the one who makes people holy and those who are made holy are of the same family. So Jesus is not ashamed to call them brothers and sisters".

Christian growth is growing up in the family of God. It is growing closer to Jesus. And the way this works is that we grow up into the likeness of Jesus.

Growing up to be like Jesus

When you become part of a family, you grow up to be like that family. You reflect the values and characteristics of that family, you grow to look and act as a Hindley, or a Smith, or a Sanchez, or whatever. I hope that when my daughters are at a friend's party or a playdate, they will show something of my values (though not my looks).

You are an adopted child, adopted into the royal family of the cosmos, the family of God. Your Father adopted you just as you are, simply because he loves you. But your Father does not want you to stay the same, and will not allow you to:

> And we know that in all things God works for the good of those who love him, who have been called according to his purpose. For those God foreknew he also predestined to be conformed to the image of his Son, that he might be the firstborn among many brothers and sisters. And those he predestined, he also called; those he called, he also justified; those he justified, he also glorified. (Romans 8 v 28-30)

God has predestined something for us. He has decided to do something in us. What is it? "To be conformed to the image of his Son." God has decided that you and I shall grow up to be like Jesus.

When I was young, I said that I wanted to be a fighter pilot. That wasn't true, but I didn't feel I could admit that the thing I really wanted to be when I grew up was a history teacher. I loved history, I had great teachers who made the subject come alive, and I wanted to do the same. Sad though this sounds, I wanted to be like the guy teaching at the front of the classroom.

But God's plan for me was more serious than teaching history and more exciting than breaking the sound barrier on the edge of space. He planned for me to be like his Son. And what God plans, he does. You and I have a big Brother, the perfect Son of God; and our growth means growing to be more and more like him.

I long more than anything to be more like Jesus, and so do you, even if you don't realise that or feel that. Let me show you. If you are anything like me, there is a tension in your life. There is the man or woman that you would like to be, that you imagine yourself to be, and that you like others to see. Then there is the real you. And the gap between the two is staggering. We are good at hiding it from ourselves, but there are times when it shows up painfully. In my mind I am winsome, erudite, witty and sharp. In reality, I am often none of those things. I remember not getting accepted by the university I had set my heart on, and suddenly realising I was neither as witty nor as sharp as I had thought. I like to think I have changed since then, but the disconnect is still there. I think of myself as a wise and considerate husband, so last week I was thrown into despondency realising how I was taking my wife for granted.

I long to be wise, gentle, courageous and full of integrity. Don't you?

And behind these longings lies one simple longing. We long to be like Jesus. We want to be like our big Brother— because that is what Jesus was and is like.

Wise

There were lots of people who wanted to discredit Jesus. They thought he was too good to be true. They were wrong. Here is one incident:

> [The Pharisees] sent their disciples to him along with the
> Herodians. "Teacher," they said, "we know that you are
> a man of integrity and that you teach the way of God in

accordance with the truth. You aren't swayed by others, because you pay no attention to who they are. Tell us then, what is your opinion? Is it right to pay the poll-tax to Caesar or not?"

But Jesus, knowing their evil intent, said, "You hypocrites, why are you trying to trap me? Show me the coin used for paying the tax." They brought him a denarius, and he asked them, "Whose image is this? And whose inscription?"

"Caesar's," they replied.

Then he said to them, "So give to Caesar what is Caesar's, and to God what is God's." When they heard this, they were amazed. So they left him and went away.

(Matthew 22 v 16-18)

Jesus' answer is so simple, and so wise. He doesn't answer the question he is asked, because he spots that the question is a trap and not asked sincerely, and also because he sees that it is a false distinction. His opponents are trying to set the authority of Caesar and God on a par and make Jesus choose. Jesus' answer is to show that the money is Caesar's, so of course he can demand it in tax. But don't let that fool you into thinking that you owe nothing to God. You owe him far more than tax. You owe him your heart, life and soul.

To the money-loving Pharisees, this is a foundation-shifting answer. Jesus isn't being clever for the sake of it; he is being wise. He is making others think. He is helping others see. I would have wanted to show off my cleverness, to jump in with both feet, to impress the listeners. Jesus' wisdom is so simple, straight and sharp. I'd love to be wise like that.

Gentle

What makes Jesus' wisdom so attractive, though, is the gentle kindness that marks how he uses it. In Luke 7, we read about a woman who comes to Jesus when he has been invited to a posh dinner in a religious leader's house. This woman is a sinner, and is known for it. Her approach to Jesus is extremely humble—she kneels at his feet and washes them with her tears before pouring her perfume on them.

The response of the religious leaders is sour, proud disapproval. They conclude that Jesus cannot really be a prophet, or he would not allow such a sinner to touch him. Jesus' response is again wise, but also gentle:

> Jesus answered him, "Simon, I have something to tell you."
>
> "Tell me, teacher," he said.
>
> "Two people owed money to a certain money-lender. One owed him five hundred denarii, and the other fifty. Neither of them had the money to pay him back, so he forgave the debts of both. Now which of them will love him more?"
>
> Simon replied, "I suppose the one who had the bigger debt forgiven."
>
> "You have judged correctly," Jesus said. Then he turned towards the woman and said to Simon, "Do you see this woman? I came into your house. You did not give me any water for my feet, but she wet my feet with her tears and wiped them with her hair. You did not give me a kiss, but this woman, from the time I entered, has not stopped kissing my feet. You did not put oil on my head, but she has poured perfume on my feet. Therefore, I tell

you, her many sins have been forgiven—as her great love has shown. But whoever has been forgiven little loves little." Then Jesus said to her, "Your sins are forgiven."

The other guests began to say among themselves, "Who is this who even forgives sins?"

Jesus said to the woman, "Your faith has saved you; go in peace." (Luke 7 v 40-50)

Jesus is gentle to Simon. He could simply rebuke his lack of love, or expose some secret sin of his and declare him a hypocrite. But Jesus leads Simon towards God's love with a simple question about debt.

It is Jesus' gentleness towards this sinful woman that is more gripping, though. In a room of men who disapprove of her, reject her and condemn her, Jesus praises her love for him. He not only doesn't shun her, he holds her up as an example of faith and love towards him. He praises her when everyone else there would insult her. His gentleness is public, affirming someone used to rejection.

It is also personal. Once he has honoured her, he turns to her. This woman is not a teaching aid to Jesus; she is not an example to use to make points about what God wants, what real love is or how empty religious goodness can be. No, she is a woman created and loved by him. Jesus declares her sins forgiven, and then turns to her to say that her sins are forgiven. Jesus wants to talk with her, not just about her. He will publicly defend her and personally affirm her hopes. Her love shows that she is his, and so he tells her that she is forgiven.

At this, there is a stir. The well-taught Pharisees at the table know that only God can forgive sins. But by this point, Jesus is not talking to them. He doesn't want their clever ideas to sow doubt in this woman's heart. So he gently reassures her of the reality of her faith, and says that she can go in peace. Jesus affirms that this least likely of people has love and faith and so there is peace between them, a relationship of wholeness and goodness.

I want to be gentle like that. To be unconcerned for my reputation. To not feel crippled with embarrassment and be unsure what to say because I care more about myself than the person I am speaking with. I want to be gentle like Jesus.

Courageous

When I am gentle, I am usually weak with it. I so fear what people think of me. But in Jesus, we see a gentleness that never lacks courage. In Luke 22 we get a glimpse into the most courageous moment in history:

> Jesus went out as usual to the Mount of Olives, and his disciples followed him. On reaching the place, he said to them, "Pray that you will not fall into temptation." He withdrew about a stone's throw beyond them, knelt down and prayed, "Father, if you are willing, take this cup from me; yet not my will, but yours be done." An angel from heaven appeared to him and strengthened him. And being in anguish, he prayed more earnestly, and his sweat was like drops of blood falling to the ground.
>
> When he rose from prayer and went back to the disciples, he found them asleep, exhausted from sorrow. "Why are you sleeping?" he asked them. "Get up and pray so that you will not fall into temptation."
>
> While he was still speaking a crowd came up, and the man who was called Judas, one of the Twelve, was leading them.   (Luke 22 v 39-47)

Jesus is facing the cup of God's wrath. He knows that he is about to be betrayed by a friend, arrested, tried by a corrupt court, declared guilty despite his complete innocence and righteousness, whipped, nailed to a cross, abandoned by his friends, scorned by his people and killed by his enemies. And he knows that as he hangs and dies, God his Father will turn his back to him as he dies the death of a sinner so that he can offer his life to sinners.

The prospect of this horrendous judgment is so awful that Jesus sweats great drops like blood and prays for the Father to spare him from this terrible fate. He is in "anguish". Imagine that—the one who should be ruling in glory on his heavenly throne, crying out in anguish on his knees. The perfect one is beginning to feel the full force of his Father's anger at human sin. And yet he does not flee it. He does not return to heaven; he walks forward to his death. He prays that he might do his Father's will.

I have never shown courage like this. I would love to be able to display just a tiny sliver of this kind of courage and selflessness for those I love.

I would love to be like Jesus.

Integrity

I lie quite often, almost without noticing. Little lies, face-saving half-truths, reputation-burnishing exaggerations. It happens like this: it is Friday night and Flick and the girls are away. A friend from church rings to ask me over for dinner. I've planned a pizza and a movie, but I don't want to sound ungrateful. It is so much easier to say: "Oh, thanks so much. But I need to work a little more. The passage I'm preaching on this Sunday is a tricky one. I'll have to pass on the dinner invitation."

One much missed but remarkable aspect of Jesus' life is that he always spoke the truth, and he lived by what he said. He was a man of complete integrity.

We see amazing examples of this throughout Jesus' life. He is the one who commanded others to: "Love your enemies and pray for those who persecute you" (Matthew 5 v 44), and then did exactly that, praying for forgiveness for the soldiers who killed him (Luke 23 v 34). He practised what he preached, and he proclaimed what was true, even when that cost him his life:

> They took Jesus to the high priest, and all the chief priests, the elders and the teachers of the law came together. Peter followed him at a distance, right into the courtyard of the high priest. There he sat with the guards and warmed himself at the fire. The chief priests and the whole Sanhedrin were looking for evidence against Jesus so that they could put him to death, but they did not find any. Many testified falsely against him, but their statements did not agree. Then some stood up and gave this false testimony against him: "We heard him say, 'I will destroy this temple made with human hands and in three days will build another, not made with hands.'" Yet even then their testimony did not agree. Then the high priest stood up before them and asked Jesus, "Are you not going to answer? What is this testimony that these men are bringing against you?" But Jesus remained silent and gave no answer. Again the high priest asked him, "Are you the Messiah, the Son of the Blessed One?"
>
> "I am," said Jesus. "And you will see the Son of Man sitting at the right hand of the Mighty One and coming on the clouds of heaven."

The high priest tore his clothes. "Why do we need any more witnesses?" he asked. "You have heard the blasphemy. What do you think?" They all condemned him as worthy of death. (Mark 14 v 53-64)

Jesus was silent as they accused him. A simple half-truth would have done, just explaining that he was a simple preacher who maybe overstated some things. The leaders wanted the problem to go away, and Jesus could have helped that to happen in a way that preserved his life, but not his integrity. So he told the truth when it was guaranteed to get him killed. He had prayed for his Father to spare him this death, but he would not bend truth to escape it. He would carry out the will of his Father with complete integrity.

Growing up as you were designed to

When I read through a Gospel, I am confronted with a man who seems so strange, alien and different. It is not that he is other-worldly or unreal. It is rather that he is more real, and truly human. He shows more wisdom, gentleness, courage, integrity, compassion, forgiveness, patience, purpose, understanding and love than anyone else I have ever met. Jesus did not float through life in this world on a cloud. He lived like us, with all the disappointments and difficulties, all the twists and turns, of life. And yet he lived so unlike us—so wonderfully well.

As we read about Jesus, we see what we all, deep down, long to be. And we see what we are growing to be.

The promise of Christian growth is that this is what you will be and what you can be. You have been adopted into the Father's family, and you will grow to be just like your big Brother. "In all things God works for the good of those who love him"

(Romans 8 v 28). In every moment, and in every circumstance, God is working for your good—and your greatest good is to "be conformed to the image of his Son" (v 29).

We will grow in God's family until we are just like Jesus, our Brother. Our Father will do this, he will do it consistently and constantly, and we will share in the glory of Jesus Christ. Growing as a Christian means something very simple. It means growing into the person you want to be. It means growing into the person you were created to be. It means growing into a person who is just like Jesus. Read a Gospel, see the wondrous man you meet there, and keep thinking: *That is who I am growing to be like.*

Now you want to grow.

3. I don't really know how to grow...

We need to grow. We want to grow. (I hope that is the case after the last chapter—but if that's the part you're stuck on, in all seriousness, I'd love you to put this book down and read one of the Gospels, looking hard at the Person God wants you to grow to be like.)

Now, how do we grow? What does it means to grow up as part of God's family, into the image of his Son and our Brother?

In one sense, it is very simple. We grow to be like Jesus as we see Jesus. So God's Spirit works to show us God's Son, so that we grow as part of the Father's family:

> ... where the Spirit of the Lord is, there is freedom. And we all, who with unveiled faces contemplate the Lord's glory, are being transformed into his image with ever-increasing glory, which comes from the Lord, who is the Spirit.   (2 Corinthians 3 v 17-18)

We had a new boiler put in a few years ago. The plumber had an apprentice who spent a lot of time getting things from the van! But when he wasn't fetching tools, he was learning. Sometimes I heard the plumber explaining what he was doing, but most of the time the apprentice simply watched his boss and learned from seeing what he did. As he watched, he learned how he himself could be a plumber.

I had a similar experience when I worked as a ministry trainee in a church, and here the analogy runs deeper than simply being about picking up skills—because I wanted to be like Simon, Roger and Will not only in what they did, but who they were. They were men of God, and I wanted to grow like them in character. As I watched, I both wanted more and more to be like them, and I saw more and more how to be like them.

This is why the Spirit shows us Jesus. He shows us the Person we want to grow to be like. And as he shows us Christ, he makes us like him. Jesus' gentleness makes us long to be like him, but as we see it, we experience it. Jesus is gentle to us, and being treated with such gentle love changes us. Seeing Jesus is how the Spirit both inspires us and changes us, growing us into the image of Jesus.

And we'll be seeing a great variety of ways in which he does this in the next set of chapters. But before we move on, there are three key truths about how we grow that we need to grasp. We must get these firmly in place before we consider the means God uses to grow us. If we don't, we'll move on to thinking about the Bible, prayer, church and so on, and turn them into a list of "things I have to do"—and that list will become a burden, which will break our growth.

Here are the three keys. I have found all of them surprising, and exciting.

We grow as love grows

Growth is rooted in love. It flows from love, and it is growth in love. Without growing in love, we will not truly grow at all.

Let me introduce you to an impressive church that has grown in all sorts of ways. At the start of Revelation, Jesus tells John in a vision to write to seven churches. First up is the church in Ephesus:

> To the angel of the church in Ephesus write: These are
> the words of him who holds the seven stars in his right
> hand and walks among the seven golden lampstands: I
> know your deeds, your hard work and your perseverance.
> I know that you cannot tolerate wicked men, that you
> have tested those who claim to be apostles but are not,
> and have found them false. You have persevered and
> have endured hardships for my name, and have not
> grown weary.   (Revelation 2 v 1-3, NIV84)

Look at everything the church family in Ephesus have in their favour—all the impressive growth. They work hard for Jesus. Their work is done in the midst of hardships. They are suffering, and yet they are persevering for Christ. They have not grown weary; they still have energy and purpose. When a new teacher comes, even one claiming to be an apostle—an inspired, chosen herald of Jesus—they test what this person teaches. This is a church which will not waver from the truth of Christ, whether tempted to by harsh suffering or sweet lies. They're working hard, they're very committed and their doctrine is straight down the line. Wouldn't you want this report card from Jesus for your church?

And all that makes what Jesus says so shocking:

> Yet I hold this against you: You have forsaken your first
> love. Remember the height from which you have fallen!
> Repent and do the things you did at first. If you do not
> repent, I will come to you and remove your lampstand
> from its place.   (v 4-5)

They do not love Jesus as they did at first. This is a church that looks as if it is growing in everything, but it is not growing in the one thing that matters: in love for Jesus. This is serious; a church that does not love Jesus is a church that has left him, and is in danger of being no church at all.

We fall into this so easily. A church that begins with joy, hope, vision and a wonder at the love of Jesus can keep on doing the right things. It can have faithful preaching, good pastoral care, excellent evangelism and an involved membership. And while all this is going on, it can stop loving Jesus.

The same thing can happen to us as individual members of a church. We move from enjoying our salvation—revelling in the new friendship we have with Jesus—to a faith defined by responsibilities or activity, ideas or experiences, conferences or books. We move from loving Jesus himself to loving ministry, or doctrine, or evangelism, or friendships—all good things, but none of them our Lord and Saviour. Presumably the Ephesian church hadn't ever decided to stop loving Jesus—they'd not had a church meeting where the proposal from the elders had been: "Let's stop loving Jesus". They had just unconsciously, slowly descended into a distant, cold relationship with him.

Jesus is telling them that without love, the rest is meaningless. Without growing in love, there will be no growing at all. Without love, there is no church—that's why Jesus threatens to take away their lampstand, the image in Revelation of a group of people in whom and through whom Christ shines his light into the world.

Jesus wants our hearts. If we do not grow in love for him, then all other growth is meaningless, because it is not Christian growth. Growth in love will lead to growth in obedience, service, evangelism, wisdom and more. But if you do not love Jesus, and out of that love others, it means nothing:

> If I speak in the tongues of men or of angels, but do not have love, I am only a resounding gong or a clanging cymbal. If I have the gift of prophecy and can fathom all mysteries and all knowledge, and if I have a faith that can move mountains, but do not have love, I am nothing. If I give all I possess to the poor and give over my body to hardship that I may boast, but do not have love, I gain nothing. (1 Corinthians 13 v 1-3)

God is a Father who wants to grow us as his children. He wants us to grow because of his love for us. And he wants us to grow into deeper love for him.

It's not just business

Imagine a family business. Let's say they instal kitchens. Jim founded the company; he does the measuring and fits the kitchens. Clare, his wife, runs the showroom and prepares the quotes. Simon and Toby, their sons, are both learning to be carpenters and work with their dad. The youngest, Lucy, is doing a plumbing course.

Over the years, the business goes from strength to strength. They work hard, build a strong reputation and enjoy a full order-book for months ahead. They all do well out of the business, and enjoy working together. They win awards for "Best Family-Owned Business". Others look on them with a mixture of awe and envy.

But... they stop hanging out together. Family meals are rare, as someone always has work to do. When they do get together, conversation invariably turns to the accounts, the new ranges, or changes in the regulations. The business is going really well; but the family has ceased to work, ceased to exist, ceased to love. It looks great, successful, wealthy, established. But it is empty. It is like the church in Ephesus.

God is our Father. We are in his family business, but we must never make the mistake of putting the business ahead of the family. We do not work for a Boss: we love a Father and a Brother.

So what about you? Is your faith a loving relationship, or has it become a business deal? If you seek to grow closer to God by performing a series of tasks (I must read my Bible more... I must pray properly... I need to do a new ministry at church...), then it has become business.

So it might be that you need to stop thinking so much about growing as a Christian and rather, start thinking about growing in love for Christ. How do you do that?

> This is love: not that we loved God, but that he loved us
> and sent his Son as an atoning sacrifice for our sins ...
> We love because he first loved us.　　(1 John 4 v 10, 19)

We will never love God, or anyone else, properly until we understand that he loves us. We never begin to grasp that love for us until we understand that his love was most clearly and wonderfully shown us at the cross.

Jesus gave his life, nailed to die on a Roman cross outside Jerusalem, to make you at one with God again. As he died, Jesus took our sin, guilt and shame into himself. He was the "atoning sacrifice", giving himself up so that we could be at one with God, and know him as our loving Father rather than our terrifying Judge. The death he died was shameful: he was naked and exposed to scorn and ridicule. It was a sinner's death: he hung between earth and heaven, with the skies as dark as night as God judged him for the sins that we, his people, have committed. He carried our guilt, took our punishment and died our death.

This is the love of God for us. This is how Jesus loves you. You!

When we see who Jesus is, and his love displayed in the brutal sacrifice he made for us, our hearts are conquered. We don't try to screw our feelings up into a ball of love for him. We don't need to—we can't help but love him. To know how you are loved, and have your heart moved to love Christ, is what it means to become a Christian. To know how you are loved, and have your heart moved to love Christ, is also how you grow as a Christian.

We grow as God works

When Paul wrote to the Philippian church, he did so with great joy. He told them:

> I thank my God every time I remember you. In all my prayers for all of you, I always pray with joy because of your partnership in the gospel from the first day until now.   (Philippians 1 v 3-5)

Here was a church whose love for Christ and for Christ's people had not grown cold. But Paul was not confident about their faith and future because of what they were like, but because of what God is like:

> I always pray with joy ... being confident of this, that he who began a good work in you will carry it on to completion until the day of Christ Jesus.   (v 6)

God will finish what he started. When he begins "a good work" in someone by making them his child, he also commits to finishing that work. He will make sure his child gets home to heaven. He will make sure that they become like Christ. He will make sure they grow. It is his work in them.

God has given us a picture of spiritual growth in our natural growth. Children grow! It takes years. We can't see it happening, but it is happening. Visit a family with little children, and you see growth recorded in photos and marks on a wall chart.

God grows children slowly, naturally and without their conscious effort. We often want our spiritual growth to be instant, but children do not suddenly shoot up two feet in a day. There are growth spurts and times of slower growth for spiritual children, but all along our Father is growing us into Christ-likeness, carefully, slowly, imperceptibly and unstoppably. God our Father causes our Christian growth and gives us everything we need to grow. He gives us love, spiritual food (as well as physical) and so much more.

God finishes what he starts. He did not begin the work by saving me, and then hand me the responsibility of keeping going and keeping growing. It is all his work, and that is why Paul, and we, can be so confident that the work will continue until it is complete.

Your part in your growth

This all suggests, though, that we just "lie back and let God". He is active, and I am passive. If growth is his job, then I must just wait for him to accomplish it, right?

Well, not according to Paul! In the same letter to the same church, he writes:

> ... continue to work out your salvation with fear
> and trembling, for it is God who works in you to
> will and to act in order to fulfil his good purpose.
>
> (Philippians 2 v 12-13)

We have to put some work in! We are commanded to "work out our salvation", to increasingly apply our saved status as children of God to every area of our lives. And we are commanded to work as God works in us. It is his work; and it is our work.

This is quite confusing, and it causes quite a lot of misunderstandings and even disagreements. It's clear that salvation is all God's work, and none of ours. But when it comes to "sanctification" (our becoming more and more pure, more and more like Jesus), it is not so clear. What part does God play? What part do I play? Can I stop God growing me? Can I slow God growing me? Does God wait to see me working before helping me grow?

The challenge of Philippians 2 is to work hard at growth. But the assurance of Philippians 1 is that God will work that growth. We will grow up. Our work depends on his, but our work is not made irrelevant by his.

The key is to remember what Christian growth is. It is growing up within a relationship of love. It is all about a father-child relationship.

Sometimes Daisy, my daughter, asks me to help her get a toy from the top of her toy cupboard. So imagine it's the day after her birthday—and for her birthday, I gave her a new jigsaw puzzle. Now I ask her if she would like to do the puzzle with me, and receive a lovely: "Yes please!" in reply. So I pick Daisy up, and as I do so, she strains towards the top to reach the puzzle. She puts every effort her little body can manage into grabbing it because she really wants that puzzle. And she will reach that puzzle.

But she will reach it because I lift her.

I could have just got the puzzle down for her. I could have lifted her high enough so that she didn't need to lift her arms at all. I could have done all the work for her, but instead I involved her, and this increased her enjoyment. Did Daisy reach the puzzle? Yes. Did I reach the puzzle? Yes. I lifted; she reached. She needed me to lift her; I didn't need her to reach. But we did it together.

This is how God grows us. He works in our hearts to show us Christ, and excite us about being like Christ; and then he shows us an area of life where we can be more like him. And then he lifts us towards Christ-likeness, as we reach for it. We grab it, but only because he made us able to grab it. He involves us in our growth. Did we do the work? Yes. Did God do the reach? Yes. We needed him to be at work to enable us to grow; he didn't need us to work to achieve that growth. But he allowed us to do it together with him.

But what if Daisy hadn't reached for the puzzle? What if she had decided, halfway up, that she didn't want the puzzle enough to bother straining her little arms towards it?

We don't know. But we do know that it would have been up to me, not her. I could have chosen to lift her all the way, so she would still have the puzzle despite her lack of effort. I could have chosen to put her down, until she realised she did want the puzzle and did want to reach for it. I could have ensured she had the toy, or ensured she did not.

Let's say I realise that I am not patient. Not like Jesus is. And I'd love to be more patient, as he is (and I know my wife and friends would like that, too). I start to try to notice when I'm being impatient, to ask God to help me at those moments to make me more like Jesus, and to work at responding patiently in my head and my words.

But... it's so much hard work! And I begin to think it isn't really worth it. Jesus-like patience still seems a long way, and a lot of effort, away! I begin to work less hard. What happens now?

We don't know. But we do know that it's up to God. He could change me anyway, despite my pitiful lack of hard work. He could leave me in my impatience for a while, not changing me at all, so that I can see all the more clearly how much I need to grow more like Jesus, and come back to God and beg him to help me and give me more desire to change. One way or another, he will put those desires in me—it is part of who I now am, the new person he has made me to be.

I can change what I do, but I cannot thwart God's purposes for me. And that's wonderfully reassuring, because it means you and I cannot get in the way of our growth. And that's wonderfully motivating, because it means that you and I can be part of the way we grow. Just as Daisy, if and as she strains as I lift her, can then have the excitement of grasping the puzzle and the joy of playing with something she grabbed, so we can have the excitement and joy of being part of the way we grow. This is how our Father works—he wants us to love him as he loves us, and so he includes us in his work of growing us. We are always dependent on him, reaching as he enables us.

We grow as God grows us. This means we work harder at our growth. He lifts, and we reach.

We grow as the church grows

Maybe you have got to this point and are confused. You do love Jesus, and you are working to grow. You know you're not doing these things perfectly, but you are doing them. And yet, as you look at your own life, growth seems sluggish at best and elusive at worst. What went wrong?!

Well, don't look at yourself. Look at your church. How are they growing?

Let's return to that Ephesian church. They receive the letter from Jesus, and they gather to hear it read out. And one of the members sits there, thinking: "Jesus' threat doesn't actually apply to me. I am loving Jesus more, and I am working hard at growing to be more like him." He nods along as Jesus accuses the church of forsaking their first love. "Right on, Jesus! I'm glad you've noticed that a lot of the others in this church are loveless. You tell 'em, Lord!"

But then the letter finishes, and it dawns on him that there is no exception. Jesus is lumping him in with them. Jesus is saying the whole church is in trouble—and he is part of that church. And he realises, with sudden, disturbing clarity, that you cannot be growing if you are growing alone. He is part of a family, a body, and it either grows together, or not at all.

We live in a culture that thinks individualistically. When the government proposes a change to the benefits it provides, we instinctively think about how this will affect us. Our first, and often only, consideration is whether we will be better or worse off. This is no surprise: it was the lie that drew the first people away from God—this idea that the centre of the world is located wherever I am standing, and that I will need to look after my own interests because I can't trust God to do so. Our physical ancestors are our spiritual ancestors, too— individualism is inbuilt in us, and it is flourishing in the way western societies currently work.

This means that Christian growth is something we consider individualistically, too. At least, it has been that way for me.

One classic "Christian growth passage" is Galatians 5 v 22-23:

> The fruit of the Spirit is love, joy, peace, forbearance,
> kindness, goodness, faithfulness, gentleness and
> self-control.

A few years ago I realised that I was not growing as a Christian. We'd just had our first daughter, so I was becoming quite friendly with a lot of times of the night that I had previously been a stranger to. So I resolved that, whenever I was looking after her, I would pray that the Spirit would grow this fruit in me. I spent big chunks of the night praying for the Spirit to grow this nine-fold fruit in my life.

And I was wrong to do so.

I was not wrong in what I prayed, but in the greater prayer I never thought to pray. Galatians 5 v 16, at the start of the section that has those wonderful words about the fruit of the Spirit right at its heart, says:

> So I say, live by the Spirit, and you will not gratify the desires of the flesh.

It continues:

> If you are led by the Spirit, you are not under the law.
>
> (v 18)

And it finishes:

> Since we live by the Spirit, let us keep in step with the Spirit. Let us not become conceited, provoking and envying each other.
>
> (v 26)

What on earth does this have to do with anything?! Every "you" in those lines is plural. Paul uses "we" and "us", and he never uses "I" or "me".

This is a section about growth, but it is about church growth, not individual growth. I was wrong to pray this for myself without praying it for my church. When I prayed about my own growth to be more like Christ, I should have prayed for my church's growth, too.

When Jesus warned the church in Ephesus, he viewed the church collectively. When Paul writes to the Galatians, he is expecting this fruit to grow among them. He would not need to interview each member of the church to see if they were growing fruit. He would simply need to see how they interacted with each other. Were they conceited, self-focused, individualistic? Were they envying others, and provoking others? Our imaginary Ephesian friend loves Jesus, and wants to be like Christ, and is working at growing into Christ—but he is conceited.

Your Christian growth is not simply between you and God; it is between your church and God. God uses the others in your church to grow you, and he uses you to grow them. He does not have millions of one-child mini-family units. He has one family, spreading through the world and up to heaven. God does not play favourites with his children; he wants to see all of us grow as his children together.

The Bible tells us the church is a family, but it is also a body—the body of Christ. And "a body, though one, has many parts, but all its many parts form one body" (1 Corinthians 12 v 12). A body where only some parts grew would be very ill. A child whose legs were getting longer, but whose arms were not, would give doctors great concern. The body of Christ grows together, or it does not grow at all. We cannot grow in a meaningful sense by ourselves.

So maybe you need to stop thinking quite so much about your own Christian life and your own Christian growth. Perhaps it's time to work harder at helping others in your church to grow. As you do that, you will find yourself growing, too.

This is how we grow. We grow together, as God lifts us and we reach. And we grow as we grow in love, by focusing on God's love for us in Christ. The Spirit shows us Jesus, and so we love more, work more, and do it for our church—and our Father gives the growth.

And this growth can happen and will happen all the time. The Hindley family children grow all the time (as the clothes budget testifies). We haven't set a time aside each morning, or an afternoon each week, and called it "growing time". No, growing time is all the time. And so with the family of God— growth is not a "sometimes event", but an "always experience". And that is what we will think about next.

4. Audacious requests

I'm guessing you don't pray very much. Or read your Bible very much. Most Christians don't.

Most members of Bible-teaching, faithful, God-honouring, good churches seldom open their Bible or their mouth to pray. I remember, when I was part of a church in Manchester, meeting up with a group of men, about fifteen of us, on a summer's evening in a pub garden by the canal. One of them, honest and brave, admitted he hadn't read his Bible for a fortnight. He felt bad, guilty, and didn't know how to make himself get going with it again. His honesty encouraged all the others to admit that none of them had read their Bibles for at least as long. I don't have the evidence for our prayer lives, but I think it would be similar.

Since I became a Christian, I have been taught the central importance of praying and reading the Bible. They are central to growth, and yet most of us neglect them; and then, when a sermon or a random thought (or a book about growth) drives us to have another go with them, we find that it doesn't seem to make any difference anyway. Perhaps one of the reasons we avoid thinking about our growth is that we know it probably involves the Bible and prayer; and we already feel as if we will never make progress, never change.

I have been a Christian for 19 years now, and since I first began following Jesus, I have been taught the crucial importance of Bible reading and prayer. I have often felt that I do not measure up to those teaching it, who clearly have it all together, with 45-minute "quiet times" of prayer and Bible reading.

Then, more recently, as a pastor I myself have taught on these topics many times. And I have done so as a hypocrite— not because I have not believed what I was saying, but because I have given the impression that I have my act together. I am sure some of those who taught me were genuine, but I guess maybe others did the same as me—they implied that their prayer life was good, and that their Bible times were regular, because they were too ashamed to admit otherwise.

Others perhaps had huge self-discipline. They were extremely regular in their devotionals. But by itself this is no better. To read the Bible as an achievement, to pray as a to-do, ticked off the list early, is to skew devotional times into being about my ability or actions, rather than about my relationship with God.

We'll think more about Bible-reading in the next chapter. But first, we are going to consider the place of prayer, because part of the answer to the problems we have with reading the Bible is to address the problems we have with prayer.

Warning: Prayer can be bad for your health

Prayer might even be bad for you. Prayer can easily stunt your growth and displease your God. God once said through the prophet Isaiah:

> ... these people come near to me with their mouth and honour me with their lips, but their hearts are far from me. Their worship of me is based on merely human rules they have been taught. (Isaiah 29 v 13)

Prayer can look and sound good from the outside, but God can still be unimpressed because it only looks good from the outside. It is possible for prayer to be about going through the motions, doing what is expected, and have nothing to do with true worship. Like a rotten egg, it looks fine, but when you get inside it, it stinks.

I struggle not to be like this. I have never been a natural pray-er, or Bible-reader. But God is changing that, because he is changing me. And he is doing it by showing me Jesus, so that I will love him, want to become more like him, and know how to be more like him. This is not a chapter that will give you steps to a good prayer life, a new way of noting your prayers, or any tips on how to engage in prayer. It is about how to view prayer. It is about seeing simple things that all Christians agree with, but that in practice we do not really believe or live by.

Let me tell you the simple, obvious truths about prayer that I am starting to believe (sometimes). There are three:

1. God answers our prayers

Jesus was a man of extraordinary prayer. Before he appointed his twelve core disciples, he spent the entire night in prayer (Luke 6 v 12-13). This is what it looks like to be the Son of God—always depending on the Father; loving, trusting and needing the Father. We are growing up in God's family to be like Jesus. Prayer like his is our goal, and seeing him on our knees is how we grow towards that goal.

Just appreciate for a moment how wonderful it would be to have a prayer life like that of Jesus. He had responsibilities, challenges and sorrows that we will never fully comprehend. But he was never grumpy, short, distracted or distant from friends, strangers or enemies. Jesus' disciples made the link between his joy, peace and hope, and his prayer life. And so they opened themselves to grow up in God's family by asking Jesus to share with them his most precious knowledge. They asked: "Lord, teach us to pray" (Luke 11 v 1)—*Teach us to pray like you.*

Jesus answered them with teaching that is extremely famous, easy to underappreciate, and that changes everything:

> He said to them, "When you pray, say: 'Father, hallowed be your name, your kingdom come. Give us each day our daily bread. Forgive us our sins, for we also forgive everyone who sins against us. And lead us not into temptation."
>
> Then Jesus said to them, "Suppose you have a friend, and you go to him at midnight and say, 'Friend, lend me three loaves of bread; a friend of mine on a journey has come to me, and I have no food to offer him.'
>
> "And suppose the one inside answers, 'Don't bother me. The door is already locked, and my children and I are in bed. I can't get up and give you anything.'
>
> "I tell you, even though he will not get up and give you the bread because of friendship, yet because of your shameless audacity he will surely get up and give you as much as you need. So I say to you: ask and it will be given to you; seek and you will find; knock and the door will be opened to you. For everyone who asks receives; the one who seeks finds; and to the one who knocks, the door will be opened." (Luke 11 v 2-10)

The first part, where Jesus tells his friends what to pray, is exciting. Here is a sweeping vision of prayer, rooted in the coming kingdom of God and focused on his glory, yet able to take in our need for breakfast, forgiveness, help to forgive and strength when tempted.

But it is the next part which stopped me in my tracks—because I naturally think of prayer as a reverent, cautious approach to the holy, all-powerful King. With baited breath and trembling hope, we walk down the shining hall, past pillars of light and warriors of fire towards the awful and glorious throne. Yes, we can approach, but we approach the one who dwells in impenetrable light. We approach the great Emperor, mighty in power and glorious in majesty.

But it seems as though Jesus pictures it very differently. Rather than me tiptoeing through a splendid throne room, he imagines me ringing on a mate's door in the small hours because some old friends have stopped by and I don't even have any food to offer them. Jesus is saying that prayer is bothering God with unreasonable demands until he answers the door. Prayer is stretching friendship to its limits. Prayer is cheeky—it is "shameless audacity".

And this prayer is answered:

> So I say to you: ask and it will be given to you; seek
> and you will find; knock and the door will be opened
> to you. For everyone who asks receives; the one who
> seeks finds; and to the one who knocks, the door will be
> opened.

Don't you think Jesus is wrong? I must have read this quite a few times in my life, but a few years ago I read it again, and realised that I did not believe him.

Jesus is saying that if you ask God for something, you will receive it. Not could receive, or might receive. Will. If you bring your cheeky, middle-of-the-night prayers to God, then he will answer.

Jesus knows what he's talking about. There never was a man who prayed like him, and there never was a man who knew more about heaven and the Father than he does. He is not being irreverent. He is not wrong. And he is not lying. Prayer is about banging on the door and asking with audacity. And prayer is answered.

This changed my prayer life, because there is so much that I can't handle in my life, let alone in my church or the wider world. But the Creator and Sustainer of all things can handle it, and he has promised to answer my prayers.

The first prayer I prayed on reading this was that my Father would help me to believe it and to live as if it was true. I asked him to change me, to make me more prayerful, and more loving of the Bible. And he did. He has answered my prayer. I still struggle, but he is working, and I am keeping on praying. Have you ever prayed for help with prayer?

Believing God answers his children's prayers changes everything. I realised that I needed to pray for my children if I wanted them to grow up enjoying Jesus. I needed to pray with them when they were happy and sad; to pray that God would give them peace when they were angry, and to pray that he would give me peace when I was angry. He changes my heart and theirs in answer.

I have lost count now of the times I have realised that my wife and I are moving into a nasty, biting, grumpy argument, and I have had no idea how to stop being so mean or salvage the situation. Now I pray (most times) for the Lord to change both our hearts, and he does.

A year or so ago, a friend at church suggested a way of growing in size so that our little church plant could take advantage of the opportunities we had. He said he thought we should ask for five more people or families to join the church.

He thought we should ask for the Lord to do it in a year, even though we had had just a couple of people join in the previous three years. I did not believe it would happen, but I was too ashamed of my lack of belief to refuse, so we prayed.

I sat with the same friend in a pub near the end of the year, and we counted the five. The exact answer. He told me he had not believed it would happen, and I admitted the same.

Because prayer is answered, prayer is what people most need, and prayer is the best thing I can give. My brother is getting married soon. I've planned a stag party (or bachelor party, if you're American!) I think he will enjoy. I will work hard as his best man so the big day (the wedding day, not the stag party) will go well. But I must keep remembering that the best thing I can do is pray for him and his bride. After all, their joy on the wedding day and for the rest of their lives is in our Father's power, and not in mine.

God answers our prayers. Jesus says so. Do you believe him?

2. God answers our prayers because he's a Father

When you think about it, prayer is shamelessly audacious. It is wandering up to the all-powerful, all-perfect Creator as a flawed, sinful creature and saying: *Do this for me, would you? Can you help me with this thing? Use your sovereign power to sort this out, would you?*

What is surprising is not so much that God can answer (though often I suspect he can't). What is amazing is that God would choose to answer.

But of course he answers! As Jesus reminds us:

> Which of you fathers, if your son asks for a fish, will give
> him a snake instead? Or if he asks for an egg, will give

him a scorpion? If you then, though you are evil, know
how to give good gifts to your children, how much more
will your Father in heaven give the Holy Spirit to those
who ask him!   (Luke 11 v 11-13)

We are God's children. Even earthly fathers listen to their
children, and answer their questions and requests. The
relationship we have with God is the basis for our confidence
in prayer, and also for our wonder and joy.

We do not walk through that heavenly throne room of
light and glory, trembling as we approach the throne and its
awesome, forbidding Lord. No, we play with a slinky spring
on its steps—because we are not merely subjects; we are sons.

God answers our prayers because he is a Father, our Father.
So he will answer even the most cheeky, irreverent and
impossible prayers. Did you notice the strange end to Jesus'
words there? On another occasion, using this same picture,
Jesus ended the teaching as we would expect:

If you, then, though you are evil, know how to give good
gifts to your children, how much more will your Father
in heaven give good gifts to those who ask him!

                              (Matthew 7 v 11)

But in the instance Luke records, Jesus twists the ending: the
Father will "give the Holy Spirit to those who ask him!" We are
being told to ask for God himself. God's Spirit will work in us
and for us, and there is nothing better.

Do you want to know peace in the middle of panic, anxiety,
stress and disaster? Ask your Father for the Spirit of peace and
he will give you him. Would you like wisdom in the difficult
client meeting you have coming up? Ask your Father for the
Spirit of wisdom to fill you, and he will (you may as well ask
for favour from your clients and a good deal, too). Want to

pray more? Ask for the Spirit to move your heart to prayer. Struggling to understand your Bible? Well, it was the Spirit who wrote it, so his help is what you need.

This gift of God's Spirit to us is the greatest present we could receive. We need to be careful with the language that Jesus uses here. When he says that we must ask for the Spirit, he is not implying that sometimes the Spirit is with us, and sometimes not. To be a Christian is to have the Spirit (Romans 8 v 9).

So to ask for the Spirit is not to ask for someone we do not have, but to ask for a closer relationship with God, to ask for the Spirit to work in specific ways in our lives and in the particular circumstances we are in. It is a circle of dependent trust—of faith. So if you are struggling to pray, then pray! Ask for the Father to give you the Spirit to move your heart to pray. This prayer has been answered in my life, and I enjoy praying now in ways I never have before.

So I pray for the Spirit many times a day. And I am growing closer to God. I mess up so often. I sin so much—lust, pride, fear of men, greed—but the Father is changing me, and he answers my prayers.

The problem is not that we have a God who doesn't answer. It is that we don't pray.

3. God answers our prayers like a Father

What about a Porsche, then?!

If God is my Father, and he answers any and every shamelessly audacious prayer, then we've just realised how to get that new sports car, or bigger house.

Or, more urgently and importantly, what about your suffering, sick sister, for whom you've been praying for years, with no change and no answer? You may, as you have read this chapter, have felt increasingly hurt, confused and angry.

How do we grapple with this tension between what Jesus says so simply and what we experience so painfully?

My daughters like to play hiding games, where they hide under a blanket and I find them. They often ask me to play this game, and sometimes we do it for ages. This morning they asked to play it and I said "no". They wanted to go to toddler group; they love it and were looking forward to it. We were running late as usual. I told them we could not play or we'd be late, and they didn't get it, because they don't understand how time works yet. They were sad not to play the game (and they let me know it!) but I answered "no" for the sake of their joy.

It is a very good thing for children playing around the throne that the King loves them enough to answer prayers according to his wisdom, and not the wisdom of children. Our sight is so limited, we know so little, and we are so wracked by sin and wrong desires. I have a friend who says that if God had answered all his prayers, he'd have married over a dozen women! Our kind Father answers for our good, for our joy, for our blessing. Always.

I know that this is not easy. I have prayed for people I love who are ill. I have seen miraculous healing, I have seen good medical healing, and I have wept over the deaths of those I love. I see one friend healed of a chronic illness, and another being crushed by the endless pain of an untreatable condition. I know this is not easy.

More than that, Jesus knew how hard it was. He designed this world to know nothing of illness, death, abuse, bullying, greed, callousness or hurt; and then he became the "Man of Sorrows", who knew all those things. One day he and his Father will wipe away every tear. When he promised answers to prayer, he knew the prayers you would pray which feel unanswered.

What do we do with that? We pray. We admit that we are toddlers and that it is nearly impossible for us to see how "in all things God works for the good of those who love him" (Romans 8 v 28). And so we ask for the Spirit, we ask for understanding, but most of all we ask for faith. We remind ourselves that there was a day of complete evil, a day when the sun was extinguished and the most innocent of men suffered guilt and judgment, a day when God bled and died—and that that darkest day of history was also the most glorious day of all.

When God says "no" to us, he may well not explain himself, but he does assure us that he loves us. When we say "no" to our children, it is not necessarily because they have done anything wrong, or have not done enough right, not loved us properly, or not asked enough. So prayers that are not answered as we want, according to how we beg, are not because we don't have enough faith, didn't find the right words, or need to become better Christians before we get answered. That would make prayer dependent on me, not on God. It would turn prayer from dependent trust to clever manipulation. It would make our Father a distant God who demands our performance, or that we use the right formula, or that we impress him.

When we do not see the answers we want or expect to our prayers, we do not look to ourselves to fix the problem. We look to our Father. We trust that God knows what we do not. And we pray.

And as we do this, we grow. Every time we pray to our Father, we are living as dependent children. We are accepting our frailty and need. Every time we ask for the Spirit's help, we live a little more like Jesus. The more we pray, the more we pray—and the more we grow.

So pray. Not because you have to. Not because you need to. But because you want to—because Jesus did, and you can. Because his Father is yours and he wants you to walk boldly, audaciously, up to his heavenly throne and say:

"Hello, Father..."

5. Bible reading can damage your health

What changed last time you read your Bible?

For most of us, the answer is: *Nothing*.

And so, for many of us, Bible reading slides into short spurts punctuating longer gaps. Others are more disciplined and optimistic. So we continue reading our Bible each day, hoping that in tomorrow's reading, it'll "work", it will all click into place, and something will change. But we never reach tomorrow.

I have struggled for years to read the Bible. Even as a full-time Christian pastor, my guilty secret was that the gaps between reading it spanned days or even weeks.

But I think I know what I was getting wrong about the Bible. First, I was reading it to help my understanding, to mould my behaviour, to guide my decisions, and to change my feelings. And second, I was reading it because it is true.

Paloma Faith wrote a song: Do you want the truth or something beautiful? and the lyric has stuck with me. I think I shared the assumption behind the title—that truth and beauty are incompatible. So the Bible was true, important, essential... but it was dry and, to be honest, a little dull. It was not beautiful.

Don't get me wrong—the Bible can help my understanding, behaviour, decisions and feelings. And it is true. But it not about me, and it is not merely truth. That's what I was getting wrong.

In fact, the Bible is about Jesus.

You probably knew that already. But do you read the Bible as if you know that? When we do, it changes everything. In Jesus, we see truth and beauty. We see the most wonderful life we could imagine, lived on the canvas of history, rather than a novel.

Do you want the truth, or something beautiful? Yes. I want both; I find them in Jesus, and so I long to read his Bible.

How to read the Bible (and enjoy it)

When my wife Flick and I were dating, we wrote each other letters. I read Flick's letters for information about what she had been doing, I read them to know how to behave as her boyfriend, and I certainly read them for the feelings they gave me. But if this was all, I would have entirely missed the point, and broken her heart. I read those letters because I loved her. I wanted to hear from Flick because of my love for her and her love for me. And as I heard from her on those pages, I grew in my love for her.

I read them because I couldn't not—because I loved her.

The Bible is first and foremost a love letter, from Christ, to his people. It is about Jesus and his love for us. Just as Flick's letters enabled me to "see" her even though she wasn't actually with me, so in the Bible we "see" Jesus. One day, we'll be just like him, because we'll be with him (1 John 3 v 2). But in this life, we become more like him as we hear from and see him in his word.

If you read a cookbook as a car manual, nothing much changes for you other than your frustration grows. If we read the Bible in a way other than as a message from our

Saviour about our Saviour's love, we miss out on what the Bible can do, how it can grow and change us. Jesus taught this with incredible simplicity in John 5. He was talking to the Pharisees, who were diligent Bible readers (they had very disciplined quiet times), but had entirely missed the point:

> You study the Scriptures diligently because you think that in them you have eternal life. These are the very Scriptures that testify about me, yet you refuse to come to me to have life ... If you believed Moses, you would believe me, for he wrote about me.   (John 5 v 39-40, 46)

The Bible is about Jesus. When Moses wrote the first five books of the Bible, he wrote about Jesus. When the Pharisees read these books, they took them primarily as a set of rules for life, a way to live out being the people of God, and in doing so to "have eternal life". They missed the point that these books were primarily about Jesus, the Lord of Israel, the Saviour of his people, and the one who bound himself to them in relationship and gave them a good and faithful way to live this out.

Bible reading never saved anyone. Bible reading never grew anyone. Hearing from Christ, about Christ, in the Bible is what saves and grows us.

To grasp that the Bible is about Jesus is to re-understand its subject, like realising that Treasure Island is a book about pirates when you first thought it was a manual on ship-handling techniques and rigging. But seeing that the Bible is about Jesus is far more than this. It is not to see the Bible as having a different subject, but to change the nature of Bible reading from information to relation, from growing in knowledge to growing in love.

That is what Paul is getting at when he tells us to:

> Let the message of Christ dwell among you richly as
> you teach and admonish one another with all wisdom
> through psalms, hymns and songs from the Spirit,
> singing to God with gratitude in your hearts.
>
> (Colossians 3 v 16)

He doesn't expect the Bible simply to inform us; he expects it to dwell in us richly. This is a picture of Bible reading as a life-transforming experience, not as an information exchange. He expects it to change us, and for us to change others with it, through admonishing and teaching.

In other words, because he knew whose the words of the Bible were, and whom they were about, Paul knew what the Bible could do. He knew there was a way to read the Bible that changes us greatly—by reading it as a love letter from Christ.

If we read the Bible like that, we will always grow. The Spirit will use it to teach us about Jesus, to remind us of him, and to set him before our eyes so that we love him, trust him, worship him and live for him. It will mean your heart will sing, and sometimes your mouth too!

The danger of Bible reading

Bible reading can be very bad for your faith.

Think of the Pharisees. Jesus himself said that they "[studied] the Scriptures diligently", which is more than could often have been said for me. Yet because of how they read it, each quiet time left them further from salvation.

It is possible to read our Bibles in a way that does not merely not help, but actually hinders, our growth. Let me show you how easy it is for this to happen. You can read your Bible and stunt your Christian growth simply by...

Reading it intellectually

We want to understand the Bible. It is true; indeed, it is the measuring line of all truth, and so we want to understand it. We want to know what it means. We want to "get a handle on" Isaiah; we want to know the "main point" of John chapter 4. We want to learn something new. And, of course, this is good and necessary. If we do not understand the Bible, we can never grow in Christ through reading it.

The problem is when we make understanding and learning the sole aim and goal of Bible reading. So we open the Bible to learn something new about God. If we manage to find something, it's a "good study". If not, we wonder why we bothered.

Of course it is exciting to learn something new about God. We should love it when we do, but when we make increased knowledge the goal of reading the Bible, we are in danger of mere cleverness. Maybe you have been in a Bible study where people have given their views of the passage and then someone, maybe the leader, carefully gives the answer, the only correct point, with the same tone as Culombo or Hercule Poirot unveiling "whodunnit".

This stunts our growth because we begin to imagine that God loves clever people. His favourite children are those who "get it". Growth is cleverness, reading the whole Bible, going to theological college or doing a correspondence course. We either trust our own intellectual abilities, or we despair because we don't have that kind of mind. We turn our Christian lives from knowing Jesus into knowing about Jesus—as though reading a biography of your mother were better than spending time with her.

But when the Bible is about Jesus, it becomes more straightforward. We can see Jesus with the Spirit's help, whether or not we have a degree. We can revel in the wonder of Christmas, the purity of Christ's life, the love of the cross, the triumph of the resurrection... even if we learned all those things years ago, in children's groups.

Reading it morally

Another way of misreading the Bible is to read it morally, looking for ways in which we must behave and things we must do. We see the Bible as a guide to life. At best, we do this because we want to obey God for his glory, or because we know a life of obedience is the most satisfying one there is. At worst, we do it because deep down we think that without our obedience, God will not bless or even forgive us. And so we approach a passage to see what we must do as a result.

If you love and trust Jesus, then of course you want to obey him for his glory and your joy (John 14 v 15). But if we approach the Bible morally, all sorts of things can go wrong. First, we end up drawing strange lessons from stories without commands, particularly when there is no hero to emulate. It might be good to "dare to be a Daniel" (see Daniel 6 for example) but I don't want my daughters to copy Delilah, and I don't want my godsons to follow much of Samson's example (read Judges 13 – 16 to see why not!). We can end up conforming the Bible to our standards as we decide which characters are to be copied and which are to be held up as moral warnings. No, the Bible will conform us to its subject, to Jesus, the one Daniel met (Daniel 10 v 5-9), loved, worshipped and risked all for.

Even worse, though, if the Bible is about how to be good, then growth is all about growth in good conduct. This exhausts us—every day's devotions just provide us with an extra line on our "moral to-do list". This crushes us—it leaves us feeling useless. It demotivates us—why open the Bible when it will only tire me out and make me feel inadequate? And most seriously, it gets God all wrong. He doesn't want children who clean up before eating a meal with him, minding their manners. He wants children who relate to him, enjoy life with him, and are honest and open with him. Read the Bible morally, and you will soon start to run from God.

Jesus says it is much simpler: "The work of God is this: to believe in the one he has sent" (John 6 v 29). When we believe in Jesus, we will love him, and our love will work itself out in a desire to trust and obey him in everything. The commands are there as part of a simple relationship of love and trust; they are there primarily to show us Jesus. Delilah and Samson, even Daniel, are there to show us our need for a Saviour, and to provide glimpses of him. Like the rest of the Bible, their stories are about him.

Reading it functionally

A third way of reading the Bible in a way that won't grow us is to do so functionally. And why not? The Bible itself promises that:

> the holy Scriptures ... are able to make you wise for salvation through faith in Christ Jesus. All Scripture is God-breathed and is useful for teaching, rebuking, correcting and training in righteousness, so that the servant of God may be thoroughly equipped for every good work. (2 Timothy 3 v 15-17)

We see that the Bible is to make us wise for salvation, and to thoroughly equip us. So we read it to be wise and thoroughly equipped! But when this is our primary view of our Bible reading, it becomes very mechanical. Some of us end up leafing through it, trying to find help with the particular issue we are facing today. We grow frustrated that the Bible isn't ordered into sections on "Anxiety about my job", "Tips on marriage" and "How to share the gospel".

Others of us make our Bible reading mechanical: The Bible does me good, it makes me grow, so I should read it for ten minutes a day. We sit down, do our quiet time and wonder why nothing is happening. We have taken the medicine, but feel no better. We put the coin in the slot in the machine, so where's the chocolate bar? We did our bit: why didn't God do his?

But this is like thinking that I will grow in love for my wife simply by spending ten minutes with her each day. Relationships are about love, engagement, trust, understanding, and not merely presence.

Reading it emotionally

So maybe we reject this thoughtful, intellectual approach and read it emotionally. Maybe we read the Bible not for knowledge but for experience. Perhaps, we reason, it is a mystical book meant to work on a more instinctive level?

I tried reading the Bible like this when I realized that the other approaches weren't doing much for me. I hoped that I would simply "get it" one day and feel closeness to God as I read it. If I could read my Bible each morning and leave it with a burning love for Jesus and a joy about life, then I would grow fast! But this approach to Bible reading makes the same fundamental mistake as all the others we have looked at. It makes the Bible about me. It just makes it about my feelings, rather than my understanding or behaviour. And it makes my feelings the ultimate judge of a "successful" time reading my Bible.

Of course we want our hearts to burn—but with the love of a real person, our Lord and Saviour.

Don't get me wrong. We need to understand the Bible. It will show us how to behave. It does equip us for life each day. It will sometimes fire up our feelings. It needs to be read diligently. But if we make it all about one of those things, we turn our Christian lives into an intellectual pursuit leading to pride, or a moral crusade doomed to failure, or a job on the to-do list, or a trip on an emotional roller coaster. Too much of any of those for too long will mean either that I give up on reading my Bible, or that I shrink by carrying on reading my Bible.

How to grow through reading your Bible

Let's read the Bible because it's about Jesus. But how can you read the Bible simply to see Jesus and avoid these mistakes we seem to fall into so easily?

Read it (not notes!)

Just read the Bible. I think that Bible-reading notes can be helpful, but if you have never read the Bible without notes, can I encourage you to ditch them, at least for a while? Get used to reading the Bible as a book you can understand. Read it as that love letter from Jesus. Read it to find him. You do not need notes to get it.

Read all of it

And this applies to all of the Bible. It is all about Jesus. It is all good, exciting, beautiful truth about our Lord and Saviour. It centres on his cross, and it sings, whispers, heralds, shouts, cries and placards his name in every chapter. For the last seven or so years, my pattern of Bible reading has been to start at Genesis, read as much as I want each morning, and when I get to the end of Revelation, start at Genesis again. Of course, that's not the only way, but it is an exciting way.

You will see Jesus everywhere, and you will see him more and more—through every king, priest, prophet, servant, warrior or shepherd. You will see glimmers of his incarnation, life, death, resurrection, ascension and return to judge and save; then you will see them played out in sparkling colours in the Gospels. You will begin to see Jesus in sacrificial systems, in the temple, in cleanness laws, in the Exodus, the exile, the return, and a thousand other images.

Read it with the Spirit alongside you and Jesus before your eyes

Earlier, I said the Bible is a love letter to us from Jesus. This is a slightly flawed image. The Bible was written as the prophets and other writers: "though human, spoke from God as they were carried along by the Holy Spirit" (2 Peter 1 v 21). It was the Spirit who guided, directed and dictated what the human authors would write. However, the love letter idea is still a helpful one, because we can't separate the work of Jesus and the Spirit; they always act together, in perfect love and unity as they obey their great Father. The Spirit's work and his delight is always to shine a light on Jesus, to bring him before our eyes and glorify him. We grow into the Son's likeness as his Spirit does this for us.

So if you get stuck reading the Bible, you can ask the Spirit. He may well not enable you immediately to understand all the cross-references in the passage, the nuances of the original Hebrew or Greek, or the structure of the book it is part of (in fact those things are very unlikely!), but he will show you Jesus. And that is the point.

Read it with your church

The Spirit gives us the Bible to show us Jesus, and he then gives us the church to help us see him more clearly and more often. That is why it is not wrong, and is often a good idea, to turn to notes, because they come from the wider church. But it makes a lot more sense to turn to the church that Jesus has put you in. It is a huge blessing to be able to own a Bible and read it ourselves, but the danger is that we forget to read it with others.

The Bible presents Jesus to us as his family, together, as we talk about it, chew it over and extract all the flavour and goodness from it. Read the Bible with your church; get together during the week to do so—in groups or in twos and threes. When you hang out with brothers or sisters for a coffee, meal or beer, tell them what you have seen about Jesus this week. Hold him before their eyes from your Bible reading, and they will love him all the more, and then they will want to do the same. After all, you grow only as your church grows.

Read it often—like a novel

Of course, unlike a novel, the Bible is true, but otherwise it is similar. A friend told me a story about his grandparents. His grandad was about to go to heaven, and was being transferred from his home to a hospice for his last few hours. And my friend's gran, whose favourite author is Jane Austen, grabbed Pride and Prejudice and said: "I think I'll take some old friends with me". Of course, Pride and Prejudice is (arguably!) beautiful, but it isn't true. But the way his Gran turned to that book was not as a manual, but as something familiar, something almost relational, where she'd meet with some old friends.

In the Bible, we meet with our oldest and best friend. And the great thing is, he's real. Doesn't that make you want to read the Bible?

Just remember who it's about

When the risen Jesus went on a walk with his friends on the day of his resurrection, they didn't recognise them, and he had to explain to them what was going on. To show them himself, he showed them the Scriptures, saying:

> "Did not the Messiah have to suffer these things and then enter his glory?" And beginning with Moses and all the Prophets, he explained to them what was said in all the Scriptures concerning himself.   (Luke 24 v 26-27)

We don't get a walk with Jesus—not yet. But we do get the Scriptures. We do get to see what is said in all the Bible concerning Jesus.

A few minutes later, those friends said to each other:

> "Were not our hearts burning within us while he talked with us on the road and opened the Scriptures to us?"
>
> (v 32)

You understand the Bible and find your feelings fired up as you meet Jesus in his word. It will change so much, and help you grow so much, if you sit down with your Bible, ask the Spirit for help, and think:

I am about to hear from Jesus, about Jesus. I am opening up his love letter. He is true, he is beautiful, and he is speaking to me.

6. Growing as your church does

For me to grow as a Christian, my church must grow. Then I will grow as part of it.

We saw this idea back in chapter 3, when we looked at Galatians 5 and 1 Corinthians 12. We are part of a family that grows together. More radically, we are actually all part of the same body. And if we seek to grow without it, we will not grow at all—we will shrink.

In his letter to the Colossians, Paul addresses a particular kind of false spirituality:

> Do not let anyone who delights in false humility and the worship of angels disqualify you. Such a person also goes into great detail about what they have seen; they are puffed up with idle notions by their unspiritual mind. They have lost connection with the head, from whom the whole body, supported and held together by its ligaments and sinews, grows as God causes it to grow.
>
> (Colossians 2 v 18-19)

Here is someone who has experienced visions of angels. They think hard about a lot of detailed theological issues. But they are disconnected from the head—from Christ. They are not part of the body that is attached to Jesus, its head. The implication of this is that they will not grow as a Christian, because the body grows together, and body parts do not grow apart from the body. The only way to grow as a Christian is to be part of a growing body attached to the head of Jesus.

To take away the "body" language, the only way to grow as a Christian is to be part of a growing church where Jesus is at work as its Lord and Saviour. This simple idea immediately throws up lots of questions for us. Surely this is too passive—don't I need to take responsibility for my growth, and not rely on those around me growing? And what if others don't grow—can't I grow anyway?

There is something right behind these questions, but the fact that they spring up so quickly in our minds indicates a deep-seated problem. Individualism, the idea that I am the master of my destiny, is in the air we breathe, carried on the airwaves into our souls. And it is dangerously wrong. It is the root of the false humility that Paul is dealing with in Colossians 2.

Mature Christian, or childish Christian?

Paul talks about this person who delights in false humility, worship of angels and going into detail about what they have seen. I think this is the sort of person we are tempted to consider mature in Christ; they certainly sound as if they have grown significantly, and so if we want to grow, they are the kind of person whom we would want to emulate.

Yet Paul calls them unspiritual, and says that they have been cut off from Jesus! Let's look at this issue a bit more closely.

This person is falsely humble. Humility is a good trait, and it is rare. To be humble is to have your vision filled with Jesus Christ. Moses was the most humble man who lived on the earth in his day (Numbers 12 v 3). This seems strange to us—after all, Moses wrote this! How can a humble man write that he is humble? And how can a humble man command God's people with the forcefulness and power that Moses did?! Surely a humble man doesn't presume to take on leadership, and talks about his weaknesses often.

But when Moses did try to turn down the position God gave him as prophet and leader of Israel, citing his slowness of speech and other weaknesses as reasons, the Lord was angry with him (Exodus 3 – 4). True humility is not having a poor view of yourself. True humility is not having any view of yourself, because your vision is filled with the glory of Christ. This allows you to have a true view of yourself: you can be honest about your sins and about your strengths—you know the former are forgiven by God, and you know the latter are given by God.

True humility is to see Jesus and live for him. False humility is a sort of pride; it is to focus on yourself, your spirituality, your growth. Pride is to look at yourself and smile at the shining saint who smirks back from the mirror. False humility is to look at yourself and list your failures and sins, and then delight in your lowliness. It is to placard your failings so that others admire your honest self-appraisal and insight. It is really a sort of pride, because it focuses on me and draws others to look at me.

That is the difference between false humility and real self-examination. Real self-examination drives us to flee to the strong tower of Jesus for forgiveness and help, while false humility enjoys living in the ramshackle shed of my failure.

False humility actually makes it all about me. So it is no surprise that this falsely humble person is intrigued by worshipping angels. They can then talk about these amazing angels (how humble!) while mentioning that they saw them (how falsely humble!) For us, it might not be the messengers of heaven that we worship, but we can easily be drawn to

Christian leaders, and go on in great detail about what we have seen, the books we have read, the sermons we have heard or the people we have met. The implication is that we are serious Christians, we are growing, we are faithful. Of course, when someone expresses such admiration to me, I quickly demur. I talk about my sin and struggles; how I could never have the faith of the pastor, or the understanding of the author I've been reading.

I keep the focus on myself and away from Jesus with an instinctive subtlety that even I hardly notice. False humility is simply pride.

The church is Christ's answer to that kind of pride. Being part of a church encourages us, sometimes forces us, to not think about ourselves too much. It makes us think about others more. It provokes us to rely on Christ increasingly. It provides others to cut us down to size when we need it, and build us up when we need it.

Growing as part of church is easy

So, how do we grow as part of a growing church? I wish it was harder, so that I could write an impressive chapter about it and show you my great (and falsely humble!) wisdom. But in fact it's very simple: to grow as part of the church, you just need to be part of a church.

It needs to be a church where Jesus is the head. Such a church will be dependent on him, and so prayerful. Such a church will want to be ruled by him, and so the Bible will be taken seriously and opened often. If your church is like this, then you probably have no idea how much you have grown since you joined, because you all grow together. When you sit with others on an express train, you don't feel as if you are moving until you look out of the window. Try to look back on where you were as a church a year or two ago, and marvel at how the Lord has grown you (plural—"y'all" is a great theological advantage that Americans with southern accents have!).

You (singular) need to be part of it. A church is a family, and you take part by spending time with each other. It is not about being at church services, meetings and activities or on courses, although these all provide opportunities to be with people. It is simply about being together. Spend time with your family, and you will grow together. A little later in his letter, Paul tells the Colossians how to do this:

> And over all these virtues [that Paul just listed] put on love, which binds them all together in perfect unity. Let the peace of Christ rule in your hearts, since as members of one body you were called to peace. And be thankful. Let the message of Christ dwell among you richly as you teach and admonish one another with all wisdom through psalms, hymns and songs from the Spirit, singing to God with gratitude in your hearts. And whatever you do, whether in word or deed, do it all in the name of the Lord Jesus, giving thanks to God the Father through him. (3 v 14-17)

We are united by Jesus. He has loved us and given us to each other as a family. Love for each other is the natural consequence of this. You need to pray for love for your brothers and sisters. It is not enough to grit our teeth and serve each other. We are to give all we are and have for one another as family, out of love for each other. I need to pray often and specifically that the Spirit would move me to love the brother or sister in church who is currently badgering me about something, or who has let me down in some way, or who for whatever reason I just naturally don't particularly get on with!

When we are part of a loving family, we simply need to let Christ's love work itself out. As we spend time together as a church, we will find ourselves talking about Jesus to each other, learning from each other, singing together, crying together, praying together... growing together.

To do this, make sure you're not only seeing your church family at organised meetings. Some families with teenage children have family meetings from time to time, where they can discuss together any issues, problems or worries. These are really helpful, as long as they're not the only time the family spend together. Families (good ones) share their lives. So as a church family eat together, go out together and pop in on each other.

This is so simple, and so attractive. We are on campaign, seeking to advance for Christ's glory and our growth. We come to our Commander, to see what difficult task he will give us. How can we move forward this week? Our commander steps up; here it comes:

> Right, I want you to go out for coffee with Ann and Jez and chat about Jesus, then tomorrow pop in on Barbara and check if she needs any shopping. You are commanded to eat her flapjacks while you are there. On Thursday, you will be invited to Samuel and Mercy's—don't eat before you go...

Growing as part of church is hard

Growing as part of the church is so easy. And it is so hard. We just need to spend time together, opening our mouths to eat and to speak of Jesus, or to our Father. Sometimes we will open our Bible to see something, read something, show something or check something. Other times, we will pray. We will do so much with each other.

But we are so scared of each other.

We fear being inconvenienced, we fear being exposed, we fear being busy, we fear being known, we fear being hurt, we fear being judged, we fear not looking good, we fear saying something silly about Jesus, we fear being honest about what we (haven't) read in the Bible lately, we fear being given something to eat that we don't like. We fear.

We fear because we are sinful. Sin is proud; it is selfish. Since God is family—Father, Son and Holy Spirit—and since we are made in his image, we long for real, giving, loving community. And we find it (or should find it) in church. But since we are fallen, and often prefer to follow the devil, who has no family and knows no community, we lapse into individualism and consumerism. We seek to get from church, instead of giving to church.

We are often like young boys playing football, all chasing the ball to be the one who scores the goal, desperate for individual glory and caring more for that than for the team to win. So what if our church loses 6-1 as long as I score that one goal?

If you want to grow up as a child of God, you need to trust him, and he put you in your church. If you're not part of one, you need to join one, because God didn't choose you to be a lone ranger, but a member of his people. If your church does not love Jesus by being committed to prayer and the Bible (including the hard parts), you might need to find a new one. But assuming you are part of a church that loves Jesus, then you are not there by mistake. He gave you these brothers and sisters as a blessing to you. The Lord of all wisdom could have placed you in any local church family across the centuries and around the world—he chose this one. Your growth is all about being part of this church. What does that mean for you?

It would be worth taking time to think about that specifically. To help with that, think about Jesus, honesty and food. To grow with your church, you need Jesus on the agenda, so risk being weird and talk about him—after the service, when you're at each other's houses, when you bump into each other while shopping. You might feel self-conscious, but I reckon others will be grateful and join in. Who knows, if your church learns to talk about Jesus together all the time, you might even find yourselves talking about him naturally with people outside the church all the time!

To grow with your church, you need to offer and accept honesty. Take down the mask, slowly if need be. The secrets and sins of the others round the table are as bad. Their desperate need for grace is as great as yours. Show it, receive it and learn to repent together.

And to grow with your church, eat. Have you ever noticed in the Gospels how many significant times of growth happened at the table as Jesus ate with people? Kitchen tables, coffee shops, pubs, picnic blankets and round the barbecue are the front line of the war for growth—fight well by eating food together.

The family meal

As with all areas of growth, church is something that God gives us and builds for us, as we receive it and live as part of it. The church is something Christ made: he is the one who promised to: "build my church, and the gates of Hades will not overcome it" (Matthew 16 v 18).

Perhaps the greatest reminders that it is Christ who builds his church are the "sacraments" of baptism and the Lord's Supper. Baptism is where we become part of the people of God—it is the door into his church. Indeed, the church was born when 3,000 obeyed Peter's command to "repent and be baptised" on the day of Pentecost (Acts 2 v 38).

If baptism is the front door in, then the Lord's Supper is the meal table; the place where Christ gathers us together to feed us... with himself. We see the importance of this family meal as Paul corrects some dangerous individualism that has crept into the Corinthian church:

> When you come together, it is not the Lord's Supper you eat, for when you are eating, some of you go ahead with your own private suppers. As a result, one person remains hungry and another gets drunk. Don't you have homes to eat and drink in? Or do you despise the church of God by humiliating those who have nothing? What shall I say to you? Shall I praise you? Certainly not in this matter! (1 Corinthians 11 v 20-22)

Paul is emphasising how the church should eat together. Christ's family grow together as they look together at Christ. They share their food, drink wine together, and enjoy it all in a way that ensures everyone can be satisfied, rather than some going home drunk and others thirsty. It is a meal to be enjoyed together, with love, singing, warm conversation, children getting treats and chairs pushed back to make room for stories and discussion.

Both baptism, as we look back at it, and the Lord's Supper, as we continue to eat it, are means of growth. They are God's gifts, given to us to help us look at Jesus, appreciate him, and be transformed as we do so. So how can you take hold of all that God is offering you through this meal? First, look back. As we break bread, as we pour wine, the Spirit shows us the love of Jesus for us. He shows us the moment when it was most clearly displayed—Jesus dying in love on the cross. Let what the sixteenth-century pastor John Calvin called the "visible words" tell you again about Jesus' death for you.

Second, look forward. It is wonderful that the result for us of Jesus' sacrifice is a feast, a joyful supper together. One day Jesus will return, and he will set the table himself, and he grows us as a church towards that day. The Spirit lifts our vision to the day when we will see Jesus face to face, the day when he will set a feast for us in the new creation.

This combination gives the bread and wine a reverential taste as we reflect on the perfect revelation of God, as he hung and suffered for us on the cross. It also gives the meal a joyful, family atmosphere as we enjoy it together. Often our churches emphasise the reverential aspect over the familial, passing out bread and wine along rows in silence. The danger is that this can make it individualistic—it becomes about my communion with God—and so we fail to observe the body, the church of God (1 Corinthians 11 v 29).

To grow in Christ through the Lord's Supper is to look back to the cross and forward to the banquet while looking around at each other. However your church is reminded of Christ's death—whether round a chaotic table of all ages, or kneeling in rows in front of the table, or passing the bread and wine down the rows of chairs—look around. As you look at the other members of your church, remember that they have been saved by Christ's death, and that you'll sit together at the great feast in the new creation.

All this is a bit much to think about at once. So maybe focus on one aspect of the Lord's Supper each time you have it—Christ's death for your sins one time; next time the feast you'll enjoy in the new creation with him; or the church he is growing you in, the brothers and sisters he has surrounded you with. The point is not to have a tick list of "prayers I must pray before I stop chewing", but a wide view of the meal that stretches back to the cross, on into eternity, and round to those God has given you to grow with.

Our growth is Jesus' work. And he grows us together. He grows us together as we eat, talk, open Bibles, cry, sing, discuss, rebuke, encourage, teach, pray, rejoice, mourn and repent together. These things come naturally as he reminds us of all he is and all he has made us with body and blood, bread and wine. Jesus will grow his church, and so although our growth as church will never be easy, it is stunningly simple.

7. Seeing Jesus in creation

I lay on my back on the grass on a warm Sunday evening, looking up at clouds tinged with the glory of the setting sun. What did I see, as I looked into the heavens?

I saw Jesus.

Well, obviously, in one sense, I didn't. I did not see the face of Christ on a piece of toast or a leaf, as someone claims to every now and then in a tabloid article.

But according to Psalm 19 v 1-6, I did see a picture of Jesus:

> The heavens declare the glory of God;
> the skies proclaim the work of his hands.
> Day after day they pour forth speech;
> night after night they reveal knowledge.
> They have no speech, they use no words;
> no sound is heard from them.
> Yet their voice goes out into all the earth,
> their words to the ends of the world.
> In the heavens God has pitched a tent for the sun.
> It is like a bridegroom coming out of his chamber,
> like a champion rejoicing to run his course.
> It rises at one end of the heavens and makes its circuit
> to the other;
> nothing is deprived of its warmth.

King David, who wrote the psalm, tells us that "the heavens declare the glory of God". This is not simply beautiful poetry; it is theology you can take hold of. The skies proclaim and pour forth speech. They reveal knowledge and their voice is heard. Most strikingly, their words go to the ends of the earth. This is language that you would normally associate with the preaching of the gospel, with people commissioned to share the message of Jesus with the world.

The word of God goes out into all the earth, declared everywhere by the heavens. The heavens show us God. As Paul puts it:

> What may be known about God is plain to them, because God has made it plain to them. For since the creation of the world God's invisible qualities—his eternal power and divine nature—have been clearly seen, being understood from what has been made, so that men are without excuse. (Romans 1 v 19-20)

So David looks to the heavens and gasps in wonder at the power and nature of the God who made them. But he sees more than that. He looks up and sees the sun as a champion, a great warrior, and a bridegroom. This is how the Bible describes Jesus: as a champion, a warrior, and the Bridegroom of his people. David, writing by the power of the Spirit, sees a picture of Jesus, God the Son. He sees his shining greatness. He sees one who loves him and who will fight his battles for him. He sees the one who guided the stone and killed the giant, and the one who forgave his sin and loved him despite it.

And David is absolutely right to see all this—because Jesus made the sun to reflect something of himself. Artists, poets, and singers put something of themselves into the work they create. And so did the One who created all things. He wrote his glory into all he made, so that we can read it.

This is amazing, and it is easy to get it the wrong way round. When I preach from the Bible, I use stories and examples to illustrate what I am saying. This is not what the Holy Spirit does. When we read a verse like Revelation 1 v 16: "His face was like the sun shining in all its brilliance", it is not that the Holy Spirit was searching for a way to describe the brightness of Jesus' face, and realised the sun would be a good image. No, the sun was made in the first place in such a way that it would declare the brightness of Christ. When you see and feel the light and warmth of the sun, you are not meant to think Jesus is a little like this; you are meant to think that the sun is a little like Jesus, and that he put it there to help you remember that and be amazed by him.

When Muhammad Ali, the boxer, said that he would "float like a butterfly and sting like a bee", he didn't mean that he had created bees and butterflies to help people understand his skill as a boxer. But when Jesus said that "the Son of Man in his day will be like the lightning, which flashes and lights up the sky from one end to the other" (Luke 17 v 24), he meant exactly that he had made lightning to tell us what he would be like in his return.

If we go back to the sun, we can see why this is important to understand. The light of the sun is indeed so dazzling that we cannot bear to stare at it. But it also draws us, warms us and delights us. Everyone is in a better mood on a warm summer's morning than in the teeth of a drizzly, grey winter's afternoon. To hear that Jesus is the light of the world might make us think of a cold and forbidding light, so he made the sun to teach us better; to teach us that his light is warm and life-giving, even though it dazzles sinful eyes.

Creation grows us by showing us Christ

Imagine you're in an art gallery, looking at a large, beautiful landscape painting of the countryside.

Initially, you are struck by the beauty of the painting. That leads your thoughts on to the skill and vision of the artist. He was clearly a master. You look at some of the details, and marvel at his ability.

Then you read the sign next to the painting that tells you a little about the artist. Strangely, it informs you that he was red-haired and bearded, a sociable man who enjoyed a good meal with his family or friends, and also a keen fisherman.

You look at the painting again. And you notice a satisfied fisherman on the banks of a river. Further to the right, there's a delicious-looking picnic being spread out by a smiling dad, joking with his family. In the corner, you even see an artist painting the scene.

The fisherman, the father and the painter all have red hair and full beards. And you realise that the artist has painted himself into his masterpiece. It is a landscape painting; it is also a self-portrait.

As we look at creation, we are drawn to see the majesty and glory of God. As we get to know Jesus better—as we hear him tell us about himself in his word—we see that the artist has painted himself into the painting. The One through whom "all things were made" (John 1 v 3) made them to show himself to us. As the Spirit tells us about the sun in Psalm 19 or lightning in Luke 17, we see more ways that the artist has painted himself into his masterpiece.

What does this have to do with our growth as Christians? Well, we grow as the Spirit shows us Jesus. It is as we think about Jesus—his love, holiness, integrity, courage, glory, the list is endless—that we grow up to be close to him and to be like him. And since Jesus has created the world in such a way that it shows him to us, we can always be growing as Christians, because his masterpiece is the canvas on which we live our lives.

The Bible, prayer and the church are central to our growth in Christ, but they are not always with us. We can pray continually, but we cannot be in concentrated, focused prayer always. We can meditate on Scripture but we cannot always have our Bible open in front of us. We can keep in touch with brothers and sisters from church by text and email, but many of us spend more time with those who don't follow Jesus—at work, maybe, or home, in our hobbies and our chores.

But we are all always in the creation. And this means that we can be seeing Jesus all the time. So we can grow all the time. Just like an oak tree, which grows so slowly that you will never see it spurt forth, we will grow as the living water of the Spirit and the light of Christ work on us through creation.

It is not that we replace the Bible or church with creation. That would be as foolish as saying: "Well, the church shows me Jesus, so I can chuck my Bible away". The generosity of our Father is so great that he gives us a full diet that grows us.

Even the ugliness, brokenness and pain of creation is part of the picture, because it reminds us that this is a picture that has been spoiled. The ground growing thistles and thorns as a result of Adam's sin was the judgment of God (Genesis 3 v 17-18). He put their spikes there so that creation would tell us that we need more than this world. And he put them there so that one day they would be jammed onto his head as he undid the curse on creation. Even the flaws of this world show us Jesus.

So living in this world is like enjoying a colossal picture that was painted by Jesus, and is about Jesus, but where different parts display slightly different aspects of his kindness, love, glory, power, gentleness or work in saving us. This is no exercise in divine vanity; it is a loving offering to us so that we can see Jesus more often, more clearly and more movingly.

Exclude atheism

What does this mean for how we live? How do we use creation to grow? The first thing we need to do is to realise what we are up against in our own heads.

Jesus is all around us, but we don't see him. We live in a world that sees creation as something to be understood without reference to God. If you ask a group of people what a star is, most would reply that it is a ball of gas, or something similar. It may well be that—but it isn't only that. A Christian sees the stars and is awed by the power of God. We see the cosmos, which he created, and it makes us amazed that God cares for seemingly insignificant people like us:

> When I consider your heavens, the work of your fingers,
> the moon and the stars, which you have set in place,
> what is mankind that you are mindful of them, human
> beings that you care for them?   (Psalm 8 v 3-4)

A star is something that tells us of the power of God. But it isn't only that. It also tells something of what it means to follow Jesus faithfully, to shine with his love in a world of bleak, dark indifference. A star is a Christian who tells other people about Jesus:

> Do everything without grumbling or arguing, so that
> you may become blameless and pure, "children of God

> without fault in a warped and crooked generation." Then
> you will shine among them like stars in the sky as you
> hold firmly to the word of life.   (Philippians 2 v 14-16)

The stars remind us that God is not impressed by size but is mindful of us; and they remind us that living publicly as a follower of Jesus, even when we might feel it makes no difference, is the difference between being a bright-shining star and being darkness. A star might be a ball of gas too, but to think you've understood what a star is by knowing what it is made of is to miss the point completely. It is as misguided as to think that a person is just a load of oxygen, carbon, hydrogen and other chemicals. A person is a sister, friend, biologist, railway enthusiast, child of God. Yes, we are made up of chemicals, but that is not a sufficient understanding of a person. A star is far more than gas.

To see Christ and so to grow in Christ through creation, we need to unlearn the atheistic way of looking at the world. This is not about whether the world was created in six days or over many millions of years; it is about whether the world was created or not. Is there a sun in the sky because Jesus put it there, or is it simply a mistake to even ask why there is a sun because there is no ultimate reason behind anything?

Of course it is legitimate for a Christian to wonder what substance a star is made from; but it is essential for a Christian to wonder why a star is there. Many Christians are rightly engaged in all fields of scientific endeavour, but we must all be involved in asking the deeper and more amazing questions of how the skies proclaim the glory of God.

The world we live in gets its priorities wrong. People think that the material questions are the most important, rather than seeing these as gateways to growth in Christ. The more we understand the creation, the more ways we will see it reflecting the light of Jesus to us. But we need to understand the water we live in, and how that water is being heated to such a temperature that it kills Christian wondering without us even realising.

We live in a world that not only does not ask these questions, but laughs at them as primitive. When we try to see Jesus in creation, people will liken us to ancient people who worshipped the sun-god. We need to realise that all we are doing is being consistent—if the world is created, then we can expect to see signs of the Creator. Remember, it is not that the Holy Spirit was wondering what to compare Jesus to and decided that the sun was a good illustration to use. No, Jesus made the sun in the first place as a reflection of some of his glory, and in Psalm 19 the Spirit simply points it out to us in case we hadn't noticed.

To fail to worship Christ through creation is dangerous, because if you don't worship Christ through creation, there is a good chance you will worship creation itself. Plenty of people have worshipped sun and moon, and many other parts of Christ's cosmos. Of course they have! The sun is a mighty light, giving warmth, light and life to all the world. If you do not know of the greater Light who made the sun to show his glory, it is natural to worship it as a god.

Our world now is not so different. Even some atheist scientists write and talk about the world with reverence and awe. They do not worship it explicitly, but their lives are dedicated to knowing and pursuing science with a zeal that fits with the most religious of people. Plenty of us seek awesome sights and sunsets, grand canyons and remote plateaus so that we can gaze on glory. We might not give the god a name, but we give it our worship.

Enjoy creation

So how do we move from one world to the other—move from teetering on the edge of worshipping the creation to letting it move us to worship the Creator? We do it by enjoying creation.

In 1 Timothy 4 v 4-5, Paul says:

> Everything God created is good, and nothing is to be rejected if it is received with thanksgiving, because it is consecrated by the word of God and prayer.

The way we avoid the opposite mistakes of worshipping creation and treating creation as merely stuff is to enjoy it thankfully.

This means we need to get out into creation and look at it. Stand gazing at the sea, looking away from the beach and pier, with the sun glinting from waves as the crystal blue waters stretch to the glorious heavens. You can feel your own smallness, and you can do so without feeling insignificant—because you can think to yourself: "What is mankind that you are mindful of them, human beings that you care for them. You have made them a little lower than the angels and crowned them with glory and honour" (Psalm 8 v 4-5). We can enjoy the sea and sun, but when we know their Maker and why he made them, they are so much more delightful.

And this means that we need to have fun with creation. If you wander through a meadow with the sun on your back and a breeze on your face, then you should enjoy it. And you should worship Christ. The simplest way to do that is to thank him.

That's enough. Receiving it with thankfulness simply increases the joy. You are not self-indulgent and selfish in that moment; you are worshipping a generous God with right gratitude. To enjoy creation with thankfulness is a huge step away from engaging with the world without thinking of

Christ. But we can go even further. You can look at the sun as David saw it, as a champion and a bridegroom. You can feel the breeze as a reminder of the way in which the Spirit goes where he sees fit (John 3 v 8). You can see a storm and think about Jesus' return: unmissable, mighty and awesome.

The way we do this is simply to read the Bible. It is full of winds and waves, darkness and light, rainbows and gold. The Bible tells us how to understand different parts of creation, and often it has a nuanced view that pushes us to mull over what we see day by day. We can worship creation, or we can use it as a signpost to Jesus.

As you read the Bible, you will come to see a treasure chest of ways in which Jesus made creation to show himself to us. Then, as you walk through your day, you will have prompts to think about Jesus all over the place. Enjoy the world, be thankful, and express your thanks in prayer and song, and then let the Bible show you the details of the picture so you enjoy it more, and feel more thankful.

This leads us to play the "What does this tell me about Jesus?" game. It's a way of making sure we look at the creation as Jesus intends us to. So walking past a tree, I remind myself that there was a tree of life, which the first humans were invited to eat from, and a tree of the knowledge of good and evil, which they were forbidden to eat from, and that humanity has always eaten of what is forbidden (Genesis 2 v 9; 3 v 6,22). And I remember that there was also a tree of death: the cross that Jesus died on (Galatians 3 v 13), taking the curse, so that we will eat from the tree of life in the new creation (Revelation 22 v 14). A simple tree can tell me the whole history and future of the world, and show me just how much I need Jesus!

All this takes practice. We do not naturally think this way. We have grown up in a world that thinks the sea or the storm or the sycamore are meaningless nothings, or they are gods. But as we learn to see the creation as Jesus' masterpiece, showing us pictures of the Master himself, we'll see him so much more, and we'll grow so much more. You may not have met anyone from church today, may not have read your Bible since this morning, and may not have prayed in a focused way for a few hours; but you can still be growing in your appreciation of Christ, and therefore growing into the likeness of Christ. All you need is what you always have—creation.

So as you finish this chapter, why not go for a walk outside? You might see all sorts of things, but if you look, you will certainly see Jesus.

8. People and their stories

We all see reflections of God, all the time.

When we meet someone—anyone—we meet a man or woman, boy or girl, who reflects the very image of God. This is the amazing glory that God gave us when he first created humanity:

> Then God said, "Let us make mankind in our image, in our likeness, so that they may rule over the fish in the sea and the birds in the sky, over the livestock and all the wild animals, and over all the creatures that move along the ground."
>
> So God created mankind in his own image,
> in the image of God he created them;
> male and female he created them.   (Genesis 1 v 26-27)

All of us were made to display the glory of God. And all of us do that—it is indelibly part of being a living human. But none of us do it perfectly, because in our sin we've marred the image. "All have sinned and fall short of the glory of God" (Romans 3 v 23). We're broken mirrors. We don't reflect perfectly. But we do still reflect God's image.

So the person at the desk next to you will spend the whole day either showing you Jesus or displaying the effects of sin. The pictures of her friends and children stuck to the cubicle walls proclaim the relational nature of someone made in the image of the God who is love. The care she shows in following up clients and checking they are satisfied proclaims the care God shows to his people. Her concern for the intern who is being badly treated makes you sense something of the outrage against injustice of the God who made her. And yet her criticism over coffee of her boss, and the way she personally attacks her and mocks her, displays to you the disloyalty and rejection of authority that marks and mars sinful humanity.

These normal interactions of life are opportunities to see what God did in creating us and what we did in turning away from him. Not only that, but they are to encourage and challenge us to live as he wants us to—as brothers and sisters displaying the family likeness of our Brother, who is "the radiance of God's glory and the exact representation of his being" (Hebrews 1 v 3).

Just as we saw that we can look at stars in different ways, so we can interact with people in different ways. We can simply allow people to impact us by making us happy or sad; we can ignore people, trying to be unaffected by them, as a defence against being hurt. Or we can look at people and wonder precisely how they are showing us the image of Christ right now, or how they are denying their Creator. When we do this, we find that we are thinking about Jesus, and growing more like him.

Beauty and brokenness

People are a particularly obvious way that creation points us to Christ, and to the depths to which we have sunk in our sin. The ordinary kindness and the everyday callousness of the same person is extraordinary. We tend to put people into "good" and "bad" boxes, and overlook the flaws of "the good" or the generosity of "the bad". When we see people as we know ourselves to be—made in the image of God, and ruined by trying to be gods—then we can see both good and bad. The contradiction within each of us—that strange mixture of beauty and brokenness that we should see in those around us—makes no sense at all unless the gospel is true.

Indeed, it is only by seeing people as broken image-bearers that we are able to see the world as Jesus does. Otherwise, we see people as bad, and withdraw into a Christian castle, living away from the rest of the world as much as possible; or we see people as good, embracing the world around us unquestioningly, and becoming just like it. By understanding this central reality about everyone we meet, we can live with the bad in "good" people and the good in "bad" people without becoming cynical or naïve. Instead, we will love people as Jesus did—as they are, but not because of all that they are.

As we see people reflecting God's image, even though they don't realise it, we will challenge ourselves: *Are my actions reflecting God in the way that person's are?* We won't dismiss non-Christian kindness with a complacent: *Yes, they're lovely— but they don't love Jesus*; we'll humbly learn from them how we might live more as a mirror of God's glory.

And when we see people messing up, sinning and failing— even great people we respect—rather than merely causing us to despair, it will remind us of how much we need Jesus, and how amazing his human perfection really is. Jesus is the Leader who never does a U-turn, the Friend who never lets anyone down, the Husband who is never harsh with his bride, the Master who first serves his servants, the God who died for sinners. The brokenness we see around us throws us in desperation on the One who, with God's image unbroken in his life, allowed himself to be utterly broken and smashed, for us. When we run to Jesus and realise that he is the Leader, Friend, Husband, Master and God we long for, we both worship him and are free to understand the mistakes and sins of others, and ourselves.

The actions, words, stories and ideas of people are always the actions, words, stories and ideas of people made in the image of God. This does not mean they are all godly actions, words, stories and ideas, but it does mean that they all point us to God. They are all either (imperfect) expressions of the gospel of Jesus, or (usually unknowingly) attacks on, or corruptions of, that gospel. This means that the actions, words, stories and ideas of everyone can point us to Christ, and can be used by the Spirit to grow us in our love of him. And stories do so most powerfully.

Once upon a time...

We all tell stories. Stories are what we use to work things through, process things, learn from and relax with. Writers, film makers, poets and singers all know that stories entertain us. So do journalists—if you want to get across the horror of a famine, it is more effective to tell the story of one family that has been devastated by it than offer endless statistics.

When we catch up with family at the end of the day, we tell the stories of work or school or home. When we see friends on a Friday evening, we regale each other with stories. We love stories.

In fact, we were created to love stories. The Bible is a book of stories, and it is a book of the great story.

This story, the gospel, is told in different ways—in letters, history, poetry and songs. It is the story of a Husband who came to find his faithless bride... of a Hero who gave his life to defeat a terrible enemy... of a Father and a Son who worked together to rebuild a broken world... of a King who captured a bandit to show him love when he deserved justice... of an Outcast who humiliated and exposed the self-serving elite... of a Shepherd who left the flock to rescue one lost sheep... of a poor Man who was far wiser and more powerful than the rich and pompous.

Because this gospel story is the most beautiful, and most true, of all stories, the other stories we write, read or pass on all reflect or distort that great story. So we can expect to learn about God from the stories we read and see, and we can expect stories to try to drag us away from Him. Every story we watch or hear will show us Jesus and help us grow in him, or it will drag us from Jesus and encourage us to grow away from him.

All stories make assumptions about the way the world is; many also aim to move our hearts and minds to align with their way of seeing the world. Every story has a worldview, a take on reality—every story can therefore shape our own worldview as we listen to it. Sometimes it is obvious; sometimes it is more subtle. So *Bridget Jones' Diary*, *What Women Want* and other rom-coms tend to tell us that finding our "one true love" is the deepest meaning and joy there is in life. When Han Solo returns to help out Luke Skywalker in the final battle of *Star Wars: A New Hope*, we're being told that friendship is more valuable than wealth or safety.

This means that we must engage with stories. We need to watch, read and listen with our eyes on Christ, so that we drink in the pictures of him, and reject the offerings of false truths.

Here are a couple of examples of how this works, positively and negatively. Recently, I watched a movie that totally fulfilled my criteria (the criteria are swords, battles and a happy ending). Called *The Eagle*, it had a scene near the beginning when a troop of Roman soldiers left the safety of their fort to rescue their comrades being held hostage by the barbarian horde they were facing. The Romans jogged towards the enemy, vastly outnumbered, and as the horde charged them, the centurion ordered his men into a *testudo*, a sort of tortoise-shaped formation, with their shields held out all around and over their heads. In the safety of this formation, they marched slowly towards the captured soldiers, bringing them into the safety of the shield wall.

I doubt the following passage of the Bible was in the director's mind when he shot this scene, but it is what came into mine:

> Put on the full armour of God so that you can take your stand against the devil's schemes. For our struggle is not against flesh and blood, but against the rulers, against the authorities, against the powers of this dark world and against the spiritual forces of evil in the heavenly realms. Therefore put on the full armour of God, so that when the day of evil comes, you may be able to stand your ground, and after you have done everything, to stand. Stand firm then, with the belt of truth buckled round your waist, with the breastplate of righteousness in place, and with your feet fitted with the readiness that comes from the gospel of peace. In addition to all this, take up the shield of faith, with which you can extinguish all the flaming arrows of the evil one. Take the helmet of salvation and the sword of the Spirit, which is the word of God. (Ephesians 6 v 11-17)

Here in this film was a picture of the church in armour, with shields of faith held tight, led by a brave and inspiring captain. As I watched, I realised that the armour of God was not describing a lone gladiator, but a church following

Christ into battle. Here was the church, protected from the attacks of the enemy by the faith of one another. Here was the church, marching through the demonic foe to save souls for Christ, with Jesus himself in the lead. The image has stuck with me, and has spurred me on to encourage the church to take the fight to Satan in evangelism. It put fire in my belly; it inspired me not to wish I was a Roman soldier, but to resolve to follow Jesus.

Of course, *The Eagle* is not the gospel, even if one part of one scene captures part of that greatest story. When you see a film that shows violence as strong and attractive, and holding back as being the weak option, it is hard to then turn the other cheek. *The Eagle* can show us great things about the gospel, but watched uncritically it could push us into the mindset that violence in pursuit of honour is a good thing.

Here is another example, this time of a message that needed to be rejected. In *The Pursuit of Happyness*, a man struggles against the odds to gain a well-paid job to lift himself and his son out of poverty. The unquestioned assumption of the story is that wealth is a saviour; it is the path to security and satisfaction. If only the Will Smith character can get the job and grab the wealth, happiness (or happyness) will follow. That is a false gospel, with money as the saviour. And I need to spot that; otherwise I will finish the film just trusting a little more in my own career or bank balance, or just a little more dissatisfied with the career and level of wealth God has chosen to give me, and just a little less like Jesus in my thoughts and attitudes. And that will all happen without me even noticing—if I don't engage with the story I am being told and the worldview I am being sold. This doesn't undo the good that seeing a beautiful father-son relationship will do me, but I need to understand both truth and lies so I grow more like Jesus, rather than away from him.

A long time ago in a land far away…

There is one more way we can engage with stories—we can use them to speak to people about the gospel by connecting that greatest story to the stories of our culture. A great example of this is Paul's speech to the Athenian leaders:

> Paul then stood up in the meeting of the Areopagus and said: "People of Athens! I see that in every way you are very religious. For as I walked around and looked carefully at your objects of worship, I even found an altar with this inscription: to an unknown god. So you are ignorant of the very thing you worship—and this is what I am going to proclaim to you.
>
> "The God who made the world and everything in it is the Lord of heaven and earth and does not live in temples built by human hands. And he is not served by human hands, as if he needed anything. Rather, he himself gives everyone life and breath and everything else. From one man he made all the nations, that they should inhabit the whole earth; and he marked out their appointed times in history and the boundaries of their lands. God did this so that they would seek him and perhaps reach out for him and find him, though he is not far from any one of us. 'For in him we live and move and have our being.' As some of your own poets have said, 'We are his offspring.'
>
> "Therefore since we are God's offspring, we should not think that the divine being is like gold or silver or

stone—an image made by human design and skill. In the past God overlooked such ignorance, but now he commands all people everywhere to repent. For he has set a day when he will judge the world with justice by the man he has appointed. He has given proof of this to everyone by raising him from the dead." (Acts 17 v 22-31)

Paul begins by connecting with an Athenian story, a worldview they have—the idea that there is a god, who is unknown. He is using a marker in the story of the city to show them a difference between his teaching and theirs—that his God is known, and that he has not come to add to their store of interesting stories, but to reveal truth to them. He then tells them the story of creation to show God's superiority. In doing so, he quotes from their own poets and philosophers. He uses the stories and ideas of the Athenians to preach the gospel to them. He knows that those he quotes and alludes to are not Christians, but they are still made in God's image, and reflecting an aspect of gospel truth. He connects their stories to the greatest story, so that they might see that what they are searching for and hoping for is nothing less than the great truth that there is a knowable God, who rose from the dead, and calls people back to him to enjoy his rule.

Happily ever after...

What you watch or read tonight will either draw you to Jesus or it will push you away from him. It will either cause you to grow in him or grow away from him. It is not simply entertainment, and it is never merely neutral. It will give you a glimpse of Jesus, the Saviour and Lord; or it will tell you that sin is great and Jesus is irrelevant; or it will do both. Watch, read, beware and enjoy, for in our stories be both dragons, and buried treasure.

9. Growing in the ordinariness

My life is full of boxes. In fact, my life is in loads of boxes.

There is my work, my home, my hobbies, time off, me-time, cave-time, date night, family night, boys' night, club night... and then there is church stuff. We all tend to compartmentalise our lives; and our faith goes into the religious box. We think that growing as a Christian is something that we do at church on a Sunday, or through going to a course or Bible study. We think that we will probably have a particular spurt if we go to a Christian conference, convention or camp.

But as we've seen, because Christian growth is about growing as a child in a family, it takes place continually. It doesn't happen in a box (or to think of it another way, it happens in every box). And it is ordinary, not extraordinary—it happens in the nitty-gritty of life far more often than in single, extraordinarily transformational ways. It comes through the small actions, the whispered prayers, the client meeting, the school pick-up, or the evening of family and TV.

Paul's letter to the Ephesians is a wonderful book for showing us where God grows us. Chapters 1 – 3 are full of enormous, eternal realities. They soar to the heights and stretch our horizons. They declare that "the God and Father of our Lord Jesus Christ ... has blessed us in the heavenly realms with every spiritual blessing in Christ" (1 v 3). They tell us that we were "dead in [our] transgressions and sins ...

deserving of wrath" (2 v 1, 3), and yet that God "who is rich in mercy, made us alive with Christ ... [and] raised us up with Christ and seated us with him in the heavenly realms in Christ Jesus" (v 4-6). They show us how the multi-ethnic worldwide church is the place where God lives on earth by his Spirit (2 v 19-22), because it is God's plan that "through the church, the manifold wisdom of God should be made known to the rulers and authorities in the heavenly realms" (3 v 10). In other words, as we meet with that friend from church to read the Bible, as we ring a sister to check if we can shop for her because her husband is in hospital, as we lead a Bible study at home group or gather on Sunday, distracted and busy, angels notice. The good and the bad of the spiritual world all stand in awe of what God has done and is doing in unlikely sinful people like you, as you meet in the middle of the week to look at the Bible.

This is awesome! We are part of God's cosmic plans, stretching from eternity to eternity. We do good works for God, prepared by God (2 v 10). We showcase his wisdom to the unseen world. What does that all look like? It looks like keeping going and keeping growing in the home and at work. It looks like being respectful to your husband when he is being grumpy, showing patience to your children when they are being loopy, and working hard even though the boss is "off sick" and working on his golf handicap.

It seems bizarre that chapters 1 – 3 are followed by chapters 4 – 6. But they are. You will wield the shield of faith and the sword of the Spirit in the office, factory, school, kitchen, park and pub. This is your battlefield. This is where you will grow up like Jesus, who was faithful to his Father whether he was hammering the nails or his enemies were.

Marriage

First Paul addresses marriage, calling wives to submit to their husbands and husbands to love their wives. This immediately strikes us as it sounds a discordant note in our modern culture. What is more striking, though, is the reason Paul gives for how we are to conduct our marriages. He keeps coming back to it through Ephesians 5 v 22-33, but it is clearest in verse 32: "I am talking about Christ and the church".

Our marriages are reflections of the marriage of Jesus with the church. So marriages are places where we can grow to be more like him. Husbands grow like Jesus as we love our wives in the way that Jesus loves his people—kindly, gently, for their good and at cost to ourselves. This comes down to simple things. I have learned to appreciate more vegetables in my meals and fewer swords in my films as I have tried to serve my wife well. These seemingly trivial choices are where we love like Christ in the daily detail of life. To love her by being home on time is much harder for many men than remembering flowers and dinner on Valentine's Day—and it is much more important.

Wives are to submit to their husbands as the church to Christ. They can grow into the same honour and trust in their husbands that the church shows to Christ, living lives of respect. Wives can grow like the servant who obeyed his Father perfectly—the Lord Jesus. It is hard to honour your husband loyally in public, especially when he lets you down in the same ways for which your friends are criticising their partners. But as you do honour him, you grow a little more like Christ as you stand by the school gate or sit in the staff-room.

None of this is easy. It is worked out in the tiredness of work, children, suffering and pain. It is worked out with niggling temptations and sometimes deep disappointments. But as we live out God's design for marriage we grow like Christ and we display Christ. Every marriage is like this; but every marriage is different, and so it will look different for you if you're married to what it will look like for me. But maybe the story of one of these people will resonate with you, and suggest how you might grow.

Joe

Joe has recently married. He met Sarah at university, and they got married last year as their studies came to an end. Joe is finding marriage wonderful, and awful, and is struggling to understand it at all. There are days when he feels completely in love with Sarah, and they enjoy each other's company, and the time flies as they talk and laugh together. Other days she seems to misunderstand him completely, almost deliberately wind him up, and see the worst in him. And he is shocked at how mean he can be: how he can put her down and hurt her simply to get his own back, or take out the frustrations of the day on her.

He did think that he simply needed to do better, to "man up", but he's realised that he can do more than that. He can understand his marriage as part of his Christian life, as an area of growth. If Christ loved a faithless bride, then Joe can love a grumpy one! He can pray for the Spirit to give him patience when he is tired and Sarah is nagging him. He can respond with love, whether it is his fault or hers. He can apologise and rebuild what he has torn down in her heart.

Joe can see that the first step has to be to see Christ as the great Husband, and then to keep looking at him prayerfully, through the whole day. The other thing Joe has realised is that he needs help if he is going to work this out. Maybe some of the other guys at church could pray for him. Stan, his Bible-study group leader, has been inviting him out for a drink for a couple of weeks—he should take him up on it and ask him for some advice.

Laura

Marriage is where Laura really struggles. She had been married for two years when Ali, a friend at work, invited her to the course to find out about Jesus. Her husband, Dave, wasn't interested in the course or Laura's conversion. She feels that she's tried every way to engage him in church. It is so hard to love a husband who doesn't love God. And she can barely read Bible passages on judgment without crying.

But to see people as made in God's image, and to let their example (when it's good) challenge her to be more Christlike in that area herself, suddenly opens up another way of seeing him at home. She does thank God that Dave is kind and good; she can see God's image in him after all, even though he doesn't know Jesus. And maybe she can help him to connect his own desire to do the right thing to the One who made him to be like that, and who always does do the right thing. That is worth praying about. It would be great to get her small group praying about this too. Maybe there are ways in which they can be more in touch, and help her to submit to her husband and show him that her love of Jesus is a blessing for him, not a rival affection.

Stan

Stan struggles in this area too. He finds the days drag, and he is so lonely as a widower. He misses Peggy terribly. Seeing marriage as a place for growing in Christ doesn't simply leave him sadder, though. It helps to explain something of the depth of his grief. Of course it is terrible for him to be separated from his wife—what is amazing is that Christ would love us as Stan loves Peggy—well, even *more* deeply than he loves Peggy. Stan can see the Spirit using even his grief to show him Jesus.

He can also enjoy seeing Christ in the marriages around him. As he watches his children live out married life, he sees pictures of the love of Christ. He sees them at church as well, and it occurs to him that there are ways the church can grow together in this. When he was a young man, he would have really appreciated some advice as he tried to work out marriage. Maybe Joe would appreciate going out for a drink and talking about Jesus and marriage? He must ask him again.

Family life

Next, Paul moves from marriage to wider family life:

> Children, obey your parents in the Lord, for this is right. "Honour your father and mother"—which is the first commandment with a promise—"so that it may go well with you and that you may enjoy long life on the earth." Fathers, do not exasperate your children; instead, bring them up in the training and instruction of the Lord.
>
> (Ephesians 6 v 1-4)

There is no age limit to verse 1's command to "honour". Just as there are terrible, abusive marriages, there are terrible, abusive parents. That is why we need the church to work out what these verses mean in some truly awful situations. But, whatever our parents are like, we will grow as we honour them. Your Christian growth is as reliant on listening to your mum on the phone on Sunday evening as it is on listening to the preacher on Sunday morning.

Having children has helped me to understand verse 4 in a way that didn't make sense before. I have realised how easily I exasperate my children. I have a tendency to want to win, or to make them pay for interrupting me, being naughty, spoiling my things or taking my time. I want to be worshipped, honoured and respected by my children—I want to be god in my house. The wonderful alternative is that I can become more and more like God, rather than thinking I should be God. I can treat my children gently, shepherding them away from sin, rather than unthinkingly goading them into it. The wonderful reality of Christian growth is that this points both them and me to the love of our Father for us. As I look to Christ and pray for the Spirit to give me patience, wisdom, and joy that I do not feel, he answers. And as I do so, I can teach my little ones that we cannot grow ourselves—we need to ask for help, to pray.

I have seen more of the goodness of Christ over the past few years in parenting than I ever imagined. His work in me gives me the grace to be like him. My failures highlight to me what a great God he is, and how gently and wisely my Father deals with me.

How else might this work itself out?

Joe

Joe and Sarah don't have any children yet, and they're not really planning on trying for a family for a few years. But they are adjusting to new ways of relating to their parents. They have their first Christmas coming up. Joe's dad is a church minister, and so if they're going to see his family around Christmas, it means driving the four hours to their house as his dad has to lead the service on Christmas Day. That would be no hardship for Joe, as he loves family Christmases and Sarah gets on well with his family. Sarah's family are only an hour away, but things aren't so easy there, for either of them. And they would both love to wake up in their own flat on their first Christmas, and go to church with all their friends. They don't really know what it looks like to honour their parents in this decision, but Laura encouraged them at the Bible study last night when they asked for advice and prayer. She said that the fact that they were wanting to honour both their parents meant they probably would. She pointed out that they had grown in this respect since they had joined the church, when they had seemed simply to want to get as far away from their parents as possible! It was really encouraging to be shown how they had grown.

Laura

Patience would be nice! She always feels so tired and near the end of her tether (or several feet beyond it!). She hates how she sometimes screams at her children and is grumpy with her husband. She knows she needs to work at actually asking God for help—he is ready to give her the Holy Spirit, but she needs to depend on him rather than herself. She knows she needs Spirit-given patience around 7pm every night. What an amazing thought, that the seemingly irrational naughtiness of the kids at times could actually be her Father's way of leading her into growth in patience. It is hard to remember at the point when the toothpaste is gleefully squeezed all over the landing carpet, but all she needs to remember then is to pray. She needs to work on relations with her in-laws too. As she pointed out the growth she'd seen in Joe and Sarah last night, she was aware that the Lord has softened her heart towards her own in-laws. Now she needs to swallow her pride and work out how to honour them. It would be quite a shock for Dave too—hopefully in a good way!

Stan

Now that he is a grandpa as well as a dad, Stan is realising that he has an entirely new way of exasperating his children, especially his sons. It seems that even well-meaning advice needs careful delivery to the father of a three-week-old! He wants to grow in this, and to see how he can become more like Jesus. So he is reading through the Gospels to see how Jesus handled people, and learning lots from his ways of asking questions and getting alongside people. He has realised that turning up at his son's house with gardening gloves, and asking how things are going over a cup of tea after tidying up the bushes, allows him more easily to offer advice and encouragement.

He has also realised that he grew hugely when he was a dad, and that it would be good to spend some more time with children to help him keep on growing. Maybe he could offer to babysit for Laura. Or he could see if her husband would appreciate a hand in the garden too—they had a good chat at the carol service last year, and it would be good for him to get to know some more guys at church.

Work

After children, Paul turns to slavery. Slavery was probably the most common form of work for the church members in Ephesus. So while Paul is addressing slaves, it is fair for us to find principles here for how we can grow in Christ as we work:

> Slaves, obey your earthly masters with respect and
> fear, and with sincerity of heart, just as you would obey

Christ. Obey them not only to win their favour when their eye is on you, but as slaves of Christ, doing the will of God from your heart. Serve wholeheartedly, as if you were serving the Lord, not people, because you know that the Lord will reward each one for whatever good they do, whether they are slave or free. And masters, treat your slaves in the same way. Do not threaten them, since you know that he who is both their Master and yours is in heaven, and there is no favouritism with him.

(Ephesians 6 v 5-9)

As we work, there is a strong temptation to work for our own benefit—either avoiding the boss's eye and doing as little as possible for an easy life, or working in a way to catch the eye of the boss and so earn that promotion, bonus or job security we want. Paul short-circuits this by telling us that the boss is always watching, because the boss is Jesus. He sees, and we can work for him. And for the church members who are masters rather than slaves, Paul points out that they still have their own Master, and that they are to act as bosses in ways that reflect the way their Boss uses his authority.

Joe

Joe started a job in a high-street bank a few weeks ago. He is excited about work and the future. He is being put through courses to learn about banking and getting experience in the different departments of the large branch where he is based. There are five of them who were taken on at the same time, and they are all hoping to move quickly into management. It is good to have others learning the ropes at the same time, but they are all aware that they won't progress at the same rate. Maybe they won't all be kept on if the economy takes another dip. It is tempting to catch the eye of the boss, and Joe smiles, thinking of how one of his colleagues has suddenly declared a deep interest in cycling, as it has become apparent that three of the managers are members of the same cycling club.

But then Joe has to be honest that he has kept quiet about his lifelong support of Manchester City after finding out that the branch director is a United season-ticket holder! Thinking about his work as a Christian, he realises that he needs to try to repent of his desire to get ahead at the expense of others. He needs simply to work hard, because Jesus notices all the time. And that will affect how he works too—he needs to take care of his colleagues, and be honest and open about who he is. Maybe he'll wear his United tie on Friday. And maybe he'll take less care to hide his Bible too.

Laura

Laura has been working in the same school for five years now, and she loves it. Her colleagues are great (for the most part!) and she has even had the chance to talk about Jesus with a few of them, just as Ali talked with her. She knows that she has become more cynical, though. Teaching for the next Ofsted inspection is a real pressure, added to that of working hard simply to get pupils though exams.

She wants to practise seeing people as made in God's image. It is so easy to dismiss the disruptive, disrespectful young people. It is even easier to join in the nasty griping about the senior management, inspectors and education officials who know nothing... but if they are all meant to point to Christ and are there for her growth, it needs more thought. Even her head, who is so fixated on results, is made in God's image. Maybe the next time when others are moaning about him, she could pray for him. After all, if Jesus prayed for the men nailing him to his cross, surely she can pray for the man who merely makes her life quite difficult! Maybe at the next staff meeting she can think of something to praise as well as something to question.

Stan

It was a long time ago that Stan installed his last fuse box, although he still enjoys helping out when friends have a problem with a light fitting or plug socket. He misses the work, and the chance it used to give him to go into all sorts of homes and talk to all sorts of people, sometimes about Jesus.

It dawned on him the other day that he needs to read the other part of Paul's teaching in Ephesians. He always worked for others, but now he is a boss. Not of a business, but he has Steph coming in to clean for him each week, and the pastor has asked him to oversee the renovation work in the church hall. What would it be like to treat people as Jesus did? He needs to be fair, and firm—but also generous and thoughtful. Maybe tomorrow he'll make some lunch for the guys working on the hall.

And then there are the others in the church. Work seems more pressured than in his day. Maybe it has always felt like that, but he's had the chance to learn a few lessons. Maybe he has something to offer to Joe and Laura and the others in his group. Maybe he can suggest to the group a couple of studies on working for Jesus. And maybe he could try to arrange his next round of coffees with group members for the end of their work-days so that it will be easy to tease out some of the challenges together.

Church

As I've written this, my little pictures of imaginary "real people" have moved towards the church. I didn't plan that when I started writing the chapter. It is no surprise, though, because it is the church that grows together in Christ. The answer to our problems with growing in Christ lies with one another. And the place where we grow is in the ordinary nitty-gritty of a standard weekday; in the unglamorous surroundings of home and work. This is where the great, cosmic purposes of God are worked out; this is where we can grow. That is exciting, because it means there is no time that is not a time to become more like Christ. But it is also challenging, because it means there is no time to clock off from striving for growth as God lifts us.

The battle for your growth is fought in your kitchen, office, school, garden, street or room and it is won by a bunch of ordinary, struggling people with mugs in one hand and Bibles in the other, supporting one another, and growing as they do so.

10. How suffering can grow us

Suffering and sin can be the soils of great growth in the Christian life.

Some of the chapter topics so far may have been fairly predictable, though I hope the actual contents of those chapters haven't been. But I guess you knew when you picked up a book on Christian growth that we'd look at reading the Bible, praying, being part of church, and so on.

Did you expect a chapter on suffering as a way in which God grows us? And one on sin? The next two chapters take us into two areas we don't tend to see as opportunities for growth; and yet God does.

The reality of suffering

Suffering is a part of normal, day-to-day life. Jesus promised his disciples two truths about this world:

> In this world you will have trouble. But take heart! I have overcome the world.   (John 16 v 33)

You don't have to be alive long, even in the west, to see the truth of this. This is a world fallen away from God, where things are broken and twisted. We suffer the pain of illness and accident. We suffer the consequences of our own sin, and the sin of others. On top of this, Christians can expect to be persecuted for following Christ.

Suffering is everywhere. In one way or another, it is a part of all our lives. Deep down we all know this, and it may well be that for you suffering is very raw and present. In the affluent west, some pain is alleviated. In our secular age, we tend to flee from it, brush over it, downplay it and avoid thinking about it. But it is there, snarling and snapping through our communities, churches and families.

The reason why society tries to ignore it is that it has woefully few answers. But Christians are different. We have amazing answers that are never glib or simplistic but which are full of hope, peace, joy and love. We do not simply grit our teeth in our suffering; we can look to grow like Christ in our suffering.

The confusion of suffering

Suffering may be normal but it is also dangerous. This is because it is confusing. We were created to live in Eden, in a world of beauty, warmth, joy and wonder—and so suffering, rightly, feels wrong. But more than this, because we don't live in Eden anymore, we're tempted to make gods of the gifts God gives. We can worship the freedom our health brings us, the security, comfort or status of the riches we have or long to have. And when suffering comes, it cuts deeply into these things.

So suffering confuses us. How can God love us, we ask, if he lets things like this happen to us? Is he angry with us? Is he even there?

As I have been writing this chapter, the news has been filled with the slaughter of Christians in Iraq, branded with an "N" as followers of the Nazarene, Jesus. They are persecuted by fighters from Islamic State simply for following Jesus. They have not turned from Christ, so why has the Lord let this happen?

You have probably felt this confusion. You visit the grave of someone you love, and you wonder why the Lord did not heal him or give him a few more years. As you go for another round of chemotherapy, the well-meaning accounts of miracles taste like dust—why not you? You find yourself wishing that the Lord didn't hate divorce; or understanding and slightly envying those who end it all, because life is just so painful.

Suffering is dangerous because it can fill our vision. It saps our ability to look to Jesus because it feels as if he has already looked away from us. And so suffering is perhaps the hardest temptation. But it is also an opportunity to see Jesus more clearly than you ever have before. It is the time when we can grow the fastest and strongest. A few years after a terrible fire, the bush often re-grows with greater life and fervour. How can that be?

The growth of suffering

I am writing this chapter against the backdrop of one of those periods of suffering in our church—illnesses that will probably end in death and those that will go on for years, desperate surgery, terrifying mental illness, difficult marriages, exhausting family worries, bereavement, redundancy. This might be easy to write if I lived in an ivory tower, but I don't. Can I really sit down with my friends, look them in the eye, and say that this is a part of God's good plan?

I can, and I must, because the Bible tells us the counter-intuitive, glorious truth that God gives us suffering for our good and our growth.

Paul teaches this in a section of Romans that is remarkable:

> Therefore, since we have been justified through faith,
> we have peace with God through our Lord Jesus Christ,
> through whom we have gained access by faith into this

> grace in which we now stand. And we rejoice in the hope
> of the glory of God. Not only so, but we also rejoice in
> our sufferings, because we know that suffering produces
> perseverance; perseverance, character; and character,
> hope. And hope does not disappoint us, because God
> has poured out his love into our hearts by the Holy
> Spirit, whom he has given us.   (Romans 5 v 1-5, NIV84)

To "rejoice in our sufferings" seems almost impossible! I can see how it is a delightful thing to rejoice in the hope of the glory of God (that is, the certainty we have now that in the future we will be with our glorious God); but can Paul really mean it when he goes on to say: "Not only so, but we also rejoice in our sufferings"? Rejoice in the midst of chemotherapy? Rejoice on the anniversary of your husband's death? Rejoice as you walk into an empty house after taking the kids back to their mum? Rejoice as you face being lashed, beaten, stoned, shipwrecked; as you face sleeplessness and starvation, as Paul himself did (2 Corinthians 11 v 24-27)?

Yes, says Paul. So does James:

> Consider it pure joy, my brothers and sisters, whenever
> you face trials of many kinds.   (James 1 v 2)

So does Peter:

> You greatly rejoice, though now for a little while you may
> have had to suffer grief in all kinds of trials. (1 Peter 1 v 6)

We do not rejoice about the suffering. But we can and do rejoice *in* the suffering, and about what God can use the suffering to do in us.

As we suffer, Paul says, we persevere. We keep trusting God even when he doesn't give us everything we want or he takes away something that we want. It means that we show that our faith is in Christ, not in the things Christ gives us.

That is why perseverance produces character. It reveals a person who is dependent on Christ alone, shaped by him. This is important, because it means that the benefits of suffering are not just for the duration of the suffering. The perseverance we are given as we suffer is not just the Lord strengthening us for that suffering; it is him growing us. The perseverance leads to a permanent growth—it produces Christ-like character.

And such a character, forged in suffering, is marked by hope—hope in the glory of God. How? Suffering makes the other treasures of life less shiny. When suffering removes a treasure from us, it reminds us that that treasure was never permanent. And when suffering threatens someone we love, it reminds us of the relative value of the treasures of this life. When my children have been ill in hospital, I could not care less about what smartphone I have, or what car I drive, or what home I live in! I care that Jesus is real, and good, and so death is not the end and eternity does lie beyond.

Suffering focuses our hopes. It shows us where to put our confidence—in Jesus. It shows us what, or who, we most need, and can never lose—our brother, Jesus. It forces our gaze forwards to the only place where pain is gone—our family home in glory.

Such a hope can never disappoint, because it is relying solely on God's love for us. This love is real, permanent and tangible, poured out into our hearts by the Holy Spirit even as we suffer; and it is then left with us when the suffering ends.

In all things

The remarkable truth is that when we suffer, it is not because God doesn't care. It is because we are his children, his beloved children, and he cares more about our eternal home and our Christian growth than he does about our present comforts.

A few months ago I had to go for some tests for possible cancer. It was no great suffering—it was not that likely I had it; and even if I did, the outcome would probably be a simple operation and then recovery. But even that suffering made me consider what really mattered in life. And I realised that it would be ok—that the worst that could happen was death, and I was amazed to see how Christ filled that horizon. I didn't want to leave my family to suffer, but even the small suffering I had in waiting for the results was a time of huge growth. The Spirit fixed my eyes on Jesus, and I saw that he was better than anything else in life.

Remember what we saw in Romans 8 back in chapter 2 of this book:

> And we know that in all things God works for the good
> of those who love him, who have been called according
> to his purpose. For those God foreknew he also
> predestined to be conformed to the image of his Son,
> that he might be the firstborn among many brothers and
> sisters.   (v 28-29)

In all things. God is at work for our good—for our growth—not only in the good times, but also in the hard ones. Not only in the joys, but in the tears. Not only in the successes, but in the setbacks. This is how it was for God's Son, who was made "perfect through what he suffered" (Hebrews 2 v 10). He was already perfect, but his perfection was tested, proved and showcased in his suffering. And this is how it will be for all of God's children, who will be conformed to Christ through suffering. We are not already perfect, but we grow towards perfection through suffering.

It is as we suffer that we show ourselves, our friends and the world that our God is all in all to us. Take my money, my health, even those I love, and you have not taken what defines me. Unless you take my Jesus, you can't take my hope, my peace, my joy or my love. And you cannot take Jesus from me, because he has suffered before me, and for me, and will never let me go, not even as I pass through death.

Suffer together

Wonderfully, for Christians suffering is never a season that we need to go through alone. Not only do we have God's Spirit within us, but we have God's people around us. Jesus gives us his church in which to grow, in good times but perhaps most of all in hard times. As Paul puts it, as church we must:

> Be devoted to one another in brotherly love ... Share with God's people who are in need. Practise hospitality ... Rejoice with those who rejoice; mourn with those who mourn. (Romans 12 v 10, 13, 15, NIV84)

We need the church to mourn with us; not to offer trite, easy answers, but to be there alongside us. When we rejoice and when we mourn, when we skip through life and when we suffer through life, we do it together. When you suffer, you will need someone to remind you that Jesus is coming, to encourage you that the Spirit is with you, to assure you that God is sovereign and loving. One day you will need a brother or sister to hold your hand and whisper that death is not the end; it is now just a doorway being opened for us to walk through with Jesus on the other side. One day you may be the one doing the reminding, the encouraging, the assuring, or the whispering.

When we suffer, the temptation is to turn in on ourselves and distance ourselves from others. But as Christians, we need to resist that; and be willing to stick close to our church family, and be humble enough to cry with them and lean on them. They, in their turn, will one day need us to provide our shoulder to cry on and our arm to lean on.

How to see suffering

Suffering will come. It may well already have come to you. You may right now be passing through a very difficult valley. The question is not: *Will it come?* but: *What will we do when it does?* Suffering brings a temptation to run away from God, as we focus on what we have lost and decide that since we no longer enjoy that, we cannot be happy and God cannot be good. It is also an opportunity to grow like God, as we learn more and more how precious he is, and as we place our hopes more and more in him.

How do you do that? You learn to see what God is doing in you, what God is planning for you, and you learn to see your suffering as part of his grand design to grow you into someone like Jesus, the someone all of us long to be. This is not easy; it is far easier for me to write this chapter than it is to put it into practice. But it is possible, and it is liberating, because it allows us to see suffering as an opportunity, rather than a disaster.

C. S. Lewis writes a lot about suffering, but one word-picture from his book *Mere Christianity* helps us see that part of our confusion at suffering is because God is doing something grander in us than we first imagined:

> Imagine yourself as a living house. God comes in to rebuild that house. At first, perhaps, you can understand what he is doing. He is getting the drains right and stopping the leaks in the roof and so on; you knew that those jobs needed

doing and so you are not surprised. But presently he starts
knocking the house about in a way that hurts abominably
and does not seem to make any sense. What on earth is
he up to? The explanation is that he is building quite a
different house from the one you thought of—throwing out
a new wing here, putting on an extra floor there, running
up towers, making courtyards. You thought you were being
made into a decent little cottage: but he is building a
palace. he intends to come and live in it himself.

If you are suffering at the moment, you need to work out how the Lord is growing you now. If you are not suffering at present, it is perhaps even more important to think about how he will grow you next time suffering hits. Whether you are suffering or not, it might be more helpful to think through past suffering as you can see the results more easily, and then apply your findings to your present sufferings. If you can grab a pencil and paper, it will probably help you to reflect more deeply on these things. Why not make a note that you can tuck in your Bible for the next time suffering cuts into your life?

Think through the temptations that suffering brought—did they lead you to doubt your Father's love or kindness towards you? Did they expose parts of your character that you wish were not there? How did they affect your relationships in your family, your church and with God?

When we suffered the death of our first child in early pregnancy (a "miscarriage"), the particular area of temptation I faced was to doubt the kindness of the Lord. I did not doubt his sovereignty over life and death, but the temptation was to see Jesus as good only in an aloof and distant way—doing good to us for our benefit, whether we like it or not, in this case by the death of my tiny child. I was tempted to see God as good in the way a judge is good, not in the way a Father is good. I needed to see how suffering could tempt me before I would be able to see how suffering might grow me.

Once you've seen the real dangers and temptations of suffering, and how they particularly affect you, you can move on to seeing the growth that suffering brings. First, what particular blessings did Christ bring in your suffering? When we were struggling with the miscarriage and I was tempted to doubt the kindness of Jesus, we had a particular awareness of his love and closeness at that time. I felt the kindness of Christ in a way that made doubting it impossible. And we were very aware of being children of God, and that both we and our child were loved by him as dear children of the most warm and generous Father. We were also blessed by many expressions of love from our church family. Along with the cards we now treasure, particularly memorable was three lads who lived opposite us turning up with flowers for my wife, saying they had got them because they didn't know what to do. The fact that Tim, Joe and Richard loved us enough to do something, and to come when they felt awkward and unsure, was a massive blessing.

Next, ask yourself: how did your Father grow you? How did you learn perseverance, Christ-like character and gospel hope during that time, which has lasted beyond that time? Since the miscarriage, the promises of the resurrection always shine more brightly for me, and death has lost its sting in even deeper ways than before. How about you? What foundations for growth has Jesus laid in the suffering you are reflecting on?

What about the suffering you are facing now? How can you apply the lessons you have learned from past suffering to the next lot? And how do the ways in which the Lord has grown you in Christ put you in a better place to grasp the opportunity for growth that your next bout of suffering will bring?

It is not easy to grow in suffering, because it is not easy to suffer. Suffering will always make us groan because it is not what we were created for. But suffering need not make us grumble about life and against God. God's children have a better response: to let suffering be the ground in which God grows us, as we appreciate Christ more, and become more and more like him. You cannot choose whether or not you will suffer, but you can grow towards Christ as you do suffer. Why not pray now that it will be him you focus on? Why not ask a friend at church to remind you that God is working for your good when suffering next comes (perhaps it's today)? Why not memorise Romans 5 v 1-5 for the day when you will need to tell it to yourself? Suffering can drag your weeping eyes from Jesus... or you can see him more clearly through the tears than you ever did in the sunshine.

11. How sin can grow us

There is one area of life in which I think we can grow even faster, and even more surprisingly, than in our suffering. It's when we sin.

If that sounds strange to you, don't worry—it should! Sin is not junk food; you have to be careful not to have too much, but it's fine as an occasional treat in an otherwise holy diet. Sin is poison. It kills us: "The wages of sin is death" (Romans 6 v 23). And that is why it is so strange, and so strangely wonderful, that times of great growth can come through our sin. Sin should kill us, but our awesome Father is so committed to helping us grow up as his children that he can and will even bend the evil of sin to his good plans. He will take the poison and make it nutritious, even as we gulp it down.

How to grow through failure

Of course, we need to avoid sin. But we also need to see how we can use the times when we do sin. Jesus explains this in one of his most famous parables, the one about two sons.

> There was a man who had two sons. The younger one said to his father, "Father, give me my share of the estate." So he divided his property between them.
>
> (Luke 15 v 11-12)

The younger son would rather have had his father's gifts than his father's presence. So he leaves home, Jesus continues, and blows his entire fortune partying. He runs out of cash just as famine hits the country and he takes a job feeding pigs, now so hungry that the pig swill looks delicious to him.

And now comes the turning point of his story:

> When he came to his senses, he said, "How many of my father's hired servants have food to spare, and here I am starving to death! I will set out and go back to my father and say to him: Father, I have sinned against heaven and against you. I am no longer worthy to be called your son; make me like one of your hired servants." So he got up and went to his father. (v 17-20)

When this son returns home, he is amazed to find that his father welcomes him with open arms. Refusing even to consider the option that his son is no longer worthy to be his son, the father immediately reinstates him in the family with joy, kisses and feasting. For this wayward son, the story has the happiest ending imaginable. He starts the day feeding the pigs alone, and ends it eating steak with his father. He ends up back home, appreciating his father in a way that he never had when all he wanted was his father's cash.

But what is it that leads the son to come home, to see the amazing love of his father, to enjoy his father's company in a way he never had before? What caused this younger son to grow in his relationship with his dad and be transformed in his own outlook?

It is seeing his sin.

It is the partying, go-hard-don't-go-home lifestyle of this young man that lands him in the gutter and leads him into growth, back to his family in repentance. Jesus' message is that God welcomes sinners home with open arms; but he is also showing that our sin is where we start when we set out home. God can use our sin to grow us.

This is not just a story; it is a reality. When Jesus talks to Simon Peter later in Luke's Gospel, the night before his death, he tells his headstrong friend:

> "Simon, Simon, Satan has asked to sift all of you as wheat. But I have prayed for you, Simon, that your faith may not fail. And when you have turned back, strengthen your brothers." But he replied, "Lord, I am ready to go with you to prison and to death." Jesus answered, "I tell you, Peter, before the cock crows today, you will deny three times that you know me."   (Luke 22 v 31-34)

Jesus knows that Simon Peter will deny that he even knows him; his courage will fail and he will betray his friend and God. And Jesus says that this sin will be part of Peter's path to church leadership, to knowing how to strengthen his brothers. Few men grow as much as Peter did between his first meetings with Jesus and his letters to the churches. And his greatest sin was one of the places of his greatest growth. After all, God is working in all things for the good of those who love him (Romans 8 v 28). We saw that this includes suffering. Now we discover it includes even sin.

How to grow when you sin

As with suffering, sin brings a great temptation to run from God, as well as a great opportunity to grow towards him. If we react to our sin by excusing it, or seeking to make up for it, then we shrink. But if we respond by owning it, and coming home from it, we are transformed. Here's how.

It is only as we see the wickedness and misery of our sin that we are amazed at the free love and forgiveness there is in Christ. I have prayed with wonder many times, thanking God that I am his child and that my sin, fresh before my eyes, is already paid for by Christ on his cross. It is as we see the pig-swill of our sin that we take the road of repentance home to our Father, and marvel at his forgiveness.

The younger son in Luke 15 had probably been hugged by his father many times. He would surely have heard words of love and delight from his dad every day as he grew up. But it was only as he limped home, desperately aware of his sin against his dad, reeking of the pigs, tattered and broken, that he understood who his father was. In that circumstance, his father's embrace and words of love and forgiveness changed everything. This is a picture of conversion, when someone becomes a Christian; but it is also a picture of every return from sin. However many times you turn for home, you will never reach the door without your Father's embrace. You will never need to get through your apology before the reassurance of Christ's love comes with bear-hugging, ring-giving, party-throwing warmth.

We can use our sin to keep leading us to Christ, and so we can use it to keep growing us. We can use it to remember all over again that we do not deserve to be children of God, but that lack of merit makes no difference to our status. It makes no difference to our Father's love. As we see our sin, we see Christ running towards us; and as we see Christ, we grow.

Let me give you an example from my experience. My prayer life is often shocking. I get on with the day without turning to the Lord, I go about all sorts of jobs at work without asking for the Spirit to fill me, and I have most conversations with family and friends without asking our Father for his wisdom.

This is despite believing everything I wrote about prayer in this book! Then I catch myself praying a prayer of desperation when a situation has got beyond my abilities, and I wonder cynically why the Lord should listen now when I have ignored him for so long. His answer shatters my cynicism: *I will listen because you are my beloved son, with whom I am well-pleased.* In my prayerless sin, my Father sees me as his son, treats me like Jesus and loves me as only a perfect Father could. He will listen and answer because my relationship with him never depends on me; it depends on Christ. With the stench of the pigs still in my nostrils, the gravy-smell of the roasting calf is so much better; it is the life-giving fragrance of Christ's love and forgiveness. I grow as I see him. I grow as I think about these truths again. And then I pray, and so grow all the more as I repent and turn once more to my Saviour.

Just reflect for a moment on when you have been most amazed at Jesus, when your eyes have been most full of his love, and when you have grown to love him and long to be like him. I wouldn't be surprised if some of those times were when you had realised the horror of your own sin. I would bet that you appreciated Christ far more in your failures than in your successes.

All this might lead us to wonder: if sin helps us grow up in the family of God, shouldn't we sin more?! Let's ask that recently-returned son the same question. He wakes up the day after the party, back in his own bed. As he lies there, he remembers how good his father's welcome was, particularly after the mess he had been in before. That warm love, spontaneous affection and powerful welcome home, not as a servant but as a son, was the best day of his life. He's never loved his Father more or felt closer to him. He would like to go on living like that.

So he decides to get some more of it. He gets up early, steals the goat his brother was hoping to enjoy, pockets any loose change lying around, and heads off to a distant country. He is already looking forward to finding a pigsty to live in and starve in, so that he can come back home again.

But of course, that's the last thing this man does! If he wants to enjoy his father's love, he doesn't need to go to the pigsty again; he just needs to go down to breakfast! The grace of God is not like badges that we can collect—it is a relationship we can enjoy. When we sin—when we experience the emptiness, disappointment and guilt it produces—we can appreciate by contrast the gracious love of God and the joy of closeness to him. And as we return, we find ourselves back home where we always needed to be, where we most enjoy life. We see sin for the pigsty it is; we resolve not to go back there; and we know God's family for what it is, and we decide to stay there. Next time the distant land and living as a stranger to God beckons, we stay home and live as a son. Of course, we don't do this all the time—often we sin, and then the Lord grows us through running down the road to meet us as we stagger back. But sometimes we resist temptation and as we do so, we live as free sons, enjoying our Father's close smile. In this sense, we grow in spite of and through our sin, and we grow when we don't sin.

How to be good and not grow

The power of God to grow us even when we sin lies in the nature of sin. At root, sin is not moral evil; it is hatred and indifference. It is turning away from loving God to a love of ourselves. This is what we see in the story of the father and his wayward son. The son did not begin to sin when he drank the ninth pint, or even the first. He did not begin to sin when he left home, or when he demanded his share of the inheritance. He began to sin long before, when he was a hard-working, obedient member of the family. He began to sin whenever it was that he stopped loving his father.

And he is not the only son who stopped loving his father. Famously, there is an older brother in the story, too. And when the younger son is accepted back into the family, the older son stays outside the family home, furious with his father:

> Look! All these years I've been slaving for you and
> never disobeyed your orders. Yet you never gave me
> even a young goat so I could celebrate with my friends.
> But when this son of yours who has squandered your
> property with prostitutes comes home, you kill the
> fattened calf for him! (Luke 15 v 29-30)

The older brother has not been partying, he has not left home, and he has not demanded money from his father. He has not failed. He has simply done what he was told. And the surprising fact is that this obedience has left him outside his father's home and his father's embrace. One son finds his dad's acceptance; the other son rejects his father.

This is because the root of sin is turning away from God, not turning towards indulgence. You can sin as deeply in a Bible study as in a brothel. God expresses this strikingly through the prophet Jeremiah:

> My people have committed two sins: They have forsaken
> me, the spring of living water, and have dug their
> own cisterns, broken cisterns that cannot hold water.
> (Jeremiah 2 v 13)

Of course it is a sin for people to worship other gods, and it will never satisfy; but the sin that comes before turning to another god is to turn away from God, the spring of living water. That is always the first sin.

The younger brother turned away from his father to the allure of the party scene. The older brother turned away from his father to self-dependent achievement. He did not obey out of love for his father, but out of love for himself. And again, this is not just a story; it is reality. Jesus was telling his parable to two groups of people—those who had failed, and those who hadn't:

> Now the tax collectors and sinners were all gathering round to hear Jesus. But the Pharisees and the teachers of the law muttered, "This man welcomes sinners, and eats with them." (Luke 15 v 1-2)

The tax collectors turned from God to worship wealth and possessions: the Pharisees turned from God to worship their self-righteous goodness. And it was the tax collectors who came home.

You do not sin only when you do wrong, nor are you righteous just because you do good. I have prayed with boredom, preached with pride, read the Bible selfishly and sung hymns with hatred in my heart. A "good" person is not necessarily a growing person. In fact, a "good" person can be busily walking out of the family home. You can "never fail", and never grow. You can repeatedly fail, and grow both despite and because of those failures.

God runs down the road

We are still sinners, and will be until Christ returns and finishes what he has begun in us. That means that we can use the times when we sin as a means of growth. It means that when you sin, don't listen to Satan. He loves to accuse

Christians. He will tell you that you've blown it with God, that there is no way back for someone as wretched as you. Or he will tell you that God will need a show of commitment now, a bit of grovelling, that you'll be in his bad books for a few days. Maybe he will whisper that now you'll never reach the potential God had for you; you're on plan B now (or plan M).

Whatever he whispers, he lies. You are a dearly loved child of God. Your sin does not have the power to undo the cosmic wonder of the cross of Christ. You are not mighty enough in your wickedness to defeat the Spirit's ability to make you a child of God. The younger son made one mistake on his way back home: he thought it was up to him to determine who his father would call a son. He only got halfway though his apology, and the point where the father cut in is hugely significant:

> The son said to him, "Father, I have sinned against heaven and against you. I am no longer worthy to be called your son." But the father said to his servants, "Quick! Bring the best robe and put it on him. Put a ring on his finger and sandals on his feet..." (Luke 15 v 21-22)

As the son declares he is not worthy to be a son, the father calls for the best robe, the ring and the sandals. The father is saying to his son: *You don't get to make that call. I do. And I say you are my son.*

You don't need to stay at a distance or work your way back into favour. God runs down the road to you in Christ and hugs you in your dirt. And as you see this, as you realise there is no country too distant for God to bring you home from, your heart is melted, you love coming home and staying home, you want to live with and like and for your Father and Brother, and you grow at a rate you would never have believed.

You and I will sin today. The question is, when we have run away, will we keep running and keep going, or will we come back and keep growing? Next time you realise you have sinned, ask God to use that sin to grow you by showing you the emptiness of life without him, by reminding you of the wonder of his forgiveness, and by thrilling you with the joy of life back home, living as his child.

We are still sinners, but God will use even our sin to grow us. That is the sort of family we are part of. That is the sort of Father we have.

12. Where we're growing to

Growing as a Christian is not a job. It is a journey.

> See what great love the Father has lavished on us, that
> we should be called children of God! And that is what we
> are! The reason the world does not know us is that it did
> not know him. Dear friends, now we are children of God,
> and what we will be has not yet been made known. But
> we know that when Christ appears, we shall be like him,
> for we shall see him as he is. All who have this hope in
> him purify themselves, just as he is pure. (1 John 3 v 1-3)

In these short verses, John tells us who we are, where we are
going, who we will be... and that we will therefore grow.

Beloved children

John begins with the love of God for us. Our Father has
lavished great love on us. How great is his love? We—you
and me—are "called children of God! And that is what we
are!" (v 1). We have been adopted into the divine royal family.
God has brought us into his family as we are, and he loves us
enough not to leave us as we are.

So everything starts with understanding who we are as loved
children—including our growth. It is my love for my children
that moves me to provide the best environment I can for their

growth—food, housing, warmth, toys, education, health care and so on. But more importantly, my love directly grows them because my love makes me delight in relating to them. As I play with them, talk with them and live with them, I open myself up and help them to grow up. I have three daughters, and I long for them to grow up happily, and the way in which my wife and I love them will be a large part of that.

To be a child is to be in a relationship, and it's a relationship that can't stay still. Babies stay children, but they don't stay babies! We grow up. Always children, and always growing. This is why the family language of the Bible is so good. It gives us both security and hope. Being children gives us the security of an unshakeable love from our Father, and the hope of ongoing growth in relationship with him.

As we come to the end of this book, it is crucial to pause here. Nothing in this book is rooted in our goodness, wisdom or strength. We do not deserve growth, earn growth or achieve growth. God our Father grows us up to be like him, in relationship with him, because he loves us.

Do you know God loves you? Do you know and live as though God is your loving Father? This is the start of everything. You will only experience growth to the extent that you appreciate the love of your Father.

We are waiting

We are growing children, and we are waiting children.

When I was young, my father had to travel away on business sometimes. I can remember waiting with my mum and brother at airports and stations for him to come home. When he came through the gate, suit carrier slung over his shoulder and tie loose, I would yell and run to him, and he would smile and kneel down and hug me and my brother.

Hundreds of times a day this scene is played out at stations and airports all over the world, as children meet parents and wives greet husbands, and I love it every time I see it, because one day I'll be doing the yelling and running again. One day our Father will come home to us. Jesus will come back for us and we will be thrilled to meet our great Husband.

And on that day, "when Christ appears, we shall be like him, for we shall see him as he is" (v 2). At the moment, we grow as the Spirit shows us Jesus, so that we see how to be like him, and long to be like him, and so grow to be like him. One day, we will see Jesus face to face. There will be no sin left in us to cloud our gaze. And we will be entirely, utterly conformed to his image. We will finally be the people God made us to be and we long to be. We will, at last, have grown up. This is the great promise of our growth—it will succeed!

You may feel as though you're in a rut. You may be frustrated with your Christian growth—it always seems to be one step forward, most of a step back. You may have forgotten all about growing until you started reading this book. But if you are trusting Christ, you are a child of God. And if you are a child of God, you shall be like him, for one day you shall see him as he is.

We are growing

A friend of mine has a two-year-old boy who recently started at pre-school. He needed a backpack to take his morning snack and change of clothes in, so his mum bought him one the week before and explained that at the very exciting pre-school he was about to start, he would get to wear this backpack. It was not just any old backpack—it was a Paddington Bear backpack, which for many two-year-old boys is quite close to the new creation.

What did this toddler do? He put the backpack on. There was a week to go until pre-school began. He would wear it the next week anyway, but he wanted to wear it *now*. It was a great backpack, it was part of being a "big boy" who went to pre-school, and so he wore it virtually every waking hour.

You will one day be just like Jesus. Today, you can become a little more like you will be that day. You can put on Christ-likeness in preparation for the day when you are totally like Christ. If you know where you are going in the future, you will be committed to and excited about growing in the present.

That is John's point at the end of this wonderful passage:

> All who have this hope in him purify themselves, just as
> he is pure. (v 3)

You know Jesus. You know what he is like. And if you know that, then you will want to be like him. And that is what Christian growth is. If eternity were boring, all about sitting around on a cloud playing a harp, we might hope that we'll like it once we're there, but it doesn't motivate us to start harp lessons! But since eternity is us being with Jesus, enjoying life in the family home, we'll want to live as a child right now!

God did not save you so you could survive as a Christian. He adopted you so you could thrive as his child. He is working each day, in so many ways, to grow you to be like Jesus. And he has invited you to be part of his work in you—to strive as he lifts. Nothing can stop it, and everything can contribute to it—even your suffering and even your sin.

Now I *ought* to grow. I know *how* to grow. I *will* grow. And, wonderfully, I *want* to grow.

How about you?

LIVEDIFFERENT

HONEST EVANGELISM

This is a book that is honest about the costs, and excited about the effects, of evangelism. And, as he draws on decades of experience, Rico shows how you—whoever you are and however you feel—can talk about Jesus with those who don't yet know him, but need to meet him.

We desperately need to read this compelling book. 'Honest Evangelism' is the 'Know and Tell the Gospel' for today. I pray that every Christian will get it and read it!

GARY MILLAR, PRINCIPAL, QUEENSLAND THEOLOGICAL COLLEGE, AUSTRALIA

LIVING WITHOUT WORRY

If you ever worry, and would love to worry less, this book is for you. You will not find trite, easy answers; but you will find real ones, as you discover what worry is, why you feel it, and how you can replace it with an experience of real, lasting peace in all the ups and downs of your life.

thegoodbook
COMPANY
Opening up the Bible

At The Good Book Company, we are dedicated to helping Christians and local churches grow. We believe that God's growth process always starts with hearing clearly what he has said to us through his timeless word—the Bible.

Ever since we opened our doors in 1991, we have been striving to produce resources that honour God in the way the Bible is used. We have grown to become an international provider of user-friendly resources to the Christian community, with believers of all backgrounds and denominations using our Bible studies, books, evangelistic resources, DVD-based courses and training events.

We want to equip ordinary Christians to live for Christ day by day, and churches to grow in their knowledge of God, their love for one another, and the effectiveness of their outreach.

Call us for a discussion of your needs or visit one of our local websites for more information on the resources and services we provide.

UK & Europe: www.thegoodbook.co.uk
North America: www.thegoodbook.com
Australia: www.thegoodbook.com.au
New Zealand: www.thegoodbook.co.nz

UK & Europe: 0333 123 0880
North America: 866 244 2165
Australia: (02) 6100 4211
New Zealand (+64) 3 343 1990

THE BLUSH

By the same author

Published by Peter Davies, Ltd.

At Mrs Lippincote's
Palladian
A View of the Harbour
A Wreath of Roses
A Game of Hide-and-Seek
The Sleeping Beauty
Hester Lilly
Angel
In a Summer Season

Published by Chatto & Windus, Ltd.

The Soul of Kindness
A Dedicated Man
Mossy Trotter
The Wedding Group

THE BLUSH

and other stories

ELIZABETH TAYLOR

LONDON : PETER DAVIES

To
WILLIAM MAXWELL

F

Printed and Bound in Great Britain by
Bookprint Limited, Crawley, Sussex

Contents

These stories have previously appeared as follows: *Cornhill Magazine* (The Letter-Writers, A Troubled State of Mind, The True Primitive, Hare Park); *Lady Cynthia Asquith's Third Ghost Book* (Poor Girl); *New Yorker* (The Blush, The Letter-Writers, Summer Schools, Perhaps a Family Failing, You'll Enjoy It When You Get There); *Vogue* New York (A Troubled State of Mind); *Woman and Beauty* (Good-bye, Good-bye); *Woman's Own* (The Ambush, The Rose, The Mauve, The White).

The Ambush

A FEW weeks after the funeral, Catherine went back to stay with the Ingrams. Uncertain, during those weeks, how much grief was suitable to her—for she and Noël had not been officially engaged and in the eyes of the world she saw her status as mourner undecided—she had shown no sign of sorrow, for one tear might release the rest and one word commit her to too many others. Her fortitude was prodigious, even alone after the funeral when all that she had keyed herself up to was over. She avoided the drawer where his letters were; the air about her, at the art school by day and with her parents at home, was full of warnings and tensions. She felt jolted and stunned, as if she had been in his car at the time of the accident, and she walked about slowly and carefully, suffering from a stiffness of her limbs and a sensation of vertigo. By the end of the first month her effort had told on her—the energy spent in fending off other people and the sympathy they might offer, the holding back of tears, left her weak and apathetic. The boredom of her grief was not its easiest part to bear—the irritation of having nothing but her loss ever enter her mind now, when once she had had so many thoughts, dulled all her days and her dreams at night. Her parents were thankful when she took herself off to the Ingrams and they could come down from their tightrope and relax.

Mrs Ingram met her at the station. Catherine saw her first, standing on the platform, scanning the carriages as the

1

doors began to open. She was wearing a mauve gingham
frock and her white hair was blown back from her forehead
and from that plane below her high cheekbone which Noël
had had, too, and which made, Catherine thought, those
two faces the most beautiful she had ever known.

"I am here," she said, setting down her suitcase for a
moment while she was kissed.

"Dear Catherine, I am so glad you came before it was
dark." Her seemingly meaningless phrases were often
found, later, to have some meaning after all.

A soldier, for Mrs Ingram's sake, not Catherine's, had
lifted the suitcase and was carrying it out to the station-yard.
A wake of devotion always followed her and Catherine
joined her own homage to the rest.

They got into Mrs Ingram's tinny little shopping car and
drove away through the red-brick Thames-side village and
down darkening lanes scented with elder-blossom.

"Esmé is still with us," Mrs Ingram said. "I wanted you
to come before his leave was over."

Esmé was Noël's elder brother, adored first-born, whom
Catherine had heard of for years, resented somewhat on
Noël's account and seen fleetingly at the funeral, to which he
had come from abroad.

"You will be someone young for him," Mrs Ingram
said.

She drove as if she were a goddess in a chariot, her white
hands confident, her head erect. Sometimes she waved to
children who pressed back against the hedges, staring.

They turned through iron gates into the tunnel of trees
leading up to the house; a haze of gnats danced under the
bitten leaves; cow-parsley was grey in the shadows. The
drive ended suddenly and they were under the high façade
of the house with its rows of Georgian windows diminishing
in height at each storey and the panelled door and rounded
fanlight. Lights were on on the ground floor and a young

man came out of the house and down the steps towards
them.

Not quite up to the shock of seeing even a slight re-
semblance to Noël, Catherine was obliged to look up at what
she had steadfastly at the funeral ignored. This brother had
the same eyes, shrewd and alert, lines from laughter
beneath them—for as a family they seemed to have laughed
a great deal. When Mrs Ingram did so, she became even
more beautiful—a rare thing in a woman; laughter en-
livened her features and never disorganised them. Esmé
was heavier than Noël; his features less defined; his colour
paler. The beautiful flatness under the cheekbone he
lacked. Catherine could imagine him in middle-age rather
puffy under the eyes and stout and inactive and even, later,
gouty as his father had been.

Catherine saw the house in the last of the light—
perhaps its most magical time. It was ashen and flat against
the dark trees. Beyond the lawns the river slid by and she
could hear and smell the tumbling water at the weir. Moths
followed them into the lighted hall. Damp had drained
colour from great patches of the crimson walls, but the
room was in brilliant contrast to outside. The tall clock only
tocked, never ticked, Noël had said. On a table was a disarray
of flowers and baskets and vases, for Mrs Ingram had left
for the station in the middle of building a great pyramid of
honeysuckle and peonies. She now, leading Catherine to
her room, looked back regretfully at her interrupted work.
Could not Esmé have fetched me, then? Catherine wondered, apologetic as always. Or wouldn't he?

From her bedroom's two long windows she would be able
to see the river when it was daylight again.

"I hope the weir won't disturb you," Mrs Ingram said,
as if Catherine had never stayed in the house before. "I
never hear it now."

When Esmé had brought in the suitcase and gone, Mrs

Ingram embraced Catherine again. "So lovely that you are here," she murmured. "Come down soon and have a drink after your long journey."

She looked round the room, pulled at a curtain and rearranged some white geraniums in a pewter mug before she left Catherine alone.

The girl had the most extraordinary feeling of dizziness from so much sudden beauty—the beauty of Mrs Ingram herself whose footsteps were now light and hastening on the oak staircase, and the house and garden and this room scented with pinks and sounding of the river.

On the wall above the writing-table hung a water-colour drawing of Esmé and Noël as children—vaguely done, insipidly pretty and not worthy of their mother's room. They sat on a sofa together and had a picture-book open across their knees. The smocking on their blouses was painstakingly tinted in and Esmé's tawny curls were carefully high-lighted though nothing much could be made of Noël's straight black hair. His eyes were round and unseeing and bright as forget-me-nots. Fond drawing by a relative, Catherine thought. She herself had never drawn Noël, either fondly or objectively. The nearest she had got to that, she reflected, was once sketching his foot when he was lying on the lawn after swimming. She had been drawing the gable of the boathouse and branches of a chestnut-tree and, for some reason turning to look at him, began on a corner of the paper to draw his foot with its bony ankle and raised veins. Then he had slapped one foot against the other to chase off a fly. She had rubbed out the sketch, blown at the paper and quickly covered up the smudge with a clump of rushes. She had trembled as if hoping to hide some misdemeanour, but was calm again when he stood up and came to look at her drawing. She had added an imaginary dragonfly above the rushes and then, at his request, a heron. What became of the drawing she could not now recall.

Mrs Ingram was in the hall when Catherine went downstairs. The uncarpeted staircase could be an ordeal, so much of it exposed to the hall, and now Mrs Ingram looking up and smiling as she stripped leaves from the peonies. Voices echoed here, and whatever Esmé said as he came from the library carrying a decanter was lost to Catherine.

She took her glass of whisky and Esmé pulled a chair out from the table for her where she could watch Mrs Ingram's flower-arranging. A pale greyhound lay on a window-seat, and Esmé sat down beside it, fingering its silky ears.

"Other women I know do the flowers in the morning," he said.

"You need not stay with me."

She tore some leaves from a stalk with an asperity to match her voice, an asperity Catherine had never heard before, but which she always had felt to be a dreaded possibility in people as decisive as Mrs Ingram.

Esmé sat far back in the shadows stroking the dog's ears, not replying.

This hall was at the heart of the house—open to the garden in fine weather, a place for casual conversations and chance meetings. The last time Catherine was there it had been filled with wreaths, cushions of carnations propped against chair-legs, Mrs Ingram's hoop of roses and camellias lying on the table. It had had a drab symmetry about it, with its suggestion of flowers bought by the dozen and Catherine had seen the glance it received, the weary contempt with which it was put aside as beyond improving.

Now Mrs Ingram carried the big soup tureen of flowers and stood it against the wall, stepped back to view it while Esmé yawned and clapped his hands, then called to his dog and went out into the garden.

Mrs Ingram sank into a chair the moment he had gone as if she had no need now to be busy.

"I shall send you to bed soon," she told Catherine. "You

look tired after your journey;" and then as Catherine was obediently finishing her whisky she asked, "How are you getting over Noël?"

At home, no one had dared to say this name and Catherine was unprepared to hear it and could think of no reply.

"Don't defer it, or try to pay off in instalments," Mrs Ingram said. "One only pays more in the end." She sat so still with her elbow among the litter of leaves on the table and her cheek resting on her hand. "I knew you would take it in this way, poor Catherine, and that is why I asked you to come here." She gave the smile that was always so much remembered when Catherine had left her and was trying to reassemble the look of her, feature by feature, in her mind. The smile was the only uncertain thing about her, wavering, pleading; deep lines broke up the smoothness of her face and her regality—the Blue Persian look, Noël had called it—vanished.

I love her, Catherine thought. I could never withstand her, no matter what she wanted of me.

When she was in bed, she wondered why such a thought had come to her, when there was no longer anything Mrs Ingram could want of her, no longer anything she could ask her to relinquish. Strangeness and the physical beauty of the place overtook her. She was under this roof again, but the old reason for being there was gone. Listening to the weir, lying in the flower-scented room, between the cool sheets (Mrs Ingram's linen was glassier than anyone else's, she thought), she fell under the spell of the family again, although the one of it she loved was dead. Missing him, it was in this place she wanted to be, no other.

She heard Esmé crossing the gravel again and calling in a low voice to the dog.

* * *

In the morning, the garden, drenched with dew, flashed

with rainbow colours; the meadows on the other side of the river gently steamed. The sun had already warmed the carpet under the windows. Catherine stood there barefoot looking down on the dazzling scene. She could hear the grating sound of oars in rowlocks before Esmé appeared round the river-bend under the silvery willows. She watched him coming up from the boathouse. His footprints were dark on the dewy grass and the dog's paw-prints ran in circles about them. He was especially tender with his dog, would be with all animals and with children, as some bachelors are, she guessed.

When Catherine had stayed in the house on other occasions, Mrs Ingram had always had breakfast in bed. She had a clever way of not being seen coming downstairs, but of being discovered later very busy about the house, at her desk or coming from the kitchen with a list in her hand, as if she had been about since daybreak, the reins gathered in her hands for hours. This morning, Catherine, coming downstairs, was surprised to hear Mrs Ingram and Esmé talking in the dining-room. "If you object, I can go to *his* place instead." That was Esmé. Then his mother said quickly, "I don't object . . ." and paused, as if she were about to add a second clause that would take the meaning from the first. She got as far as saying 'but' and then heard the footsteps in the hall and Catherine came into the room to a tense silence and rearranged expressions.

Mrs Ingram was standing by the window, drinking coffee. Esmé rose from the table and, doing so, scattered some pages of a letter over the carpet. His mother glanced, then glanced away. She really does look as if she has been up since dawn, Catherine thought. Perhaps *she* doesn't sleep, either.

The warmth of Mrs Ingram's smile welcomed her and Catherine regretted the stiffness and timidity of her own that answered it. She felt full of a jerky vagueness, and the beginning of a fear that the house with its associations might undermine her and expose some nerve in an intolerable way. She was constantly alarmed at the possibility of behaving badly and trembled to think of the presumption of not holding back a grief that Mrs Ingram herself seemed able to contain. The strain was not merely of never being herself, but of not knowing who she any longer was.

She took a chair opposite Esmé's and Mrs Ingram came back to the table to pour out coffee, but without sitting down.

"Are you going out sketching this morning?" she asked Catherine; for that was how she had spent her mornings on other visits.

Catherine stared down at her boiled egg as if she were wondering what curious object she had been given, so dismayed was her expression. Esmé, who had put away his letter, looked across at her but wished that he had not. There was a sign of a crack in her sedate composure.

She said: "Yes, I think I will do that."

"Then we shall all meet at luncheon."

Mrs Ingram was brisk, as if now Catherine was disposed of for the morning. This was unlike her, Esmé thought: but his mother was definitely up to something and he wondered for whom ill was boded, Catherine or himself. Some wonderful ill, no doubt, he thought; done for one's good; a great, bracing, visionary ill. Even if I want to paint again, Catherine thought, I don't want to be in the painting *mood* —so exposed and inviting. She had brought her painting materials with her and knew that she must rouse herself to work again and better here, perhaps, than at her own home with its too patent watchfulness, the irritating parental concentration upon her and all her doings and the secret discussions she could imagine just as if she had overheard them. "Now she is painting again. Such a good sign. We will pretend not to have noticed."

So after breakfast she went down to the river and along the bank until she reached the lock. Much about the Thames Valley is Victorian—the canopied steamers and the red brick lock-keepers' houses and the little shelters with spiked edges to their wooden roofs like miniature railway platforms. The garden beds of marguerites, calceolarias, were edged with whitewashed stones and slung about with whitened chains; all was neat and two-dimensional, like a primitive painting, captivating, bright and unconvincing.

Beyond the lock was a stretch of river, darkened and smothered by dusty, summer chestnuts; the oily, olive-green water slid by, was brown when the sun went in; a boat tied up in the rushes had no reflection. The other bank, in contrast, was silvery with aspens and willows, with shifting white leaves and light.

She sat on the bank and unpacked her water-colours. The sun was strong now, the light banal, she thought fretfully, narrowing her eyes to blur what she saw too sharply and with too many irrelevances. She felt a deep reluctance to begin painting on this lulled and buzzing mid-morning, and felt too that she had been expelled, excluded from Mrs Ingram's presence where she wanted to be, and sent off to do her painting as a child might be sent to practise scales.

She slapped at the horse-flies biting her bare legs. They were always a plague—the towing-path flies—and on other summer days Noël had sat beside her and waved them away with his handkerchief while she painted. Her irritation suddenly heeled over into grief and she dropped her brush, stunned, appalled, as the monstrous pain leapt upon her. Her painting—the faint washes of grey and green which had lifted the paper—dried in the sun, the jar of water was scarcely coloured. She rested her elbows on the drawing-board and covered her eyes with her hands, waiting for this moment to pass. Esmé, going along the tow-path to the pub, saw her before she heard his footsteps and would have turned back, but as he hesitated he thought that she had heard him. He was a reticent man but could see no reason for turning his back on sorrow, so against his inclination he went over to her. His dog, following him, sniffed at the paint water and stretched himself out in the shade of some rushes.

Catherine kept her head bent, and began to pack up her painting things as Esmé sat down beside her. She had not been crying. Her face was pale, but her cheek-bones were red where her hands had pressed against them. In a few seconds this colour receded and she seemed more in command of herself.

She unpinned the drawing-paper from the board and tore it across.

"Not a good morning?" he asked.

"I am bitten to death by horse-flies."

"Come with me to the pub and have a drink. I will carry all the paraphernalia."

He had Noël's voice, though he talked too rapidly and stumbled over words. His tongue was not quick enough to keep up with his desire to have the words done with and his part of the conversation over. His manner of speaking was, from nervousness, over-decisive and just when he meant to be tender he sounded stern.

They walked along the towing-path in silence until they reached The Rose and Crown—there, the bar was empty until a woman came through from the kitchen, drying her hands, to serve them. She drew the beer and went back to her cooking. Catherine and Esmé sat on the varnished window-seat and looked out at the river. Conversation was uneasy between them. What they had in common was felt by both to be taboo and he, from lack of interest and living abroad, had no idea of what sort of girl she was. This morning, he began to be moved by her forlornness and blamed his mother for letting her mope: something strenuous and gay should surely have been arranged—though he could not think what.

"Would you like to play darts?" he asked her. She did not in the least want to play darts and did not know how, but his solicitude was so masked, his voice was so abrupt that she timidly agreed. He was patient and encouraging as her darts struck the brick wall, once a tin lamp-shade, but rarely the board, until, as part of her haphazard throwing—and she had no idea that such a thing could happen—two darts landed together in the bull's-eye. She glowed at his amazement and praise. He called in the landlord's wife to draw them some more beer and to see Catherine's score and said that he had never done such a thing in his life and would never do it.

"But I didn't *know*," Catherine said happily. "They might just as easily have gone out of the window." She could not have imagined that doing something well in a game could be so stimulating.

They left the pub and walked back along the towing-path. Mrs Ingram was sitting on the steps in the sun and she, too, listened to Esmé's account of Catherine's first game of darts and she smiled radiantly, as if this was the nicest, gayest thing that could happen. At luncheon, the three of them were drawn together: by some simple magic, which Catherine could not understand, Mrs Ingram no longer seemed cross or embarrassed with her son, but rather as if she were acquiescing to some delightful plan he had for the future. Only when they were drinking coffee on the terrace and Esmé suggested an afternoon on the river did she detach herself from them again, making too many excuses—a little headache and a letter to write and a vague notion that one of her friends might call. She would not let them delay one moment. They must go alone and if they wanted tea it could be packed for them.

Catherine was disappointed, for it was Mrs Ingram she

loved and admired, not Esmé; and Esmé himself looked sulky again. He watched his mother going away from them along the terrace and his eyes were full of contempt, as if he knew some secret she had, which he despised. He stood up and said "Well, then," in a hearty voice, trying to seem gaily anticipatory, but not managing it.

Mrs Ingram had a small motor launch which was used for visiting her friends up and down the river, and in this, sitting beside one another in wicker chairs, Esmé and Catherine drove sedately under the summer darkness of the trees. The easy gaiety had gone and Catherine felt helplessly that Mrs Ingram had pushed her off alone with Esmé against his inclination, and she was puzzled to think what motive she could have for doing such a thing. If it was simply to be rid of her, then she need never have invited her; that she might be trying to lay the foundations of something deeper between Esmé and Catherine than this slight acquaintance they had was not in character with her rôle of possessive mother. Noël had once said: "It is lucky for you that you love me, not Esmé. Mamma never allows any girls within yards of her darling. They are just to be devoted to one another." Equally, that Mrs Ingram simply had, as she said, a headache was unthinkable. She was not a woman who would be likely to have headaches or confess to such frailty if she had. She was ordinarily so proudly direct that excuses were alien to her. She would not deign to dissemble or explain. When she did so, Catherine felt uneasily compelled to wonder why.

Some cloud was between mother and son. In other circumstances, Catherine would have thought that it gathered from Mrs Ingram's jealousy. Her coldness might have been caused by Catherine and Esmé wishing to escape together, not from the reverse. For the second time that day Esmé set out to dispel the melancholy his mother had induced in Catherine. She recognised along the river features of the landscape she had discovered with Noël, and Esmé pointed them out to her as if she had never seen them before. Soon, his discourse became more than a commentary upon the river banks and the late Victorian and Edwardian houses, gabled and balconied, the rustic summer-houses, the lawns with urns of geraniums and flag-poles, and weeping copper-beeches, and began to be an excursion back through time; for here, he said, Noël had rammed the boat into the mooring-posts, ("Yes, he told me," Catherine whispered) and on that island disturbed a wasps' nest in a hollow tree.

They were held up outside the lock, and at last the keeper came out and opened the gates. The peace and heat inside the lock were intense. As the water went down, Catherine, grasping a slimy chain looked long at Esmé who stood up with the painter over a bollard and was lighting a a cigarette. The most veiled of men, she suddenly thought him; his in some ways handsome face expressionless with discretion, the speed of his talk overcoming his reluctance to talk at all, and his easiness, his courtesy—with the lock-keeper at this moment—proclaiming almost that beyond this he was far removed and could not love, be loved, or have any exchange at all that courtesy or kindness did not dictate.

Beyond the lock, she found herself thinking: We shall have to come back through it, in an echo of the triumph with which she used to say this aloud to Noël. Each lock had prolonged their aloneness, as indeed it prolonged her time with Esmé, but it was so much as an echo of an old thought that it came to her that she found herself telling Esmé now how once it had been.

At first, she thought his courtesy had deserted him. "Oh, look, a kingfisher," he said.

She looked in the wrong place and it was gone. "Another thing about the river," he said. "We can quite safely bring our unhappiness here. No one can reach it or be contaminated by it, as on dry land. I have felt that I was in quarantine with it these last weeks."

"But at home . . . ?" Catherine began.

"No, I don't think we can be safe there," he said rapidly. "I mean that other people would not be safe from *us*."

"I wonder if your mother wishes now that she hadn't invited me."

"My dear little Cathy, what an odd thing to wonder. Or should I not call you 'Cathy'?"

"I liked to hear it." She had blushed with pleasure and surprise. "I wondered if the sight of me depresses her," she said humbly. "I suppose that we have only Noël in common. By the fact of just being myself I can only go on and on reminding her of him."

"You remind her of yourself and that she loves you. The dead can become too important, just by dying. Any ordeal is yours surely? Coming back to the house and the river and so much obviously that only you and Noël knew about." He spoke rather aloofly, to imply that being in love was not in his province, though he acknowledged it in hers. "But I understand," he added, "that it was probably now or never."

"I shouldn't have liked it to be never. I love it here, being with your mother and seeing the house again—the *beautiful* house . . ."

"Yes, I think it is the only nice one on the river," he said. He turned the boat round in mid-stream. "All of those rose-red villas with their fretwork balconies and the conservatories and so much wistaria . . . yet I miss it when I'm away, and it comes at me with a dismaying, not wholly depressing rush, when I return. Living in one place all of one's youth makes being an expatriate very difficult. I think I shall go and live in London for a bit before I go abroad again. Go by instalments, as it were. It may halve the

pains of departure. I must tell Mamma. Until I have done
so, know nothing of it, please."

"Of course not," Catherine whispered.

*   *   *

"Has Esmé said anything to you about leaving here?"
Mrs Ingram asked Catherine a day or two later.

"No."

'Wide-eyed surprise, poorly done,' thought Mrs Ingram.
"I know he feels concerned about leaving me and may not
like to mention it; but he will have to go in the end. He
mustn't be tied to my apron-strings for ever."

'Apron-strings' had too homely a connotation altogether
—Esmé and his mother were not just pottering cosily about
a kitchen. So fine that they were invisible were the threads
with which she drew him to her: it was by the most delicate
influence that she had had him break off his long-ago
engagement and had later tried to stop him from going
abroad, though seeming all the time to speed him on his
way. I know that she sometimes does wrong, Catherine
thought. But I love her and I should be happy if she cared
to dominate me, too. She had wanted to be her daughter-in-
law and part of the enchantment. She and Noël would have
lived nearby, and come often to the house. "The children
are coming to luncheon," Mrs Ingram would say. Once, the
summer before, Catherine, sitting out on the steps in front
of the house had heard Mrs Ingram in the hall, telephoning
a friend. "Do come over. I shall be alone. The children are
going to the cinema." Bliss had flowed through Catherine.
She had shut her eyes, feeling the sun, hearing the sounds
of the garden—the birds and insects and the weir. Yes, it
was bliss in those days, she thought, and she still sensed the
magic of this quieter house, though the river was more
melancholy to her and the family diminished and Mrs
Ingram's composure no longer completely holding.

Someone called Freddie began to be talked of—a friend of
Esmé's, a painter, of whose painting Mrs Ingram disapproved.
She compared it unfavourably with Catherine's. It had, she
said, that detestable ingredient, virtuosity. "It allows one to
see how clever he has been, and that should never be. I
don't want to see the wheels go round or to feel called upon
to shout, 'Bravo', as if he were some sweating Italian tenor.
One should really feel, 'How easy it must be! How effortless!' I should think—don't you, Catherine?—that an
artist must seem too proud to have tried, too careless to have
thought of succeeding." Esmé said nothing, so Catherine
could not judge if he agreed.

Freddie was expected for luncheon, but did not come.

"Perhaps he didn't feel hungry today," Mrs Ingram said.
So Freddie himself was out of favour along with his
paintings, Catherine thought. Mrs Ingram had glanced at
Esmé when she had spoken and his face betrayed him by its
impassivity.

In the afternoon, Catherine made another attempt to
paint, in a tangled part of the garden behind the old stables.
In the shade, the nettles and docks were a dark and bitter
green and this greenness seemed to tinge the curdy white
flowers of elder and cow-parsley. She became gradually
absorbed in the shapes and the textures of the leaves—the
feathery, the ribbed and spade-like, the giant fern weighted
down by a heavy snail. She was pleased with what she was
doing and just painting in a bright poppy among the green
and silvery green, for contrast, when she saw a snake lying
on the path before her at the edge of the shade. It was green,
too, of an olive-green to enhance her picture and in a
curious way she realised this before she took fright, tiptoeing backwards away from it until she felt safe to turn and
run.

She sped up the steps and into the hall, calling for Esmé,
then the wonderful sunny slumbrance of the house checked

her and she felt disconcerted. A young man came to the drawing-room door, saying, "I wanted Esmé, too."

Oh, I am glad, for Esmé's sake, that he came at last, thought Catherine, pulling up too suddenly and slipping on a rug.

"Scatter-rugs they call these in America," said Freddie, coming to steady her. "A good name. I should like to scatter them all in the river."

He seemed a very neat young man at a first glance. His suit exactly matched his fawn hair and his blue bow-tie matched his pullover and socks. His voice and his Cockney accent were pert and gay, his small eyes very bright. A second impression revealed his bitten nails and dirty shoes and the fact that his slight build and his clothes made him seem more boyish than he was.

"You sound as if you wanted Esmé in a great hurry," he said.

"Yes, I saw a snake round by the stables and I think it is an adder."

"Isn't there a gardener or something?" Freddie asked, looking vaguely out at the terrace.

"I just thought of Esmé first. I left all my painting things there."

"I shouldn't think a snake would harm them. Did you want me to kill it or something?" he asked reluctantly.

"You see, I am sure they are deadly."

"Is that supposed to encourage me?"

He went into the back hall and chose a walking-stick from the umbrella-stand. "Oh, dear, this isn't really up my street. I just hope it's gone away by now. It would have been much better if you had asked a gardener."

They set out towards the stables and he said: "My name is Freddie Bassett. I was expected to lunch. Was there much hard feeling?"

"I am a guest. It isn't for me to say."

"So there was! I ran out of petrol miles from anywhere. So what could I do?"

"You could have telephoned, I suppose."

"Splendid! I knew I was right to try the story out on you first. You spotted the flaw as Mrs Ingram would have done. How can I get round that one? I telephoned, but the silly girl at the exchange said there was no reply. I don't know what these girls are coming to."

"No one would believe you."

"Mrs Ingram will not dare to say so. All right, then, I lost my way."

"This way," said Catherine coldly, taking another path.

"As a matter of fact, I did." He seemed surprised to find himself speaking the truth. "I stopped for a quick one and fell in with a little party. You know how that can be done—complete strangers, but something happens, there is some clemency in the smoke-haze, so that they seem the dearest companions one ever had, one almost weeps with gratitude that they are so sympathetic, so much one's own sort. So helpful in helping one to forget anxiety. I could not tear myself away from them and now I have forgotten them and shall never see them again—only similar ones. When it was closing-time we stayed on, because the landlord was the same sort as well. I felt dreadfully guilty about Esmé, and they were all so sympathetic and so full of condolences and advice about what his mother would say. They came out to see me off and wish me good luck. Then I took the wrong road."

"Wouldn't it have been better not to have come at all?"

"Surely not? I can stay to dinner instead."

Catherine felt frightened. I am not his accomplice, she thought. It is nothing to do with me.

"Do you know when Esmé went out?" he asked. "I want to say that I arrived the minute after."

"I didn't know that he had gone."

"He has taken his mother to a meeting. I hope it is a nice long one and that my head will feel better before she comes back."

They crossed the stables courtyard and Catherine peered through the archway at the path where her painting things were lying beside her folding stool.

"Have I really got to?" Freddie asked. "Oughtn't I to be wearing puttees or something? I am sure it has kindly gone away."

But the snake had only moved farther into the sun. Catherine shrank back and for some strange reason put her hands over her ears. "Oh, Lord!" grumbled Freddie, going forward with the stick held high. Catherine stayed in the courtyard. She heard the stick beating the ground and Freddie swearing, but she would not look. When he came back, he was carrying the stool and the drawing-board and his face was white. "I take it you don't want to go on with this at the moment," he said, handing her the unfinished water-colour without glancing at it. "I just left it there— the snake."

"You did kill it?"

"Yes, I suddenly went mad with fear. It was a dreadful thing to ask someone from London to do. Are you the girl Noël was engaged to?"

"We weren't engaged."

"And now, I understand, Mamma wants you to marry Esmé?"

"I think you are rude and absurd," Catherine said. "It is none of my business, but I don't know how Esmé can tolerate you."

She hurried on ahead of him and turned the corner of the house. There was Esmé walking on the lawn, his head down, his hands in his pockets. He paced up and down dejectedly. When he saw Catherine he smiled and then his smile warmed and he came forward eagerly, quite transformed by the sight of Freddie trailing behind, carrying the folding stool.

* * *

"It was a poor grass snake," Mrs Ingram said. "It would have done no harm to anyone and great good to the garden."

"I am just a Cockney. How should I know?" said Freddie. "I did as I was told."

Catherine could only keep saying how sorry she was.

"I am surprised at you," Mrs Ingram said teasingly. "So meticulous in your painting, and to make such a mistake."

It seemed to be Catherine who had failed. Freddie was triumphantly eating dinner instead of lunch, although Catherine would have staked a great deal against such a possibility. She had listened to his long apology with outraged astonishment . . . "tramping along in the blazing heat with my little petrol can in my hand. . . . I went all round some village looking for the Post Office. Wonderful honeysuckle all over it and jars of bull's-eyes in the window. I should have thought there would be some regulation against calling them that, when they are nothing of the kind . . ."

He is putting off the weak part of his story, about the telephone, Catherine thought with interest.

". . . the phone-box was just outside the door and the exchange itself just inside by the bacon-slicing machine. The same pop-eyed old codger who was selling the bull's-eyes went to the switchboard. Twice he got the wrong number. 'Skates the Fishmongers here' was one. The third time I truly thought would be lucky, but there was no reply. 'There is always someone there. There are hundreds of servants. They are moneyed folk,' I said. 'Comfortably *placed*, as you might say.' 'I daresay,' he said, sarcastically, as if I were a child, or drunk. 'All the same, they're not answering.' "

Esmé bent down and stroked his dog, trying to hide a smile.

"You *might* have answered," Freddie whined complainingly. "After I had trudged so far and had such a horrible time and my hands were so *sore* with carrying the petrol can." He glanced at them, wincing.

"It *is* only pretending, isn't it?" said Mrs Ingram, her voice as sweet as honey. As if she thought that Freddie was over-exciting himself, she changed the conversation.

So Freddie triumphed. He triumphed over his headache and he stayed to dinner and Catherine thought that he would manage to stay the night as well. Esmé was quiet and full of a peace that Catherine could understand. She remembered the contentment of saying those words to herself, "We are under the same roof." She had known how beautiful it can be to come to the close of the day and lie down in bed, thinking those words. Then the house itself became haunted, enchanted, spellbound with love.

Her heart began to ache again and her throat almost shut. The flesh is endlessly martyred by grief, humiliated by nausea and vomitings, bothered and alarmed; breath checked and the heart belaboured; the eyes stabbed viciously until they unload their tears and the tongue as bitter as if it had tasted poison. 'This Freddie does not know,' Catherine thought, and she felt pity for Esmé and kinship with him.

*   *   *

Dinner was soon over, for there was hardly any conversation to prolong it. Once Mrs Ingram said to Freddie: "Catherine paints, too," and Freddie answered, "So I saw."

Beset by midges they drank coffee out on the terrace above the steps. "An irritating noise," Freddie said, referring to the weir, and Catherine thought, So it is. The sound is what you are yourself at the moment: if you are in despair, it sounds despairing; tumultuous if you are angry; romantic when you are in love.

Esmé and Freddie never exchanged remarks or glances and when Mrs Ingram went indoors Catherine felt herself so much in the way that she followed her and was conscious of their nervous silence as she walked away.

Mrs Ingram came from the back hall carrying a bunch of roses. "I was going to ask you if you would like to come, but don't if you aren't up to it. To Noël's grave, I mean. No, you would rather not, I am sure," she said quickly. "It is difficult to guess how other people feel about such a thing. I know it is old-fashioned and unimaginative of me, but I feel comforted when I go there."

Catherine did not know herself how she felt or would feel, but she went with Mrs Ingram and carried the roses for her. They walked slowly along the scented lane to the church by the river; then through the lych-gate under the limes. She began to be afraid. She remembered the church-yard carpeted with wreaths and the raw earth mounded up ready for its dreadful purpose; the groups of black figures standing, as if stunned, among the graves and the lime-trees only just in leaf which now were ready to flower. She wondered if she would have to face some overpowering monument, for death is alien enough in itself without some of the things which are done afterwards as being appropriate. She hung back on the gravel path as she had done once before and Mrs Ingram, humming peacefully, her pink cardigan hung over her shoulders, stepped quickly across the grass. Following her, raising her eyes only to look at a safely eighteenth-century headstone with a cherub's head and wings and saffron rosettes of lichen all over the crumbling stone, Catherine saw the name 'Ingram' with a sense of shock. But there were groves of Ingrams, among them Noël's father, who was to share the roses. Unlike most of the other riverside families, this had kept its bones in one

place for at least two hundred years. The last Ingram had,
Catherine was relieved to find, only a simple white wooden
cross with his name painted in black. She faced this steadily,
feeling that she had been spared an awkwardness. "Only
until the ground has sunk," Mrs Ingram said, throwing
away stale water and going to fetch fresh.

Catherine took a step back, as if she might otherwise
sink with the earth. She felt obscenity, not peace, around
her.

"I suppose that little liar will be staying the night," said
Mrs Ingram, returning from the water tap. "I can't
pretend that I fancy having him under my roof."

She knelt down and began to strip leaves off the roses and
break off the big blood-red thorns.

When her plans have failed, there are always the
flowers to do, Catherine thought. The night I arrived, I
suppose that she left them until late as an excuse for sending
Esmé to the station—to make us be together from the start.
But Esmé wouldn't fall in with the plan—a new habit in
him, I should think.

Then the words 'my darling Noël' broke across her
reflections. For a second, she wondered if she had said them
aloud, caught on the in-breath of a sob. But Mrs Ingram
finished the flowers calmly and then they walked home
along the towing-path. The river was bronze in the sunset
and the fluffy meadow-grasses filled with a pinkish light.

Esmé and Freddie were still sitting on the terrace.
Freddie was now in Mrs Ingram's wicker chaise-longue, his
hands clasped behind his head and his legs stretched out
comfortably. Esmé sat, rather awkwardly, with his greyhound across his lap. They both struggled to rise when they
saw Mrs Ingram and Catherine crossing the lawn, but Mrs
Ingram ignored them and went round the house by a side-
way and Catherine followed her.

*   *   *

Catherine went up to bed and stood by the open window, looking out into the dark garden. A misty moonlight furred the grass, like rime, and white ghosts rose off the weir. 'I have been to the churchyard,' she thought, 'and now I have had enough.'

She drew one of the heavy velvet curtains round her like a cloak. 'I cannot *not* feel when I am here,' she thought. 'Especially when I am so *meant* to feel.' Was not Mrs Ingram, she wondered, trying to make her realise the extent of her loss, as if nothing could be accomplished until this was done or any other part of her plan proceeded with.

Mrs Ingram came in to say good night and found Catherine wound up in the curtain.

"So Freddie went—as if he overheard me and meant to prove me wrong."

She came to the window and they both looked out at the garden, listening to the weir.

On the blanched terrace below Esmé's greyhound appeared, then Esmé. He went down the steps and was lost in the dark garden. Sometimes he reminded Catherine of his brother. Family likenesses in gestures are stranger than those of feature or build and often more poignant and she had sometimes been moved by such a slight thing as the inclination of his head as he walked, so mysteriously the same as Noël.

"He is going away next week," Mrs Ingram said.

"And I," said Catherine quickly. "I must go too." She was struggling with tears and her voice was rough and abrupt. She breathed very steadily and presently the tears receded and she said: "I must get back to work, you know. I must. . . ."

"What makes it difficult for living here may make it good for painting," Mrs Ingram said.

"Too beautiful," Catherine began. She put her hands over her face and tears ran down her wrists and the insides of her arms. Mrs Ingram waited, as if she were measuring the fall of tears and knew when the limit of grief was reached and only then put out her hand and touched Catherine's shoulder.

"You see, I can't stay. You do see?" Her heart had been twice ambushed in this house and now she was desperate to escape. Yet did Mrs Ingram understand? She said nothing. She simply took Catherine in her arms and kissed her—but with a welcoming, a gathering-in gesture as if to one who has come home at last rather than to someone preparing to go away.

The Blush

THEY were the same age—Mrs Allen and the woman who came every day to do the housework. "I shall never have children now," Mrs Allen had begun to tell herself. Something had not come true; the essential part of her life. She had always imagined her children in fleeting scenes and intimations; that was how they had come to her, like snatches of a film. She had seen them plainly, their chins tilted up as she tied on their bibs at meal-times; their naked bodies had darted in and out of the water-sprinkler on the lawn; and she had listened to their voices in the garden and in the mornings from their beds. She had even cried a little dreaming of the day when the eldest boy would go off to boarding-school; she pictured the train going out of the station; she raised her hand and her throat contracted and her lips trembled as she smiled. The years passing by had slowly filched from her the reality of these scenes—the gay sounds; the grave peace she had longed for; even the pride of grief.

She listened—as they worked together in the kitchen—to Mrs Lacey's troubles with her family, her grumblings about her grown-up son who would not get up till dinner-time on Sundays and then expected his mother to have cleaned his shoes for him; about the girl of eighteen who was a hair-dresser and too full of dainty ways which she picked up from the women's magazines, and the adolescent girl who moped and glowered and answered back.

27

My children wouldn't have turned out like that, Mrs Allen thought, as she made her murmured replies. "The more you do for some, the more you may," said Mrs Lacey. But from gossip in the village which Mrs Allen heard, she had done all too little. The children, one night after another, for years and years, had had to run out for parcels of fish and chips while their mother sat in The Horse & Jockey drinking brown ale. On summer evenings, when they were younger, they had hung about outside the pub: when they were bored they pressed their foreheads to the window and looked in at the dark little bar, hearing the jolly laughter, their mother's the loudest of all. Seeing their faces, she would swing at once from the violence of hilarity to that of extreme annoyance and, although ginger-beer and packets of potato crisps would be handed out through the window, her anger went out with them and threatened the children as they ate and drank.

"And she doesn't always care who she goes there *with*," Mrs Allen's gardener told her.

"She works hard and deserves a little pleasure—she has her anxieties," said Mrs Allen, who, alas, had none.

She had never been inside The Horse & Jockey, although it was nearer to her house than The Chequers at the other end of the village where she and her husband went sometimes for a glass of sherry on Sunday mornings. The Horse & Jockey attracted a different set of customers—for instance, people who sat down and drank, at tables all round the wall. At The Chequers no one ever sat down, but stood and sipped and chatted as at a cocktail-party, and luncheons and dinners were served, which made it so much more respectable: no children hung about outside, because they were all at home with their Nannies.

Sometimes in the evenings—so many of them—when her husband was kept late in London, Mrs Allen wished that she could go down to The Chequers and drink a glass of sherry and exchange a little conversation with someone; but she was too shy to open the door and go in alone: she imagined heads turning, a surprised welcome from her friends, who would all be safely in married pairs; and then, when she left, eyes meeting with unspoken messages and conjecture in the air.

Mrs Lacey left her at midday and then there was gardening to do and the dog to be taken for a walk. After six o'clock, she began to pace restlessly about the house, glancing at the clocks in one room after another, listening for her husband's car—the sound she knew so well because she had awaited it for such a large part of her married life. She would hear, at last, the tyres turning on the soft gravel, the door being slammed, then his footsteps hurrying towards the porch. She knew that it was a wasteful way of spending her years—and, looking back, she was unable to tell one of them from another—but she could not think what else she might do. Humphrey went on earning more and more money and there was no stopping him now. Her acquaintances, in wretched quandaries about where the next term's school-fees were to come from, would turn to her and say cruelly: "Oh, *you're* all right, Ruth. You've no idea what you are spared."

And Mrs Lacey would be glad when Maureen could leave school and "get out earning". "I've got my geometry to do," she says, when it's time to wash-up the tea-things. "I'll geometry you, my girl," I said. "When I was your age, I was out earning."

Mrs Allen was fascinated by the life going on in that house and the children seemed real to her, although she had never seen them. Only Mr Lacey remained blurred and unimaginable. No one knew him. He worked in the town in the valley, six miles away and he kept himself to himself; had never been known to show his face in The Horse & Jockey. "I've got my own set," Mrs Lacey said airily.

"After all, he's nearly twenty years older than me. I'll make sure neither of my girls follow my mistake. 'I'd rather see you dead at my feet,' I said to Vera." Ron's young lady was lucky; having Ron, she added. Mrs Allen found this strange, for Ron had always been painted so black; was, she had been led to believe, oafish, ungrateful, greedy and slow to put his hands in his pockets if there was any paying out to do. There was also the matter of his shoe-cleaning, for no young woman would do what his mother did for him—or said she did. Always, Mrs Lacey would sigh and say: "Goodness me, if only I was their age and knew what I know now."

She was an envious woman: she envied Mrs Allen her pretty house and her clothes and she envied her own daughters their youth. "If I had your figure," she would say to Mrs Allen. Her own had gone: what else could be expected, she asked, when she had had three children? Mrs Allen thought, too, of all the brown ale she drank at The Horse & Jockey and of the reminiscences of meals past which came so much into her conversations. Whatever the cause was, her flesh, slackly corseted, shook as she trod heavily about the kitchen. In summer, with bare arms and legs she looked larger than ever. Although her skin was very white, the impression she gave was at once colourful—from her orange hair and bright lips and the floral patterns that she always wore. Her red-painted toe-nails poked through the straps of her fancy sandals; turquoise-blue beads were wound round her throat.

Humphrey Allen had never seen her; he had always left for the station before she arrived, and that was a good thing, his wife thought. When she spoke of Mrs Lacey, she wondered if he visualised a neat, homely woman in a clean white overall. She did not deliberately mislead him, but she took advantage of his indifference. Her relationship with Mrs Lacey and the intimacy of their conversations in the kitchen he would not have approved, and the sight of those calloused feet with their chipped nail-varnish and yellowing heels would have sickened him.

One Monday morning, Mrs Lacey was later than usual. She was never very punctual and had many excuses about flat bicycle-tyres or Maureen being poorly. Mrs Allen, waiting for her, sorted out all the washing. When she took another look at the clock, she decided that it was far too late for her to be expected at all. For some time lately Mrs Lacey had seemed ill and depressed; her eyelids, which were chronically rather inflamed, had been more angrily red than ever and, at the sink or ironing-board, she would fall into unusual silences, was absent-minded and full of sighs. She had always liked to talk about the "change" and did so more than ever as if with a desperate hopefulness.

"I'm sorry, but I was ever so sick," she told Mrs Allen, when she arrived the next morning. "I still feel queerish. Such heartburn. I don't like the signs, I can tell you. All I crave is pickled walnuts, just the same as I did with Maureen. I don't like the signs one bit. I feel I'll throw myself into the river if I'm taken that way again."

Mrs Allen felt stunned and antagonistic. "Surely not at your age," she said crossly.

"You can't be more astonished than me," Mrs Lacey said, belching loudly. "Oh, pardon. I'm afraid I can't help myself."

Not being able to help herself, she continued to belch and hiccough as she turned on taps and shook soap-powder into the washing-up bowl. It was because of this that Mrs Allen decided to take the dog for a walk. Feeling consciously fastidious and aloof she made her way across the fields, trying to disengage her thoughts from Mrs Lacey and her troubles; but unable to. "Poor woman," she thought again and again with bitter animosity.

She turned back when she noticed how the sky had

darkened with racing, sharp-edged clouds. Before she could reach home, the rain began. Her hair, soaking wet, shrank into tight curls against her head; her woollen suit smelt like a damp animal. "Oh, I am drenched," she called out, as she threw open the kitchen door.

She knew at once that Mrs Lacey had gone, that she must have put on her coat and left almost as soon as Mrs Allen had started out on her walk, for nothing was done; the washing-up was hardly started and the floor was unswept. Among the stacked-up crockery a note was propped; she had come over funny, felt dizzy and, leaving her apologies and respects, had gone.

Angrily, but methodically, Mrs Allen set about making good the wasted morning. By afternoon, the grim look was fixed upon her face. "How dare she?" she found herself whispering, without allowing herself to wonder what it was the woman had dared.

She had her own little ways of cosseting herself through the lonely hours, comforts which were growing more important to her as she grew older, so that the time would come when not to have her cup of tea at four-thirty would seem a prelude to disaster. This afternoon, disorganised as it already was, she fell out of her usual habit and instead of carrying the tray to the low table by the fire, she poured out her tea in the kitchen and drank it there, leaning tiredly against the dresser. Then she went upstairs to make herself tidy. She was trying to brush her frizzed hair smooth again when she heard the door-bell ringing.

When she opened the door, she saw quite plainly a look of astonishment take the place of anxiety on the man's face. Something about herself surprised him, was not what he had expected. "Mrs Allen?" he asked uncertainly and the astonishment remained when she had answered him.

"Well, I'm calling about the wife," he said. "Mrs Lacey that works here."

"I was worried about her," said Mrs Allen.

She knew that she must face the embarrassment of hearing about Mrs Lacey's condition and invited the man into her husband's study, where she thought he might look less out-of-place than in her brocade-smothered drawing-room. He looked about him resentfully and glared down at the floor which his wife had polished. With this thought in his mind, he said abruptly: "It's all taken its toll."

He sat down on a leather couch with his cap and his bicycle-clips beside him.

"I came home to my tea and found her in bed, crying," he said. This was true. Mrs Lacey had succumbed to despair and gone to lie down. Feeling better at four o'clock, she went downstairs to find some food to comfort herself with; but the slice of dough-cake was ill-chosen and brought on more heartburn and floods of bitter tears.

"If she carries on here for a while, it's all got to be very different," Mr Lacey said threateningly. He was nervous at saying what he must and could only bring out the words with the impetus of anger. "You may or may not know that she's expecting."

"Yes," said Mrs Allen humbly. "This morning she told me that she thought. . . ."

"There's no 'thought' about it. It's as plain as a pike-staff." Yet in his eyes she could see disbelief and bafflement and he frowned and looked down again at the polished floor.

Twenty years older than his wife—or so his wife had said —he really, to Mrs Allen, looked quite ageless, a crooked, bow-legged little man who might have been a jockey once. The expression about his blue eyes was like a child's: he was both stubborn and pathetic.

Mrs Allen's fat spaniel came into the room and went straight to the stranger's chair and began to sniff at his corduroy trousers.

"It's too much for her," Mr Lacey said. "It's too much to expect."

To Mrs Allen's horror she saw the blue eyes filling with tears. Hoping to hide his emotion, he bent down and fondled the dog, making playful thrusts at it with his fist closed.

He was a man utterly, bewilderedly at sea. His married life had been too much for him, with so much in it that he could not understand.

"Now I know, I will do what I can," Mrs Allen told him. "I will try to get someone else in to do the rough."

"It's the late nights that are the trouble," he said. "She comes in dog-tired. Night after night. It's not good enough. 'Let them stay at home and mind their own children once in a while,' I told her. 'We don't need the money.' "

"I can't understand," Mrs Allen began. She was at sea herself now, but felt perilously near a barbarous, unknown shore and was afraid to make any movement towards it.

"I earn good money. For her to come out at all was only for extras. She likes new clothes. In the daytimes I never had any objection. Then all these cocktail-parties begin. It beats me how people can drink like it night after night and pay out for someone else to mind their kids. Perhaps you're thinking that it's not my business, but I'm the one who has to sit at home alone till all hours and get my own supper and see next to nothing of my wife. I'm boiling over some nights. Once I nearly rushed out when I heard the car stop down the road. I wanted to tell your husband what I thought of you both."

"My husband?" murmured Mrs Allen.

"What am I supposed to have, I would have asked him? Is she my wife or your sitter-in? Bringing her back at this time of night. And it's no use saying she could have refused. She never would."

Mrs Allen's quietness at last defeated him and dispelled

the anger he had tried to rouse in himself. The look of her, too, filled him with doubts, her grave, uncertain demeanour and the shock her age had been to him. He had imagined someone so much younger and—because of the cocktail-parties—flighty. Instead, he recognised something of himself in her, a yearning disappointment. He picked up his cap and his bicycle-clips and sat looking down at them, turning them round in his hands. "I had to come," he said.

"Yes," said Mrs Allen.

"So you won't ask her again?" he pleaded. "It isn't right for her. Not now."

"No, I won't," Mrs Allen promised and she stood up as he did and walked over to the door. He stooped and gave the spaniel a final pat. "You'll excuse my coming, I hope."

"Of course."

"It was no use saying any more to her. Whatever she's asked, she won't refuse. It's her way."

Mrs Allen shut the front door after him and stood in the hall, listening to him wheeling his bicycle across the gravel. Then she felt herself beginning to blush. She was glad that she was alone, for she could feel her face, her throat, even the tops of her arms burning, and she went over to a looking-glass and studied with great interest this strange phenomenon.

The Letter-Writers

AT eleven o'clock, Emily went down to the village to fetch the lobsters. The heat unsteadied the air, light shimmered and glanced off leaves and telegraph wires and the flag on the church tower spreading out in a small breeze, then dropping, wavered against the sky, as if it were flapping under water.

She wore an old cotton frock, and meant to change it at the last moment, when the food was all ready and the table laid. Over her bare arms, the warm air flowed, her skirt seemed to divide as she walked, pressed in a hollow between her legs, like drapery on a statue. The sun seemed to touch her bones —her spine, her shoulder-blades, her skull. In her thoughts, she walked nakedly, picking her way, over dry-as-dust cow-dung, along the lane. All over the hedges, trumpets of large white convolvulus were turned upwards towards the sky— the first flowers she could remember; something about them had, in her early childhood, surprised her with astonishment and awe, a sense of magic that had lasted, like so little else, repeating itself again and again, most of the summers of her forty years.

From the wide-open windows of the village school came the sound of a tinny piano. "We'll rant, and we'll roar, like true British sailors," sang all the little girls.

Emily, smiling to herself as she passed by, had thoughts so delightful that she began to tidy them into sentences to put in a letter to Edmund. Her days were not full or busy and the gathering in of little things to write to him about took up a large part of her time. She would have made a paragraph or two about the children singing, the hot weather—so rare in England—the scent of the lime and privet blossom, the pieces of tin glinting among the branches of the cherry trees. But the instinctive thought was at once checked by the truth that there would be no letter-writing that evening after all. She stood before an alarming crisis, one that she had hoped to avoid for as long as ever she lived; the crisis of meeting for the first time the person whom she knew best in the world.

'What will he be like?' did not worry her. She knew what he was like. If he turned out differently, it would be a mistake. She would be getting a false impression of him and she would know that it was temporary and would fade. She was more afraid of herself, and wondered if he would know how to discount the temporary, and false, in her. Too much was at stake and, for herself, she would not have taken the risk. "I agree that we have gone beyond meeting now. It would be retracing our steps," he had once written to her. "Although, perhaps if we were ever in the same country, it would be absurd to make a point of *not* meeting." This, however, was what she had done when she went to Italy the next year.

In Rome, some instinct of self-preservation kept her from giving him her aunt's address there. She would telephone, she thought; but each time she tried to—her heart banging erratically within a suddenly hollow breast—she was checked by thoughts of the booby-trap lying before her. In the end, she skirted it. She discovered the little street where he lived, and felt the strangeness of reading its name, which she had written hundreds of times on envelopes. Walking past his house on the opposite pavement, she had glanced timidly at the peeling apricot-coloured plaster. The truth of the situation made her feel quite faint. It was frightening, like seeing a ghost in reverse—the insubstantial suddenly solidifying into a patchy and shabby reality. At the window on the first floor, one of the shutters was open; there was the darkness of the room beyond, an edge of yellow curtain and, hanging over the back of a chair set near the window, what looked like a white skirt. Even if Edmund himself threw open the other shutter and came out on to the balcony, he would never have known that the woman across the road was one of his dearest friends, but, all the same, she hastened away from the neighbourhood. At dinner, her aunt thought she might be ill. Her visitors from England so often were—from the heat and sight-seeing and the change of diet.

The odd thing to Emily about the escapade was its vanishing from her mind—the house became its own ghost again, the house of her imagination, lying on the other side of the road, where she had always pictured it, with its plaster unspoilt and Edmund inside in his tidied-up room, writing to her.

He had not chided her when she sent a letter from a safer place, explaining her lack of courage—and explain it she could, so fluently, half-touchingly yet wholly amusingly—on paper. He teased her gently, understanding her decision. In him, curiosity and adventurousness would have overcome his hesitation. Disillusionment would have deprived him of less than it might have deprived her; her letters were a relaxation to him; to her, his were an excitement, and her fingers often trembled as she tore open their envelopes.

They had written to one another for ten years. She had admired his novels since she was a young woman, but would not have thought of writing to tell him so; that he could conceivably be interested in the opinion of a complete stranger did not occur to her. Yet, sometimes, she felt that without her as their reader the novels could not have had a fair existence. She was so sensitive to what he wrote, that she felt her own reading half created it. Her triumph at the end of each book had something added of a sense of accomplishment on her part. She felt it, to a lesser degree, with some other writers, but they were dead; if they had been living, she would not have written to them, either.

Then one day she read in a magazine an essay he had written about the boyhood of Tennyson. His conjecture on some point she could confirm, for she had letters from one of the poet's brothers. She looked for them among her grandfather's papers and (she was never impulsive save when the impulse was generosity) sent them to Edmund, with a little note to tell him that they were a present to repay some of the pleasure his books had given her.

Edmund, who loved old letters and papers of every kind, found these especially delightful. So the first of many letters from him came to her, beginning, 'Dear Miss Fairchild'. His handwriting was very large and untidy and difficult to decipher, and this always pleased her, because his letters took longer to read; the enjoyment was drawn out, and often a word or two had to be puzzled over for days. Back, again and again, she would go to the letter, trying to take the problem by surprise—and that was usually how she solved it.

Sometimes, she wondered why he wrote to her—and was flattered when he asked for a letter to cheer him up when he was depressed, or to calm him when he was unhappy. Although he could not any longer work well in England— for a dullness came over him, from the climate and old, vexatious associations—he still liked to have some foothold there, and Emily's letters refreshed his memories.

At first, he thought her a novelist manqué, then he realised that letter-writing is an art by itself, a different kind of skill, though, with perhaps a similar motive—and one at which Englishwomen have excelled.

As she wrote, the landscape, flowers, children, cats and dogs, sprang to life memorably. He knew her neighbours and her relation to them, and also knew people, who were dead now, whom she had loved. He called them by their Christian names when he wrote to her and re-evoked them for her, so that, being allowed at last to mention them, she felt that they became light and free again in her mind, and not an intolerable suppression, as they had been for years.

*   *   *

Coming to the village, on this hot morning, she was more agitated than she could ever remember being, and she began to blame Edmund for creating such an ordeal. She was angry with herself for acquiescing, when he had suggested that he, being at last in England for a week or two, should come to see her. "For an hour, or three at most. I want to look at the flowers in the *very* garden, and stroke the cat, and peep between the curtains at Mrs Waterlow going by."

'He knows too much about me, so where can we begin?' she wondered. She had confided such intimacies in him. At that distance, he was as safe as the confessional, with the added freedom from hearing any words said aloud. She had written to his mind only. He seemed to have no face, and certainly no voice. Although photographs had once passed between them, they had seemed meaningless.

She had been so safe with him. They could not have wounded one another, but now they might. In *ten* years, there had been no inadvertent hurts, of rivalry, jealousy, or neglect. It had not occurred to either to wonder if the other would sometimes cease to write; the letters would come, as surely as the sun.

"But will they now?" Emily was wondering.

She turned the familiar bend of the road and the sea lay glittering below—its wrinkled surface looking solid and without movement, like a great sheet of metal. Now and then a light breeze came off the water and rasped together the dried grasses on the banks; when it dropped, the late morning silence held, drugging the brain and slowing the limbs.

*   *   *

For years, Emily had looked into mirrors only to see if her hair were tidy or her petticoat showing below her dress. This morning, she tried to take herself by surprise, to see herself as a stranger might, but failed.

He would expect a younger woman from the photograph of some years back. Since that was taken, wings of white hair at her temples had given her a different appearance. The photograph would not, in any case, show how poor her complexion was, unevenly pitted, from an illness when she was a child. As a girl, she had looked at her reflection and thought 'No one will ever want to marry me' and no one had.

When she went back to the living-room, the cat was walking about, smelling lobster in the air; balked troubled by desire, he went restlessly about the little room, the pupils of his eyes two thin lines of suspicion and contempt. But the lobster was high up on the dresser, above the Rockingham cups, and covered with a piece of muslin.

Emily went over to the table and touched the knives and forks, shook the salt in the cellar nicely level, lifted a wine glass to the light. She poured out a glass of sherry and stood, well back from the window—looking out between holly-hocks at the lane.

Unless the train was late, he should be there. At any moment, the station taxi would come slowly along the lane and stop, with terrible inevitability, outside the cottage. She wondered how tall he was—how would he measure against the hollyhocks? Would he be obliged to stoop under the low oak beams?

The sherry heartened her a little—at least, her hands stopped shaking—and she filled her glass again. The wine was cooling in a bucket down the well and she thought that perhaps it was time to fetch it in, or it might be too cold to taste.

The well had pretty little ferns of a very bright green growing out of the bricks at its sides, and when she lifted the cover, the ice-cold air struck her. She was unused to drinking much, and the glasses of sherry had, first, steadied her; then, almost numbed her. With difficulty, she drew up the bucket; but her movements were clumsy and uncertain, and greenish slime came off the rope on to her clean dress. Her hair fell forward untidily. Far, far below, as if at the wrong end of a telescope, she saw her own tiny face looking back at her. As she was taking the bottle of wine from the bucket, she heard a crash inside the cottage.

She knew what must have happened, but she felt too muddled to act quickly. When she opened the door of the living-room she saw, as she expected, the cat and the lobster and the Rockingham cups spread in disorder about the floor.

She grabbed the cat first—though the damage was done now—and ran to the front door to throw him out into the garden; but, opening the door, was confronted by Edmund, whose arm was raised, just about to pull on the old iron bell. At the sight of the distraught woman with untidy hair and her eyes full of tears, he took a pace back.

"There's no lunch," she said quickly. "Nothing." The cat struggled against her shoulder, frantic for the remains of the lobster, and a long scratch slowly ripened across her cheek; then the cat bounded from her and sat down behind the hollyhocks to wash his paws.

"How do you do," Emily said. She took her hand away from his almost as soon as she touched him and put it up to her cheek, brushing blood across her face.

"Let us go in and bathe you," he suggested.

"Oh, no, please don't bother. It is nothing at all. But, yes, of course, come in. I'm afraid . . ." She was incoherent and he could not follow what she was saying.

At the sight of the lobster and the china on the floor, he understood a little. All the same, she seemed to him to be rather drunk.

"Such wonderful cups and saucers," he said, going down on his knees and filling his hands with fragments. "I don't know how you can bear it."

"It's nothing. It doesn't matter. It's the lobster that matters. There is nothing else in the house."

"Eggs?" he suggested.

"I don't get the eggs till Friday," she said wildly.

"Well, cheese."

"It's gone hard and sweaty. The weather's so . . ."

"Not that it isn't too hot to eat anything," he said quickly. "Hotter than Rome. And I was longing for an English drizzle."

"We had a little shower on Monday evening. Did you get that in London?"

"Monday? No, Sunday we had a few spots."

"It was Monday here, I remember. The gardens needed it, but it didn't do much good."

He looked round for somewhere to put the broken china. "No, I suppose not."

"It hardly penetrated. Do put that in the wastepaper-basket."

"This cup is fairly neatly broken in half, it could be riveted. I can take it back to London with me."

"I won't hear of it. But it is so kind . . . I suppose the cat may as well have the remains of this—though not straight away. He must be shown that I am cross with him. Oh, dear, and I fetched it last thing from the village so that it should be fresh. But that's not much use to you, as it's turned out."

She disappeared into the kitchen with her hands full of lobster shells.

He looked round the room and so much of it seemed familiar to him. A stout woman passing by in the lane and trying to see in through the window might be Mrs Waterlow herself, who came so amusingly into Emily's letters.

He hoped things were soon going to get better, for he had never seen anyone so distracted as Emily when he arrived. He had been prepared for shyness, and had thought he could deal with that, but her frenzied look, with the blood on her face and the bits of lobster in her hands, made him feel that he had done some damage which, like the china, was quite beyond his repairing.

She was a long time gone, but shouted from the kitchen that he must take a glass of sherry, as he was glad to do.

"May I bring some out to you?" he asked.

"No, no thank you. Just pour it out and I will come."

When she returned at last, he saw that she had washed her face and combed her hair. What the great stain all across her skirt was, he could not guess. She was carrying a little dish of sardines, all neatly wedged together as they had been lying in their tin.

"It is so dreadful," she began. "You will never forget being given a tin of sardines, but they will go better with the wine than the baked beans, which is the only other thing I can find."

"I am *very* fond of sardines," he said.

She put the dish on the table and then, for the first time, looked at him. He was of medium height after all, with broader shoulders than she had imagined. His hair was a surprise to her. From his photograph, she had imagined it white—he was, after all, ten years older than she—but instead, it was blond and bleached by the sun. 'And I always thought I was writing to a white-haired man,' she thought.

Her look lasted only a second or two and then she drank her sherry quickly, with her eyes cast down.

"I hope you forgive me for coming here," he said gravely. Only by seriousness could he hope to bring them back to the relationship in which they really stood. He approached her so fearfully, but she shied away.

"Of course," she said. "It is *so* nice. After all these years. But I am sure you must be starving. Will you sit here?"

How are we to continue? he wondered.

She was garrulous with small talk through lunch, pausing only to take up her wine-glass. Then, at the end, when she had handed him his coffee, she failed. There was no more to say, not a word more to be wrung out of the weather, or the restaurant in Rome they had found they had in common, or the annoyances of travel—the train that was late and the cabin that was stuffy. Worn-out, she still cast about for a subject to embark on. The silence was unendurable. If it continued, might he not suddenly say, "You are so different from all I had imagined", or their eyes might meet and they would see in one another's nakedness and total loss.

*　　　*　　　*

"I *did* say Wednesday," said Mrs Waterlow.

"No, Thursday," Emily insisted. If she could not bar the doorway with forbidding arms, she did so with malevolent thoughts. Gentle and patient neighbour she had always been and Mrs Waterlow, who had the sharp nose of the total abstainer and could smell alcohol on Emily's breath, was quite astonished

The front door of the cottage opened straight into the living-room and Edmund was exposed to Mrs Waterlow, sitting forward in his chair, staring into a coffee-cup.

"I'll just leave the poster for the Jumble Sale then," said

Mrs Waterlow. "We shall have to talk about the refreshments another time. I think, don't you, that half a pound of tea does fifty people. Mrs Harris will see to the slab cake. But if you're busy, I mustn't keep you. Though since I am here, I wonder if I could look up something in your Encyclopaedia. I won't interrupt. I promise."

"May I introduce Mr Fabry?" Emily said, for Mrs Waterlow was somehow or other in the room.

"Not Mr *Edmund* Fabry?"

Edmund, still holding his coffee cup and saucer, managed to stand up quickly and shake hands.

"The author? I could recognise you from your photo. Oh, my daughter will be so interested. I must write at once to tell her. I'm afraid I've never read any of your books."

Edmund found this, as he always found it, unanswerable. He gave an apologetic murmur, and smiled ingratiatingly.

"But I always read the reviews of them in the Sunday papers." Mrs Waterlow went on, "I'm afraid we're rather a booky family."

So far, she had said nothing to which he could find any reply. Emily stood helplessly beside him, saying nothing. She was not wringing her hands, but he thought that if they had not been clasped so tightly together, that was what would have happened.

"You've *really* kept Mr Fabry in the dark, Emily," said Mrs Waterlow.

Not so *you* to *me*; Edmund thought. He had met her many times before in Emily's letters, already knew that her family was 'booky' and had had her preposterous opinions on many things.

She was a woman of fifty-five, whose children had grown up and gone thankfully away. They left their mother almost permanently, it seemed to them, behind the tea-urn at the village hall—and a good watching-place it was. She had, as

Emily once put it, the over-alert look of a ventriloquist's dummy. Her head, cocked slightly, turned to and fro between Emily and Edmund. 'Dyed hair' she thought, glancing away from him. She was often wrong about people.

"Now, don't let me interrupt you. You get on with your coffee. I'll just sit quiet in my corner and bury myself in the Encyclopaedia."

"Would you like some coffee?" Emily asked. "I'm afraid it may be rather cold."

"If there *is* some going begging, nothing would be nicer. 'Shuva to Tom-Tom', that's the one I want." She pulled out the Encyclopaedia and rather ostentatiously pretended to wipe dust from her fingers.

She has presence of mind, Edmund decided, watching her turn the pages with speed, and authority. She has really thought of something to look up. He was sure that he could not have done so as quickly himself. He wondered what it was that she had hit upon. She had come to a page of photographs of Tapestry and began to study them intently. There appeared to be pages of close print on the subject. So clever, Edmund thought.

She knew that he was staring at her and looked up and smiled; her finger marking the place. "To settle an argument," she said. "I'm afraid we are a very argumentative family."

Edmund bowed.

A silence fell. He and Emily looked at one another, but she looked away first. She sat on the arm of a chair, as if she were waiting to spring up to see Mrs Waterlow out—as indeed she was.

The hot afternoon was a spell they had fallen under. A bluebottle zig-zagged about the room, hit the window-pane, then went suddenly out of the door. A petal dropped off a geranium on the window-sill—occasionally—but not often enough for Edmund—a page was turned, the thin paper rustling silkily over. Edmund drew his wrist out of his sleeve and glanced secretly at his watch, and Emily saw him do it. It was a long journey he had made to see her, and soon he must be returning.

Mrs Waterlow looked up again. She had an amused smile, as if they were a couple of shy children whom she had just introduced to one another. "Oh, dear, why the silence? I'm not listening, you know. You will make me feel that I am in the way."

You preposterous old trollop, Edmund thought viciously. He leant back, put his finger-tips together and said, looking across at Emily; "Did I tell you that cousin Joseph had a nasty accident? Out bicycling. *Both* of them, you know. Such a deprivation. No heir, either. But Constance very soon consoled herself. With one of the Army padres out there. They were discovered by Joseph's batman in the most unusual circumstances. The Orient's insidious influence, I suppose. So strangely exotic for Constance, though." He guessed—though he did not look—that Mrs Waterlow had flushed and, pretending not to be listening, was struggling hard *not* to flush.

"Cousin Constance's Thousand and One Nights," he said. "The padre had courage. Like engaging with a boa-constrictor, I'd have thought."

If only Emily had not looked so alarmed. He began to warm to his inventions, which grew more macabre and outrageous—and, as he did so, he could hear the pages turning quickly and at last the book was closed with a loud thump. "That's clinched *that* argument," said Mrs Waterlow. "Hubert is so often inaccurate, but won't have it that he can ever be wrong." She tried to sound unconcerned, but her face was set in lines of disapproval.

"You are triumphant, then?" Edmund asked and he stood up and held out his hand.

When she had gone, Emily closed the door and leant against it. She looked exhausted.

"Thank you," she said. "She would never have gone otherwise. And now it is nearly time for *you* to go."

"I am sorry about Cousin Joseph. I could think of no other way."

In Emily's letters, Mrs Waterlow had been funny; but she was not in real life and he wondered how Emily could suffer so much, before transforming it.

"My dear, if you are sorry I came, then I am sorry, too."

"Don't say anything. Don't talk of it," she begged him, standing with her hands pressed hard against the door behind her. She shrank from words, thinking of the scars they leave, which she would be left to tend when he had gone. If he spoke the truth, she could not bear it; if he tried to muffle it with tenderness, she would look upon it as pity. He had made such efforts, she knew; but he could never have protected her from herself.

He, facing her, turned his eyes for a moment towards the window; then he looked back at her. He said nothing; but she knew that he had seen the station-car drawing to a standstill beyond the hollyhocks.

"You have to go?" she asked.

He nodded.

Perhaps the worst has happened, she thought. I have fallen in love with him—the one thing from which I felt I was completely safe.

Before she moved aside from the door, she said quickly, as if the words were red-hot coals over which she must pick her way—"If you write to me again, will you leave out today, and let it be as if you had not moved out of Rome?"

"Perhaps I didn't," he said.

At the door, he took her hand and held it against his cheek for a second—a gesture both consoling and conciliatory.

When he had gone, she carried her grief decently upstairs

to her little bedroom and there allowed herself some tears. When they were dried and over, she sat down by the open window.

She had not noticed how clouds had been crowding into the sky. A wind had sprung up and bushes and branches were jigging and swaying.

The hollyhocks nodded together. A spot of rain as big as a halfpenny dropped on to the stone sill, others fell over leaves down below, and a sharp cool smell began to rise at once from the earth.

She put her head out of the window, her elbows on the outside sill. The soft rain, falling steadily now, calmed her. Down below in the garden the cat wove its way through a flower-bed. At the door, he began to cry piteously to be let in and she shut the window a little and went downstairs. It was dark in the living-room; the two windows were fringed with dripping leaves; there were shadows and silence.

While she was washing up, the cat, turning a figure-of-eight round her feet, brushed her legs with his wet fur. She began to talk to him, as she often did, for they were alone so much together. "If you were a dog," she said, "we could go for a nice walk in the rain."

As it was, she gave him his supper and took an apple for herself. Walking about, eating it, she tidied the room. The sound of the rain in the garden was very peaceful. She carried her writing-things to the table by the window and there, in the last of the light, dipped her goose-quill pen in the ink, and wrote, in her fine and flowing hand, her address, and then, "Dear Edmund."

A Troubled State of Mind

IN the old part of the town, between the castle and the cathedral, were some steep and cobbled streets whose pavements were broken open by the roots of plane trees. The tall and narrow houses stood back, beyond the walls of gardens and courtyards, but there were glimpses of them through wrought-iron gates. The quiet here was something that country people found unbelievable. Except for the times when the cathedral bells were ringing, the silence was broken only by the rooks in the castle trees or, as on this afternoon, by the sound of rain.

Lalage left the car in the garage at the foot of the hill and the two girls—Lalage herself and her step-daughter, Sophy—walked as quickly as they could towards home, carrying the smaller pieces of Sophy's luggage, Lalage, already hostess-like (Sophy thought), bowed over to one side with the weight of the bigger suitcase, and the other arm thrust out shoulder-high to right her balance.

The road narrowed gradually to less than a car's width and rain ran fast down the cobbles, swirling into drains. Reaching the gate in the wall, Sophy swung her skis off her back and turned the iron handle. The scraping, rusty sound of it was suddenly remembered and was as strange to her as anything else in a world where every familiar thing had moved into a pattern too fantastic ever—she was sure—to be dealt with or understood. She and Lalla, for instance, going in through this gate as they had done so often before; but

Sophy now at a loss to guess what might be waiting for her inside, in her own home.

Her father, Colonel Vellacott, had always loved Italy and everything Italian and had tried to make a Venetian court-yard in wet England. Its sadness was appalling, Sophy thought. The paving-stones were dark with rain and drops fell heavily from the vine and the magnolia, off statues and urns and, in a sudden gust of wind, rattled like bullets on the broad fig leaves by the wall. In the seats of some iron chairs puddles reflected the cloudy sky.

"John will be back for dinner," Lalage said, as they picked their way across the wet stones—"He had to go because he was in the chair."

Ah yes, 'John', of course, Sophy thought.

The front door opened and Miss Sully came out to take the case from Lalage, primly eager to wring all she could from the peculiar situation. "It is just like old times," she said to Sophy, "when Madam used to come to stay with you in the holidays and I used to listen to hear the gate so that I could run out with a welcome."

'Madam' had been a shock and a calculated one, Sophy thought. She smiled and shook hands. "In the old days, you always said we had grown. Not any more, I hope."

"Grown *up*, I should say."

"Isn't she brown?" said Lalla.

"As brown as a berry."

They went into the dark hall where the Italian influence continued in glass and marble, trailing leaves and a wrought-iron screen which served no purpose. Nothing visible had been altered since Sophy was here last, a year ago, but everything invisible had been. At Sophy's bedroom door, Miss Sully turned away, with promises of tea in five minutes and a fire in the drawing-room. Sophy, standing in the middle of the room, looking about her, but not at Lalla, asked: "How do you get on with *her*?"

"As I always did, trying to be as nice as pie, wearing myself out, really, but not getting anywhere. She is, as we always found her, a mystery woman."

"Kind . . ." Sophy began.

"Kindness itself. Thoughtful, considerate, efficient. But what lies underneath, who knows? Something does. She's learning Italian now."

"Perhaps that's what's underneath. Not enough goes on here for her. She's too intelligent to be a housekeeper, and too ambitious."

"Then why go on?"

Sophy could not now say "I think because she hoped to marry my father." She had sometimes thought it in the past and suddenly wondered if she had ever told Lalla. She felt that she must have done, for she had told her everything, though she no longer could.

"What was Switzerland *like*?" Lalla asked, "I mean really."

"It went on too long."

Sophy put her fingers to the locks of her suitcase, about to spring them open, and then could not be bothered, and straightened her back, thinking, She will wonder why, if I found it too long, I did not come back earlier, as I could have done, and should have done and would have done, if it had not been for *that*. It was always 'that' in her mind—the marriage of her father and her dearest friend. The other questions—Sophy's questions—that hovered between them were too unseemly to be spoken—for instance 'why?' and 'how?' and 'where did it begin?' The only question in the least possible Sophy was turning over in her mind and beginning to make a shape of it in words, when Lalla, before it could be spoken, answered it. Since early girlhood, they had often found their thoughts arriving at the same point without the promptings of speech.

"I am so happy, you know," Lalla said. "It is all so lovely

in this house and now to have you in it with me at last!
Though," she added quickly, "it is you who have always
been here and I who has at last arrived."

"But, Lalla dear, you always seemed *part* of the house to
me. We never called the spare room anything but 'Lalla's
room'. When other people came to stay, it seemed wrong
to me that they should hang their clothes in your cupboard."

Then she suddenly bent down and unclicked her suitcase
after all, to have something to do with her trembling fingers,
and wondered, what is the spare room called now? I have
made another booby-trap for us, where there already were
too many.

"Did you notice," Lalage asked, as if she had not heard,
"how eagerly Miss Sully ran out to greet you? She has been
quite excited all the week."

"I can understand that." Sophy lifted the lid of the
suitcase and looked gloomily at her creased and folded
clothes. "She loves situations and she wanted to see how I
was facing this one."

"Yes, to see if you were jealous of me, hoping perhaps,
that life here from now on would be full of interesting little
scenes between us, something to sustain and nourish her
while she chops the parsley—which she does—doesn't she?
—with not just *kitchen* venom?"

"She will analyse everything we say and fit it into her
conception of our relationship."

"She has already tried to haunt me with your mother—
so beautiful she was and you are growing up to be her
image."

Sophy lifted her head from the unpacking and could not
help giving a quick look into the mirror before her. "How
absurd!" she said. "If she could throw up a woman so long
dead, how impatiently she must have waited for *me* to
throw *myself* up."

"She longs for incidents. I am sure she will hover to see who pours out the tea and whether, from habit, you will go to your old place at the table."

This was brave of Lalage and seemed to clear the air.

"It is a good thing," Sophy said, "that you and I have read so many novels. The hackneyed dangers we should be safe from."

"We shall be safe *together*," Lalla said. "Loving one another," she added, so quietly that she seemed to be talking to herself.

"Demurrings and deprecations will not escape notice either," said Sophy. "Saying '*you* do it, please,' or 'you go first'. We must beware of every one of those. I will be a straightforward daughter to you, I think. It may be ageing for you, but I think it will be safer than for us to try to be like sisters. I thought of that in Switzerland, and I decided that a daughter has privileges and a rôle to play, which a younger or inferior sister has not."

"As long as I am never called 'Mamma'."

Miss Sully, hovering at the foot of the stairs, heard laughter as the bedroom door opened and Lalage's voice saying with great gaiety "Who—a year ago—would have believed that we could come to this?"

They were on the stairs now, and Miss Sully hurried back to the kitchen for the hot scones. She wanted to watch the approach to the tea table.

This turned out to be disappointing. Sophy went straight to the drawing-room window and, with her back turned to the room, said; "Since last I saw you, Lalla, I've given up milk and sugar. What father used to call 'puppy-fat' turned out just to be fat."

"Then I must do the same," said Lalla and sat down before the tray and took up the tea-pot. "And every time John goes out, we will have those slimming meals I am always reading about at the hairdresser's—meagre things like tomato jellies and stuffed cucumbers and lettuce juice. Meanwhile, you could have a scone, couldn't you?"

Sophy turned from the window and sat down in a chair, opposite the one where she had always sat before.

"Only this time," she said.

Miss Sully, having very slowly put a log on the fire and rearranged the tongs, was now obliged to go. At the door, she heard Sophy say, "Just to celebrate the occasion."

By the time Colonel Vellacott returned from his meeting, a mode of behaviour was established between the two girls. It had often been tried out in their minds during their separation, suggested and explored with nervous tact in their letters to one another.

He found them by the drawing-room fire, Lalage winding wool from Sophy's outstretched hands. Kneeling on the rug, Sophy rocked from side to side, and swayed her arms, turning her wrists deftly as the wool slipped off them. So often, bemused and patient, she had held Lalla's wool for her: the knitting craze came and went, jerseys were seldom finished and, if they were, were sorry things. From past experience, neither had high hopes for this new skein.

"A charming sight," Colonel Vellacott said. They had settled down together already, he was relieved to see. It was like bringing a new dog into a house where another had reigned alone for a long time. The scene might have been prearranged—the girls were so tangled up in wool that they could not extricate themselves and the kisses he gave each on the top of her head were almost simultaneous, Lalla hardly first at all.

That's *that* over, he thought, and for no reason felt self-congratulatory. 'That' for him, was his embarrassment. Now, it was as easy as could be to talk about Switzerland and Sophy most brilliantly took the lead with her descriptions of the school and the lunacy of its inhabitants.

"Don't!" Lalage half-sobbed, gasping with laughter, and wiped her eyes on the ball of wool.

"Ah, you are going into fits," her husband said. He remembered all the holiday laughter in this house, Lalla's cries of "Don't" and her collapsed state, his teasing of them both and his mocking echoes of their girlish phrases. He had felt in those days wonderfully indulgent. "Bring Lalla back with you," he always told Sophy. "It is sad for you to be alone—and sad for her, too." Lalla—the poor orphan child—lived with an aunt, but was more often, in school holidays, at Ancaster, with Sophy.

"Now, Lalla!" he said, in a severe voice. He leant back in his chair and folded his arms with a show of excessive patience. "If you snort again, you must be sent away."

"Oh, please, I *ache*," she implored Sophy, holding the ball of wool tight to her ribs, her beautiful eyes glittering with tears.

"Oh, please, I *ache*, Sophy," said Colonel Vellacott.

"I am only telling you what happened," Sophy said, with what Lalla called her straight face.

"The experience seems to have been worth every penny," her father said.

"Yes, I am truly finished."

The end of the wool slipped from her fingers, she sank back on her heels and looked up at her father, at last returning his gaze, smiling with love and delight, but with a reserve of mischief, too, and that pleased him most of all, it was what gave reality to her warm-heartedness. If she were dissembling her gaiety and friendliness, she would not have dissembled *that*, he thought. It would not have occurred to her as a necessary ingredient of mirth.

*   *   *

Sophy kept up her spirits throughout dinner and then flagged. It was her long journey, the other two said and she agreed. "And you miss the clarity of that air," her father added.

But there were other exhaustions she could less easily endure and the chief was, she saw, that she had cast herself in a rôle that would take too much from her.

She remembered—and this was after she had said good-night and gone to her room—long ago and when her mother was alive, she herself perhaps five or six years old, being taken on a train journey, from Edinburgh, her mother's old home it may have been. Kneeling in her corner seat, breathing on the window, breathing and wiping, in stupefying boredom, she had begun suddenly to talk in baby talk, demanding, for no reason she could now recall, in a lispy, whiny voice that had never been her own, a "chocky bikky." Her mother, gently remonstrating, had made publicly clear that this odd voice was to be regarded as a game. "Icky chocky bikky," Sophy had insisted pouting. It was then that she had first realised her own power of mimicry; power it was and went to her head. She had *become* the nauseating infant she impersonated. Other people in the compartment took the lead from her mother and laughed. Sophy herself had pretended not to hear this and turned her back and breathed on the window again, but soon she could not help herself. "Pitty gee-gees", she said, pointing. When she had tired of talking, she let her eyelids droop and began to suck her thumb as she had scornfully watched other children doing. Her mother, who knew that things were going too far, but was never brisk with her in public, tried to distract her attention, but could not. The performance had been tiring, like playing Lady Macbeth with heart and soul and, in the end, Sophy had become sickened by her own creation, caught in its tentacles and quite unable to escape. Everyone else was tired, too; she knew that her mother was desperate and that glances were exchanged; but she seemed powerless to end the misery. It was too late to speak suddenly in her own voice. What voice was it, and what things did it say? She could remember putting her forehead to the cool window-pane and counting to herself 'One, two, then three and then I'll speak again as I used and they will all know the other voice has gone.' But her shyness was too great, she was too committed to the other character and had no way of breaking loose from it. Badgered, exhausted and embarrassed, she had at last burst into tears, taking refuge, as she wept, against her mother's arm. "Over-tired," the grown-ups said. "Such a long journey. She's stood up to it very well."

Lalla and her father had said goodnight and used the same words, though now the climate was to blame as well. They were no more true than when she was a child. The acting had exhausted her, and nothing else. She could have cried, as she had when a young girl, "Oh, my darling Mamma, why did you have to die?" The words were so loud in her head and her breast that she might have said them aloud. They returned with the aching familiarity of a long time ago, when she had lain in bed after lights-out at boarding-school, or on their first Christmas Eve alone, with her father trying to remember everything her mother had always done, so that Sophy should not be deprived of one sprig of holly or Christmas tree candle. In the end, unbelievably, the words had become a habit and lost their pain. Her life without her mother was different from before, but it was, after all, the same life. If Mamma had been here, she sometimes thought, accepting that she could not be.

This evening the phrase sprang at her with a sudden freshness, the first time for years. She sat down on the edge of her bed and her hands dropped into her lap, palms upwards in a gesture of hopeless inertia. 'If she were alive,' she thought, 'she would be downstairs with father, and Lalla here with me, as she ought to be. Or not under this roof at

all. And I should be relieved of this tiring pretence, that
won't end with the end of the train journey, as it did
before. It will be there waiting for me in the morning and
all the mornings after—having to be gay and unself-
conscious—as if it were a perfectly normal thing for one's
father to marry one's school-friend—fifty-three and
eighteen and all plotted and planned with me safely out of
the way in a foreign country,' she added, feeling self-pity.
'I must be gracious and hand over my home and my place
in it and have, day in, day out, my constant companion
chosen for me.'

Sometimes, at school, Lalla had stolen marches on her.
She could remember well the case of the borrowed treasure
and the broken promise, the forgotten appointment, the
betrayed confidence. Many instances came to her mind
from the dark place where they had long ago been thrust
impatiently away.

'I must get away,' she thought, and her hands sprang to
life and were clenched tight, drumming on her knees. 'I
must run away from my own home, as soon as I have come
back to it.' In Switzerland, she had longed for it so much, in
that clear air her father had mentioned, faced for months at
a time with the monotony of the snow, and the dark trees
that never shed their leaves, as trees ought, she was sure.
"Write to me about England," she had begged her father
and Lalage. "Describe a nice drizzle, a beautiful muggy
evening with the fallen leaves sticking to the pavements.
You describe it for me, though; not I to you."

Instead, they had written to say that they were getting
married. They had met several times in London, for both
had been lonely, missing Sophy. In their loneliness they had
flown together, and clung, and wished to remain so for
ever. The loneliness had been much stressed—orphan and
widower, as they constantly referred to themselves.
Companionship (and Sophy was to share in this, too) and

common interests (both liked going to plays, but seldom did so) were enlarged upon. Love itself was not once mentioned and Sophy was glad that it was not. She was to fly home for the wedding—very quiet, just the three of them and Lalage's aunt. But Sophy would not go. She was on her way up to a chalet for the winter sports and had made arrangements which she could not confuse. She knew that they were glad to have her stay in Switzerland and she was glad to do so, although she was sure that if she had not gone there in the first place, she could have prevented things from reaching such a pass.

Her bedroom, above her father's, overlooked the courtyard and when she heard footsteps out there, she went across to the window and looked out. It was almost dark. Lalage and her father were going for a walk in the rain. He opened the courtyard door into the street and as Lalage passed through it, put his hand on her shoulder.

'Ah, yes, and bedtime, too,' Sophy thought turning away. 'Beyond one's imagination, thank God. I hope I can hide my revulsion from her. I daresay there's nothing to stop her having a baby even. It is perfectly possible.'

Their footsteps and voices faded away down the street. The drizzle continued, and downstairs Miss Sully was singing 'Oh, what a Beautiful Morning.'

'I must get a job,' Sophy thought. 'Without a day's delay.'

*   *   *

"Sophy's job", was soon a great topic of conversation.

Colonel Vellacott was full of facetious suggestions. At every meal some new one came to mind, and Sophy grinned, and wondered if her face would crack in two, as her heart must.

"Oh, hush, I can't hear of it," Lalage would beg her husband, and stuff her fingers in her ears. "Sophy, please!

You will make me think you are running away from *me*
and it will be as Miss Sully predicted." She kept her hands
pressed to her cheekbones, ready to make herself deaf again,
if necessary. Her bracelets slid down her thin arms to her
elbows. Her eyes were full of pleading.

'Affected,' Sophy thought. 'She used not to be. Father
loves it.'

"I always meant to get a job," she said. "I couldn't have
just stayed here and looked after the house—which Miss
Sully does much better anyhow." But this was dangerous
ground and she stepped from it quickly. "I should have
taken the Secretarial course with you, Lalla, if Father hadn't
made me go to Switzerland first."

"*Made?*" said Colonel Vellacott.

"Persuaded, then."

"Your French was horrible."

"Well, 'made' me, then."

"You'd have loathed the Secretarial School," Lalla said
complacently. "I hated every moment."

'And was glad to leave it and get married,' Sophy thought.
'So it was typing and shorthand that drove you to it. He
hasn't after all, a spectacular enough amount of money to
be married for. And love? If you love him, you show none
of it. Perhaps I inhibit you and force you to keep it for when
you are alone. In which case, the sooner I go, the better.'

She felt absurdly in the way, but also shut out that they
should turn to secrecy because of her.

*   *   *

It was not easy to slip away from Lalage, her too-constant
companion, but, one morning, she managed to, and set out,
as if on an illicit errand, through wet alleyways towards the
Market Place. It had rained for all of the fortnight she had
been at home, but had this morning stopped. The clouds
had lifted and broken open and bright light, though not yet

quite sunshine, poured down over the puddles and dripping eaves. Slate roofs dried rapidly and pavements steamed. It was the end of April.

"We begin the second of May," said the Principal of the Secretarial School in Market Street. She underlined this date on the application form. "Your father will complete this for you." She thought it strange for the girl to come there on her own, making enquiries. Sophy stared at her hands, which were a dark plum colour, scarred from broken chilblains. Clumsy as they were, she used them affectedly, drawing attention to them with hooked fingers as she wrote, and then by twisting round an engagement ring of dull little diamonds.

"I know your father very well," Miss Priestley said. "Although I don't suppose he would be able to place *me*. I was a reporter once upon a time on the *Ancaster Herald* and used to cover some of the Court cases when he was on the bench. And my late fiancé was in his regiment in the war. He didn't come back," she added, in an affectedly casual voice she had learnt at the cinema.

"I'm so sorry," Sophy murmured.

"Yes, we had been engaged for eleven years. But you don't want to listen to all my sad affairs."

Although this was true, Sophy felt obliged to make a sound which she hoped suggested denial as well as a certain amount of discouragement. If only there were something amusing in this she thought. Something with which to decorate the plain statement when I tell them at lunch. But there was not: the bereaved Miss Priestley with her chilblains was saddening and unattractive and the office was stuffy and untidy, not a good example to the pupils.

The sun was shining when Sophy stood, dazed by its brightness, on the steps in Market Street. The Town Hall clock struck twelve. She hurried back home and was there before Lalla returned from the hairdresser's.

"Just *see* what they've done," was Lalla's piteous cry at luncheon. They had always done the same thing and Sophy only briefly glanced.

"Why don't you tell them?" asked Colonel Vellacott and seemed to have an edge of exasperation to his voice.

"I tell them and tell them. As smooth as smooth, I always say. Not a kink or a curl or I shall be so cross."

"It will settle down," Sophy said. "It always does."

They had just finished what Miss Sully called "chicken and all the trimmings."

"They've caught that man," Miss Sully said, as she lifted the dishes off the table. "They gave it out on the one o'clock news."

"What man?" asked Lalla, still fidgeting with her hair.

"The one that assaulted that little boy and then smothered him."

"Oh dear!" Lalage frowned.

"I shouldn't have mentioned it, only I thought you'd like to know. It isn't very nice at mealtimes, I'm afraid." She stacked the plates and carried them away.

"This is a very rum Baba," said Colonel Vellacott, as he always did when given this pudding, and Sophy felt the usual embarrassment, wondering—as she was also used to wondering—just how tedious her friend found this heavy jocularity. Then she remembered that her father was much more Lalage's responsibility. The old situation was reversed. It should be Lalla's task to try to prevent the inevitable phrases, to turn the conversations as deftly as she could as the stale quip rose ominously before them.

'And I shall enjoy seeing how she does it, as time goes on,' she thought. At present, Lalla was merely smiling her bright, usual smile, a guest's smile, vaguely willing.

"I met someone this morning who knows you, Father," Sophy suddenly told him, deciding that as any kind of approach to her embarrassment would lead to it, this would do as well as any. "In fact, I did not so much meet her as go to see her."

Colonel Vellacott waited—with the calm of a man who has nothing to fear—for the mystery to unfold, but Lalla stopped eating, put her fork down on her plate and glanced anxiously at Sophy, who went on: "Though she says you would never be able to place *her. Can* you place someone called Miss Priestley, who has a secretarial school—no, college, so sorry—in Market Street?"

"No. She is right. I can't."

"Is she from your past?" Lalla asked. "Poor Miss Priestley! I am glad that I am in your present."

"No, she simply wrote down in shorthand things you said in Court," Sophy explained. "And her fiancé was in the regiment and was killed, but I don't think she blamed you for it."

"It was generous of her. Especially as I survived. I should have thought she would have resented that."

"Why did you go to see her?" Lalla asked, taking up her fork again.

"She is going to teach me to be a secretary."

"Oh no! Then I shall come too, I won't be left here on my own. May I go, too, John?"

"You know that we agreed not to be sisters," Sophy told her. "You have to learn to be my Mamma and stay at home while I go off to school."

"I shall be lonely."

"Mothers are. Though perhaps they get used to it, and even rather like it in the end."

"Why did you go about the business in so odd a way?" her father asked. "There was no necessity to be secretive. If you wanted to do it at all, you should have said so."

"I said, and said."

"We thought you were joking."

"Yes, I knew you thought that."

"And I might have been consulted, I should have thought. I could have done much better for you than this Miss Whatshername, of whom I certainly have never heard."

"Then why did you do nothing?"

"Now, Sophy, don't try to be cool with me. You are only just home from Switzerland and there was all the time in the world to make arrangements."

"I never like to do things at a leisurely pace," Sophy said, looking calmly at him. "One may as well get on with life." As you did, her voice implied.

"But we know nothing of this Miss Thingummy. She seems a strange end to your education."

"It is what I want, Father."

Lalla, murmuring 'coffee', left the room.

"I was bringing it," said Miss Sully, who was never caught out. The tray was in her hands.

Instead of going ahead to the drawing-room, Lalla ran upstairs murmuring 'handkerchief'.

In the dining-room Colonel Vellacott and his daughter were arguing. "Unlike you, Sophy," Miss Sully heard.

"I've put the coffee in the drawing-room," she said, then hurried forward to rearrange the fire. But there was nothing for her to listen to but the sound of their chairs being pushed back. "Madam will be down directly," she added.

This was unanswerable and unanswered. Sophy crossed the hall to the drawing-room and without sitting down, carelessly poured out her father's coffee and her own. She took hers over to the window-seat and began to sip it, lifting the cup only a little from its brimming saucer. She Supposed that Lalla was upstairs, waiting for them to finish their quarrel.

*   *   *

Displeased and austere Colonel Vellacott remained for days, wearing what Sophy called his Doge's face. With

Lalage, too, and in private, he was reserved. Rebellion was in the air—a youthful contagion that he intended should not spread. Don't *you* go running to some Miss Thingummy, or even worse, his mood seemed to warn her.

That Sophy's action was hardly drastic he constantly reminded himself, but her way of taking it had been cold and secretive. For her to earn her own living was nothing other than he intended and desired, but it seemed to him that there was no desperate need and that for a month or two she might have helped him out with Lalla. 'Helped me out' was his own phrase. He had seen what he called 'Bride's despondency' in Lalage's eyes, in spite of her bright smiles and her laughter. He did not know how to cheer her up; his time was so much given over to public work and there was no theatre here in Ancaster. She was lonely and suffering reaction from the sudden adventure of their courtship and wedding. He could not hide his anxiety that the house was dull and silent and—with all his Italian décor long ago perfected—too completed. She had simply taken over what was there and had had nothing to contribute. Although he was pleased with what he had done, he began to wonder if it was what a bride would hope for. "One day, we will have a change," he had promised, but could not bring himself to move one fern or sconce. She had insisted—not knowing what was good for her—that nothing should be touched and that she loved it exactly as it was.

Sophy's home-coming had raised her spirits and he himself had felt freer and happier and less anxious. He looked forward to entering the house when he returned from his meetings. People who have had the best of both worlds are the crossest of all when the best in one is lost, and he knew this and scolded himself, but the Doge's face remained and, inhibited by his new habit of sternness, he found himself unable to make love to Lalage. The marriage, Miss Sully thought, was crumbling even more quickly than she had predicted.

*   *   *

At Miss Priestley's, Sophy was by far the eldest girl and the slowest one at learning, too. Miserably, she bowed her head over the abominable hooks and dots of her shorthand, or touch-typed rows of percentage signs or fractions where should have been 'Dear Sirs, We beg to confirm receipt of your esteemed order.'

The other girls had left school at sixteen and seemed as quick as birds with their taking down and reading back, always put their carbon paper in the right way round and never typed addresses on upside-down envelopes.

The class-rooms were on the first floor of the old house, a building now given over to offices. The boards were bare and the long tables were ribbed and splintered and ink-stained. Miss Priestley felt the cold and even in May the windows were kept shut, so that the air was chalk-laden and smelt of lead pencils and glue and india-rubber and girls. The windows faced south, over the top branches of budding lilac trees. Below was a tangled garden into which Sophy found herself more and more inclined to stare. At twelve and four, the heavy notes of the Town Hall clock descended on the roof tops in the most gracious—Sophy thought— signal of release. She was the first to have her books closed, knowing before the chimes began that they were imminent; she could feel the air growing tense and the clock gathering itself to strike, and her face would put on its bright, good- bye look, turned expectantly towards Miss Priestley for dismissal.

Then, being free, she was suddenly loth to go home to Lalla's 'I knew you'd hate it!' The other girls clustered together and showed one another their work, but Sophy took down her jacket from its peg. She knew that the others exchanged looks when she left them and when she called out 'goodbye' only one or two answered her, and then in a surprised tone as if it were strange of her to address them.

Sometimes, instead of going home to tea, she would buy an evening paper and read it in a little café in Market Street. The idea of punishment being in the air, it suited her to think of her teacup on the tray at home, unfilled. There, in the Oak Beams Tea Shop, she met Graham Dennis again. He was working in a solicitor's office nearby and had so grown up that she had not recognised him.

*   *   *

The Dennis's parties were famous in Ancaster, and Sophy had been going to them for as long as she could remember. Mrs Dennis always described herself as putting herself out for her young people and was not content with Christmas and birthday parties. There were Hallowe'en parties and garden parties, and parties at the New Year and on Guy Fawkes' Day. Her husband could find no escape. If there were not children bobbing for apples in the hall, they were playing charades in several rooms, or hunting for treasure all over the house. "I shall rope Herbert in," Mrs Dennis told her friends, who, rather aggrieved because she put themselves so much to shame, wondered how she could manage it. Herbert had been roped in to let off fireworks or be Father Christmas. Lately, as Denise and Graham were no longer children, he was roped in to make claret cup or dance with an odd girl out.

Sophy remembered even the first parties, when she was a little girl. After the exquisite orderliness of her own home, the great, shabby, untidy house with its lighted windows and its noise infected her with delicious excitement.

Mrs Dennis was always kindness itself. "You are only young once," she often told her children and their friends and made sure that, as well as youth, they had as many other delights lavished on them as she could find time and money to bestow. At the back of her mind, she knew that the two most important parties of all would come at the end: even in nursery days, watching the little ones departing with their balloons and presents, she felt that she was only rehearsing for the culmination of it all—Denise's wedding and Graham's twenty-first birthday. Now, both were looming in the same year and 'loom' was her own word for their approach. She was confident that she would surpass herself—the Dennis wedding would be talked about for years; but, for the last time of many, Denise would say, as she drove away: "Thank you for doing it all." Beyond, lay a blank future for her mother. But first would come Graham's twenty-first birthday and any champagne left over from that would come in later for the wedding. Only one thing perplexed her, as they went over the list of invitations. Lalage, when staying with Sophy, as she so often was, had always been invited too. For years and years, she had attended the Dennis parties.

"We couldn't leave her out now," Mrs Dennis said.

"And how possibly ask her?" Graham said. "Husbands and wives go to parties together. You'd have to ask that old man."

"He is only your father's age," Mrs Dennis said, but she knew that that was what Graham meant. It was an awkward situation. She realised that she and Herbert were only at the parties themselves in order to see that the food and drink were plentiful and available. Herbert knew his place and preferring it, made off to his study as soon as he was able, and Mrs Dennis was always in and out of the kitchen.

"How sad to leave her out, after all these years, poor girl," she said.

*   *   *

Lalage felt both sad and embarrassed when Sophy's invitation came. Her husband, watching her show of unconcern, realised for the first time the consequences of their romance. The marriage, surviving important hazards, seemed now as likely as not to founder upon trivial matters, on this invitation, for instance, and others that would follow. Lalage had been ardent and generous in her love, to come first in someone's life exalted her and, radiant and incredulous, she had given herself in gratitude. Yet, at the sight of an invitation to a party, she appeared to falter, she glanced away and was confused and could not hide her feeling that she had placed herself in a special position with her contemporaries, was being markedly pushed by them into the ranks of the middle-aged.

Sophy, her father realised, was no longer making things easier, but worsening them. The sooner she could go away and leave them, the better for them all. He could perfectly see this now and wondered how he could hasten what he had so lately tried to prevent.

"As you seem so sure about your typing and shorthand," he said one day, with a great show of tolerance, "and are really settled to it, I am quite willing for you to do the thing properly, to go up to London and train at some reputable place."

But Sophy had not settled to her shorthand and typing; every day she fell back, as the other girls progressed; and now she no longer wanted to go away from Ancaster, having at the twenty-first birthday party, fallen in love with Graham Dennis.

Graham and Sophy had rediscovered one another, as young people do who have lived in the same neighbourhood for years and then been separated by school, so that, meeting in the holidays, they seem almost total strangers. Violent changes of height and voice and manner were bewildering and shyness descended. Now, with all the changes made—as they thought—quite grown-up and likely to remain the same for ever, they could sum one another up, and come to a conclusion. Sophy and Graham concluded that they were in love, that they must always have loved, though first immaturity and then separation had hindered their acceptance of the fact.

To Colonel Vellacott, Graham's National Service had not made the man of him it should. Nonchalant and without ambition, he had spent the two years cheerfully peeling potatoes or drinking in the Naafi. Promotion had seemed to him quite as undesirable as it was unlikely. To Colonel Vellacott's questions, on their first meeting after some years, he gave unsatisfactory answers. Nor did Colonel Vellacott like his clothes—his dirty cord trousers and suède shoes and vivid pullovers. Particularly he disliked—and in a cathedral city it was out of place, as Graham himself was—the car he drove. It was an old London taxi painted yellow, with window-boxes and lace curtains. Once, Graham had had written across the back "Do not laugh, Madam, your daughter may be inside." In love, and serious at last, he had painted this over.

Even so, that *his* daughter should be inside annoyed Colonel Vellacott considerably.

"Lots of young men have cars like it," Sophy told him. "It isn't smart to have a new one. The older and funnier the better."

"Not in a place like this."

"We can't *help* living in a place like this. And I think it's amusing. You were young once yourself, remember."

Lalage who could not easily escape these much dreaded discussions, turned aside.

*   *   *

Sophy and Lalla found their so gallantly planned relationship beginning to wear threadbare. It was difficult to keep up, especially as it was so unproductive of in-credulity in others—its primary aim. Their affection for one another was too easily taken for granted and few of their friends or acquaintances seemed to find it at all remarkable. Their laughter about the hackneyed jealousies that might have threatened them was joined in by their guests, who—so infectious was the gaiety—did not realise how much of relief it contained.

Sophy was the first to find the ordeal going on too long. It had become a mere routine of good behaviour, with no congratulation in it for herself. Miss Sully thought, observ-ing the minute omens, that soon the situation would have more piquancy. Lalla seemed dull and puzzled, with nothing to do but mend her clothes, change her library books and water all the ferns—too often, for they began to droop and rot away.

One morning, when Colonel Vellacott was in Court and Sophy at her Typing School, Lalage, feeling more restless than ever, wandered into the kitchen, where Miss Sully was making stuffing for green peppers. Lalla sat on a corner of the table and watched, picking up bits of parsley and chewing them, holding pepper-seeds on the tip of her tongue until it tingled.

Miss Sully, mixing raisins and rice, was talking of the days when she was companion to an old lady whose footman had interfered with one of the gardener's boys. She brought in many a Freudian phrase along with those of the cheapest newspapers and her voice dropped to its cathedral hush as it did when she talked of sex. One side of her neck was a bright red. Deftly her fingers worked and when she took up a large knife and began to chop some mushrooms, she abandoned herself almost obscenely to the job. "What's for pudding?" Lalla asked, like a little girl, as soon as there was quiet again. It had never occurred to her that she might order meals herself. She had once timidly put forward a

suggestion that Colonel Vellacott would like jugged hare,
but had been told that hare was out of season.

"Well, what *shall* we have?" Miss Sully asked suddenly
indulgent. The names of puddings at once went from Lalla's
head, although Miss Sully had such a repertoire of them—
there was Cabinet Pudding and High Church Pudding and
Guardsman's Pudding and even Railway Pudding—they
were mostly sponge mixtures, differing with a dash of spice
or jam, or a handful of candied peel. Lalla could never
remember which was which.

"What about rice pudding?" she asked. "I haven't had
that since I was at school."

"Well, we can't very well have rice two courses running,
can we?" Miss Sully asked, laughing gently and pointing at
the dish of peppers, now ready for the oven. "And you will
have to give me plenty of warning for rice pudding, because
the grain must soak at least an hour, you know."

Lalage hadn't known.

"Is there anything I can do?" she asked, jumping down
from the table. It was only eleven o'clock.

"Well, now, you could run the ribbon through the hem
of Miss Sophy's petticoat. I know she'll be wanting it this
evening. Then I can get on with some scones for tea."
("Without you under my feet," she seemed to imply.) By
the time she had told Lalla where to find the petticoat and
then the ribbon and the bodkin, she thought that she could
have done the job herself.

"The shiny side of the ribbon facing you, mind," she
warned her, thinking, "Really, she's as useless as a little
doll."

When Lalla had finished that small task, she carried the
petticoat to Sophy's room and laid it carefully on the bed,
hoping she would be touched and grateful when she discovered it there. And I would do anything for her, she
thought, if there were anything else to do.

She went over to the window and looked down into the courtyard—so still and full of heat and the scent of honeysuckle this sunny morning. On the wall below her, was the starry jasmine that framed her own bedroom window. She leaned out, resting her elbows on the rough stone sill, feeling insecurely attached to space and time—the seconds would never tick on till luncheon, or the silence be broken, or the sun ever again go in.

It was the room behind her that overcame, at last, her sense of unreality—though she had turned her back upon it, she felt it awaiting her attention—Sophy's room, where Sophy shut the door on all that she pretended downstairs and where she was confronted by her own thoughts, which she kept imprisoned in this place. They were almost palpably imprisoned, Lalla suddenly felt, ands he spun round quickly from the window as if to catch them unawares.

The room was menacing to her now and laden with treachery, its air heavy with secrets. The clock ticked slyly and a curtain lifted slowly and sank back full of warning. It was an alien territory and one where Lalla knew she had no right to be. Even the way the towels hung by the basin expressed hostility, she thought, and so did the truculent angle of the looking-glass. It did not seem too fanciful to imagine mute things infected by Sophy's own antagonism.

A letter addressed to Graham lay on the writing-table, the envelope unsealed and the pages sticking out from it as if as a reminder that they were to be added to, or something else enclosed.

In terror, Lalla thought, I could find out if I cared to, just where I stand with her and why, for weeks, she has shrugged me aside in that bright, cold way.

She recoiled and then, almost immediately, stepped quickly forward and drew the pages from the envelope, very careful to make no sound, lest Miss Sully, far below in the kitchen, would prick up her ears and sense the treachery.

'It is the worst thing people can do to one another,' she told herself, 'and I knew nothing about myself, when I believed that I could not.'

The first lines—Sophy's lament at Graham's absence for five whole days—Lalla passed over. She was looking only for her own name and, sure that she would find it, turned to the second page.

"Father, of course, will disapprove and say that I should not go, for he gets more stuffy and morose each day. Anyone young is what he can't bear nowadays, and all that we two do is vulgar and absurd. I wish that Lalla would try to be a wife to him and not a romping schoolgirl still. I should think he would like to be quiet for a while and serious, and so should I. To see him all the time exposed to her high spirits—that gather *me* in, but exclude him—and in any case they are far beyond his powers—is quite painful. He is less and less in the house, and when he is, is so sour and gruff. But he can't—so far—be gruff with *her*, so is with me instead. Where can it end? But all the same, I'll brave his wrath and tell him that I'll go away with you."

There was no more. Very gently, Lalla folded the pages and put them inside the envelope. Then she tiptoed from the room. Her heart beat so loudly that she thought it would betray her. Her hands were icy-cold, and hurt, as if they had touched poison.

*   *   *

She tried to eat luncheon, but failed. The sight of the dish of peppers reminded her of how short a time ago she had been sitting in the kitchen, bored and restless, but still innocent and loving.

Perhaps it is a baby already, Sophy thought, when Lalla, too sick to stay, had left the room. She now had her father to herself and in a nonchalant voice said: "Graham and I think of going to France in August, as soon as Denise's wedding is over!"

"You couldn't choose a worse month," said Colonel Vellacott and threw down his napkin and stood up. "I'm worried about Lalla. I think I'll go up to her." Sophy sat alone. Her eyebrows were raised and she looked down at her plate with an air of surprise and curiosity.

*   *   *

Afterwards she went to her bedroom. The petticoat threaded with its scarlet ribbon lay on the bed, and she wondered if Lalla had done it. She could imagine her trying to while away her mornings with one trivial task after another, spending as long upon them as she could. She pictured her standing in this sunny room, with the petticoat over her arm, feeling lonely and out-of-place. Then a fearful intuition sprang upon Sophy and she swung round and looked for the letter she had so carelessly left on the table. It lay there, just as she expected, and with a trembling hand she picked it up and stared at it. 'I have been read' it seemed to say.

*   *   *

Miss Sully could now watch things worsening daily. The laughter had worn off: it was strange to her that it had lasted so long.

Lalla recovered from her sickness, but was dispirited. Her attitude towards her husband changed, was appealing and conciliatory and over-anxious. With Sophy she was reserved. They had drawn a long way apart and the distance was clouded with suspicions and mistrust.

Colonel Vellacott, as the letter had stated, was less and less in the house, and when she was alone, Lalla paced up and down, clasping her hands tight to her breast, and then the other words of the letter echoed over and over in her mind, with burning emphasis—"Where can it end? Where can it end?"

"You are run down," her husband told her. He was wonderfully solicitous, yet bored. She seemed unreal to him, but he would do his best for her. This summer he was feeling his age; marriage had drawn too much attention to it, and so much youth in the house underlined it. Once, he had thought it would have the opposite effect.

"You need a holiday, poor Lalla. And you shall have one. In September I should be able to get away for a couple of weeks. How would you like to go to Florence?"

Yes, she would like to go to Florence and she smiled and nodded; but she thought, 'I am not really used to him *here*, and now I must try to get used to him in a foreign country.'

She tried hard to be more wifely to him, but when she made attempts at serious discussion, he smiled so fondly, so indulgently, that she was aggravated. Sophy watched her attempts with grim understanding. 'I know what *this* is all about,' she thought.

So they were all going abroad—Lalla and her husband sedately to Florence, and Sophy and Graham, full of secrecy and excitement to France. There was a great difference, Lalla thought.

*   *   *

"I neglect you shamefully," said Colonel Vellacott. "I promise I will mend my ways after our holiday. I will come off some of my committees."

"But couldn't I go with you?" Lalla asked. "I should be so interested to hear you speak. Just this once?"

"You would be bored to death and, in any case, I'm afraid tonight's meeting is in camera."

To her own distress, her eyes filled with tears. She was most dreadfully sorry for herself and grieved that no one else was.

She knew that the tears were a pity and that he would think her more childish than ever. "Where will it end?" she wondered, as he patted her cheek, saying "goodbye".

Sophy was out with Graham, Miss Sully listening to a Murder play on the wireless in her sitting-room. 'I could teach myself Italian, perhaps,' Lalla thought, and she went to the study and looked along the shelves, but, though there were many books written in Italian, she could find none to teach the language to her. One was expected to know it already.

'In Florence, they will all gabble away and leave me out of it,' she thought, growing sorrier and sorrier for herself. 'It really is too bad.' Now, they were to be joined in Italy by Major and Mrs Mallett, old friends of the Colonel's, a pleasant elderly couple, who still regarded the Colonel as of a younger generation.

'They are only going because he would be so bored with just me,' Lalla thought, crossly. 'Oh, I have been complaisant for too long'; she decided. 'I have tried hard and given in and got nowhere.'

She thought that, instead of meekly waiting up for him she would go up to bed, without telling Miss Sully even. She would turn out the lights and if she were not asleep when he came home, she would pretend to be.

A long drawn-out scream came from Miss Sully's wireless-set as Lalla crossed the hall and went softly upstairs.

*   *   *

When she awoke it was dark and she was still alone. She got out of bed and went to the window. Lamplight shone over leaves in the street beyond the wall and fell over the courtyard. The statues and urns looked blanched. In the centre was an ornamental stand for plants. Its wrought-iron lilies threw slanting shadows across the paving-stones; she could even see the shadows of the fuchsia blossoms—real flowers, these—swinging upon the ground.

It was a romantic place in this light, and she knelt by the window looking down at it, quite awake now and refreshed by her sleep. Then she saw that Sophy and Graham found the place romantic too. She had not noticed them at first, under the dark wall, clasped close together, as still as the tree beyond them. But before Lalla could turn away, she saw them move—they swayed lightly, like the fuchsia blossoms, as if rocked by the same faint air, of which they were so heedless.

She went back to bed and lay down and drew the covers over her, her eyes wide open to the darkness. 'Defend me from envy, God', she prayed. But the poison of it gathered in her against her will and when it had filled her and she was overflowing with despair, tears broke in her like waves. Even Miss Sully, coming upstairs when the play was over, could hear her.

The True Primitive

LILY had not considered culture—as a word or anything else—until she fell in love. As soon as that happened it, culture, descended on her. It was as if all the books Mr Ransome had ever read were thrown at her one after the other—Voltaire, Tolstoi, Balzac—the sharp names came at her, brutal spondees, brutally pronounced. She thought, though, that she hated Dostoievski most of all. "Yes, Dad," Mr Ransome's two sons continually said, agreeing to rate Zola higher than Dickens if he wished them to, promising to remember what he had told them about Michelangelo. Painters names were also part of the attack, but Lily thought they sounded gentler. She had felt curiosity about someone called Leonardo when first she heard him mentioned and had wondered if he were Harry's cousin. When she asked Harry he laughed and referred her to his father, which meant three-quarters of an hour wasted, sitting in the kitchen listening, and then it was too late for them to go for their walk. Trembling with frustrated desire, she had learnt her lesson; she asked no more questions and sat sullenly quiet whenever the enemy names began again.

Only winter courting seemed to be allowed: then, with the Thames Valley giving off impenetrable vapours or taking in, day after day, torrents of rain until the river rose and spread over the fields, Harry was free to take her out; except, of course, for his two evenings at the Art School. They held hands coming back in the bus from the cinema, kissed beneath dripping trees in the muddy lane, choked and whispered in the fog.

"Silly notion, venturing out tonight," Mr Ransome would tell them. "You've no right, letting her catch her death, Harry."

"I think it's easing up now," Lily would say. "Just the clearing-up shower. And a spot or two of rain doesn't do anyone any harm."

Mr Ransome, with a daunting-looking book open in front of him, would be hurriedly unfolding his spectacles.

"We ought to be going," Lily whispered.

"Man is a political animal," boomed Mr Ransome, wanting to throw as many words at them as he could before they escaped, but Lily had gone, was through the scullery and already standing in the wet garden and Harry sent an apologetic smile back at his father and followed her.

"Good Lord," said Lily. "Once he gets going."

"He's a wonderful old man," Harry said.

"You're both afraid of him, I think—you and Godfrey."

"We *respect* him," Harry said sententiously. "He's been a good father and since Mother died he has no one to read to in the evenings. He misses that."

'She did the best thing, dying,' Lily thought.

Mr Ransome was a lock-keeper. He and his sons lived in a red-brick cottage at the side of the lock. On hot summer afternoons, the garden was what people going through in their boats called a riot of colour. The primary colours assaulted the eye—salvias, geraniums, lobelias, calceolarias were made all the more dazzling by everything being white-washed that Mr Ransome could lay his brush on—flower-tubs, step-edges, the boulders round flower-beds, the swinging chains round the little lawns. In winter-time, it seemed that it could not really have been so bright.

Now, when all the locks down the river were closed, the cottage was lost in a cauldron of steam and the sad sound of the weir came drearily through the fog. Mr Ransome wondered how Harry and Lily could prefer the sodden lanes to a nice fire and a book to read beside it. He read so much about great passions, of men and women crossing continents because of love, and enduring hardship and peril, not just the discomforts of a dark, wet night—but he could not see Harry and Lily go out without feeling utter exasperation at their fecklessness.

"It will be lovely when the summer comes," Lily sometimes said; but Harry knew that it would not be, if by 'lovely' she meant they would have long evenings together in the golden meadows or walking along the towing-path. "He does like us to get out with our sketching, Godfrey and me," he said.

"I don't mind. We can go miles away. You can sketch with one hand and I'll sit beside you and hold the other."

"We couldn't very well do that, you see, because Dad likes to come out with us."

"I can't think why you bother with it when you've got such a nice job."

Harry knew why he bothered. His father, self-taught painter, had once had a picture hung in a local exhibition— an oil-painting, moreover. "I jib at nothing," he had explained. The bright, varnished scene hung in the parlour now. "It was not for sale," he said, when no one bought it. Jibbing at nothing, he had used a great deal of paint and had, in some way, caught the hard, venomous colours of his own garden. 'The Towing Path of A Sunday' was inscribed carefully on the frame. The white chains stood out thickly, like icing piped on the canvas; the chestnut-trees had pink cones of blossom stuck about them and dropped down sharp ovals of shadow on the emerald grass. "If I had of had tuition," Mr Ramsay so often said. He would see to it, he added, that his sons should not look back and have to say the same. In their earliest days they had been given paint-boxes and sketching-blocks; he had taken them to London to the National Gallery and shown them the Virgin of the Rocks and, standing in front of it, lectured them on Leonardo. They had not known which was most painful—their embarrassment or their shame at their own disloyalty in suffering it. Young as they were at the time, they realised that he was much stared at—the thin, fierce man with his square beard and so old-fashioned clothes—but they could not help feeling that he deserved it, booming away as he did in the echoing gallery. They even began to think that he expected to be noticed and took pleasure from it.

Harry and Godfrey, articled in respectable offices in the nearby town, were not quite yet a disappointment to him; for many great men mature late, their father reminded them, reach their height after middle age: Voltaire, for one. They went on with their art classes at evening school and were painstaking enough in their desire to please; but, sometimes, looking at them and then at their feeble paintings, Mr Ransome could not help thinking that passion was missing from them.

'They are not on fire,' he mourned. 'As I have been.'

Then Harry met Lily and seemed, to his father, to be less on fire than ever. "But it will come," he encouraged his sons. It must come. What had been in him so powerful a desire, so bitterly a failed attempt, could not be wasted, must be passed on, and in greater strength, too, if things were to turn out as he considered just.

Lily, impinging on his plan with her sly, mincing manner, her pout and her impatient sighs, was the eternal female enemy. He had built a bastion, a treasure-house for his sons, with all the great names they had heard from the cradle, the learning he had struggled for to make their inheritance. It had come too easily, he realised now, and

Harry would rather spend an evening talking inanities, lowering his mind to Lily's level. His attitude towards her was vexing, suggesting that he was willing, eager to learn something from her and even that she might be able to teach it: suppliant, receptive he was with her; yet it was surely for him to instruct, who knew so much, and dominate, being a man, and to concede, whatsoever he felt inclined to concede; not beg for favours.

Mr Ransome thought of his own happy married life—the woman, so gentle and conciliatory listening to him as he read. Into those readings he had put the expression of his pleasure at being able to share with her the best he had discovered. She had sat and sewed and, when she raised her eyes to look for her scissors, she would also glance across at him and he, conscious of her doing so would pause to meet this glance, knowing that it would be full of humble gratitude. She had never been able to comprehend half of what he had offered her, she had muddled the great names and once dozed off after a few pages of Stendhal; but something, he thought, must have seeped into her, something of the lofty music of prose, as she listened, evening after evening of her married life. Now he missed her and so much of the sound of his own voice that had gone with her.

How different was Lily. The moment he began to read aloud, or even to quote something, down came her eyelids to half-mast. An invisible curtain dropped over her and behind it she was without any response, as if heavily drugged. He would have liked to have stuck pins in her to see if she would cry out: instead, he assaulted her—indecently, she thought, and that was why she would not listen—with Cicero and Goethe, Ibsen and Nietzsche and a French poet, one of his specials, called Bawdyleer. Having removed herself, as it were, she would then glance at the clock, wind a curl round her finger and suddenly loosen it to spring back against her cheek. Distracted by this, Harry

would murmur, "Yes, Dad, I remember you telling us."
So Mr Ransome had lost them both. 'Come here,' Lily
seemed to be enticing his son. 'Come behind my invisible
curtain and we can think of other things and play with my
hair and be alone together.'

Sometimes, but very rarely, Mr Ransome would manage
to catch her unawares and force one of the names on her
before she had time to bring down the curtain. Then her
manner was rude and retaliatory instead of vague. "And
who, pray, is Dosty what's-is-name when he's at home?"
She knew that Mr Ransome was her enemy and felt not only
malice in his attitude towards her, but something she might
have defined as obscenity if she had known the meaning
of the word.

He—for he was at heart puritanical—had once or twice
delighted to indulge in a bout of broad-mindedness. She
should learn that he and some of the great thinkers of the
world could face the truth unflinchingly and even some of
the words the truth must be described in. To the pure, he
said, all things are pure: he watched Lily's look of prim
annoyance, implying that to her they obviously were not.
He was defeated, however, by the silence that fell—Lily's
and his son's. His remark, made to seem blatant by being
isolated and ignored, repeated itself in his own head and he
felt his cheeks and brow darkening. He did not want to
appear to have any impurity in his own mind and quickly
bent down and rearranged the coals on the fire.

The spring was beginning; the puddles along the rutted
lanes were blue, reflecting the bright sky, and lilac-trees in
cottage-gardens bore buds as small as grape-pips. Although
the darkness fell later, the interval of daylight after tea was
of no use to Lily, for Mr Ransome had his two sons out,
white-washing and weeding and trimming. "We shall have
no time to do it once the season has begun," he said.

"But what about us?" Lily asked Harry.

"I can't help but give him a hand of an evening. It wouldn't be right to leave it all to Godfrey."

"It sounds as if the summer's going to be just as bad as the winter."

All along, Harry had known it would be worse.

In the summer, the lock was always full, boats jostled together, smart women in motor launches stared through their dark glasses at men in rowing-boats wearing braces and knotted handkerchiefs on their heads: in the narrowness of the lock they were all resentful of their proximity to one another, and were glad, when the water had finished rising or falling, to see the gates opening slowly. The locks were an ordeal to be negotiated, not made easier by the passers-by on the tow-path who stopped to watch them lying exposed below and hoped that they would ram their craft into the gates, or take the paint off one of the white launches.

Steamers came through at intervals and then the lock was a well of noise with someone thumping at the piano in the saloon and cheery messages thrown from deck to towing-path; glasses of beer were held up to tantalise and the funny man of the party, wearing a yachting cap, sang 'A life on the ocean wave is better than going to sea.'

The pretty stretch of river with its willows hanging down to the water and the brilliance of the lock garden brought artists, with folding stools and easels, who took up much of Mr Ransome's time. Such an odd character they thought him, forgetting—as, of all people, the English should not—that characters are encouraged at the cost of their families' destruction. He showed them his own painting of the same scene and they were enraptured, they called him a true primitive and talked of the Douanier Rousseau.

On summer evenings, after days of advising these amateur artists, talking about himself, bringing in a great deal about Leonardo, Mr Ransome behaved as if he had been drinking too much. He boasted, belaboured his son

with words and then, from too much excitement, sur-
rendered to self-pity. It suddenly seemed to him that he had
wasted his life: he had seen this on the face of one stranger
after another. 'You!' they had been thinking, 'a man who
has all the great Masters at his finger-tips and can summon
from memory one thundering phrase after another, who
would expect to find you in such a backwater, living so
humbly?'

"You two, my sons, shall make up for me," he told them.
"Then I have not lived in vain." "I am the teacher of
athletes," he intoned. "He that by me spreads a wider
breast than my own proves the width of my own. He
most knows my style who learns under it to destroy the
teacher."

"Yes, father," said his sons.

"Walt Whitman," he added, giving credit where credit
was due.

Lily, who had given up working in a shop to become a
laundress, now had Saturday afternoons free. The full
significance of this she told Harry when they were lingering
over, postponing from minute to minute, their farewell
embrace in the dark lane near her home. To draw apart was
so painful to them that, as soon as they attempted it, they
suffered too much and flew together again for comfort.

"It must be gone eleven," she said. "Dad's tongue
will curdle the milk. But guess what, though. Did you
realise?"

"Realise what?" he mumbled, and lifted her hair from
her shoulders and kissed underneath it, along the back of
her neck, with busy little nibbling kisses. In a curious and
contradictory way, she felt that he was so intent on her that
she no longer existed.

"Why, Saturday afternoons, of course," she said. "You'll
be free: now I'll be free as well." She could not help
noticing that the kissing stopped at once.

"Well, you do know week-ends in the season I have to give Dad a hand," Harry said.

"It isn't the season yet. We'll have a fortnight before that. I can meet you any time after dinner. Sooner the better," she whispered and raised herself on tiptoe and put her warm mouth against his. He was unhappy and she became angry.

"Say about tea-time," he suggested.

"Why not earlier?"

She knew, although of course she could not see, that he was blushing.

"Ever since we were little, Dad's liked us to be together on Saturday afternoons."

"What for, pray?"

"Just to have a quiet time together. It's a family custom."

Now she could feel him blushing.

"If you ask me, he's round the bend," she said loudly. "And even if you don't ask me, he is."

She pushed Harry away and began to walk down the lane towards her home. He followed her. "And so are you," she added. She did not turn her head as she spoke, but the words came back to him clearly. "No wonder that girl Vera Webster gave up going out with Godfrey. She could see the way the wind was blowing. 'Dad likes this and Dad likes that.' I'm sick and tired of Dad and one of these days I'll tell him so. 'You and your Bawdyleer', I'll say, 'you boring old . . .'" her voice rose and trembled, "'codger'" she cried. "And you, too," she had reached her gate, threw it open and hurried up the path.

"Saturday tea-time then?" he called after her anxiously.

"Saturday nothing," she shouted back, and she lifted the latch and went in boldly to face her father's sarcasm.

"You're in early this morning," he said. "The milkman hasn't been yet."

The next day her beautiful anger had dissolved. She had

enjoyed it while she indulged in it, but now her words haunted and alarmed her. Perhaps they had meant the end of Harry's love for her and, so, of all her hopes. Her future life with him dissolved—a whole council-house full of day-dreams; trousseau, wedding-presents, pots and pans, dainty supper-dishes, baby-clothes; cradle, even a kitten asleep on a cushion. She imagined him going to work and then on to his evening class, his head tilted proudly back, the stain of anger on his cheeks. The day after would be Saturday and if it turned out that he had taken her at her furious word, she could not endure to go on living.

"Not going out with Harry?" her mother asked her, when Lily began to wash her hair at the kitchen sink on Saturday afternoon.

"I think love's sweet song has run into a few discords," her father said. "*Very* hoity-toity words coming up the path the night before last."

Lily poured a jug of water over her head and so her tears were hidden.

By four o'clock her hair was quite dry. Harry had not come. She was restless and felt herself watched by her mother and father. Soon she decided that there was, after all, nothing to stop her walking along the towing-path for a breath of fresh air. It was a public way and there was no one who could stop her. It would be a sorry thing if, just because of Harry Ransome, she could never walk along the river bank again.

It was a bright and blowy evening. She met no one. At every bend in the lane, she expected to see Harry come hastening, full of apologies, towards her. Then she came to the river and still no one was in sight. The water was high, after the winter's rain, and flowed fast, covered with bubbles, bearing away scum and twigs and last year's leaves. The sound and look of it completed her depression.

With her head turned towards the river and not in the

direction of the cottage, she walked along the lock-side. She
went on beyond it a little way and then turned and
sauntered back. The kitchen window was dark, but from
the parlour a light fell faintly through the wooden shutters
which had been drawn across the outside of the window.
This seemed quite strange to Lily, for it would not be dark
for some hours to come and in all the months she had known
Harry she had never seen anyone go into the parlour except
to fetch a book. She remembered Harry's shame and
reluctance when she had tried to make plans for this afternoon and an unreasonable suspicion overtook her that he
was in that shuttered room making love to someone, that he
had k. own beforehand that he would be doing so, and
knowing, had gone on kissing Lily; though he had had, she
admitted, the decency to blush. She stepped quietly on to
the little plot of grass and hesitated, glancing round her.
There was no one in sight and not a sound except for the
river. She went softly across to the window and listened
there; but there was a shameful silence from within. Her
heart beating with great violence unnerved her and only the
extreme tension of her jealousy enabled her to lay her hand
on the shutter and move it gently towards her.

The light in the room was not so very bright; but standing
upright in a strange stiff pose with hand on hip and one knee
slightly bent, she could see Mr Ransome facing her not two
yards away, his beard jutting forward and his expression
fixed. A rosy glow from an oil-stove close beside him fell
over his completely naked body.

Their eyes met, his widened with surprise, Lily's with
horror. Then she slammed back the shutter and leant against
it for a moment, sick and trembling. Through the narrow
slit between the shutters she had not seen the two sons,
sitting unwillingly but dutifully behind their easels. Terror,
in any case, had quite put the thought of Harry out of her
mind. She was afraid that Mr Ransome would come

leaping out of the house after her and chase her down the towing-path, naked and mad as he was, shouting Balzac and Voltaire after her. She summoned all her strength and turned and ran across the lawn, as fast as she could go, away from the cottages and her legs were as heavy as lead, as if she were running in a nightmare.

The Rose, The Mauve, The White

In the morning, Charles went down the garden to practise calling for three cheers. When he came to the place farthest of all from the house and near to the lake, he paused among clumps of rhubarb and mounds of lawn-clippings, and glanced about him. His voice had broken years before, but was still uncertain in volume; sometimes it wavered, and lost its way and he could never predict if it would follow his intention or not. If his voice was to come out in a great bellow or perhaps frenziedly high-pitched, people would turn towards him in surprise, even astonishment, but how, if it sank too low would he claim anyone's attention after the boisterous confusions of Auld Lang Syne? He could hardly be held responsible for it, he felt, and had often wished that he might climb to the top of a mountain and there, alone, make its acquaintance and come to terms with it. As he could not, this morning in the garden at home, he put on what he hoped was an expression of exultant gaiety, snatched off his spectacles and, waving them in the air, cried out: "And now three cheers for Mrs Frensham-Bowater." He was about to begin 'Hip, hip hooray', when a bush nearby was filled with laughter; all the branches were disturbed with mirth. Then there were two splashes as his little sisters leapt into the lake for safety. "And now three cheers for Charles," they called, as they swam as fast as they could away from the bank.

If he went after them, he could only stand at the edge of the water and shake his fist or make some other ineffectual protest, so he put his spectacles on again and walked slowly back to the house. It was a set-back to the day, with Natalie arriving that afternoon and likely to hear at once from the twins how foolishly he had behaved.

"Mother, could you make them be quiet?" he asked desperately, finding her at work in the rose-garden. When he told her the story, she threw back her head and laughed for what seemed to him to be about five minutes. "Oh, poor old Charles. I wish I'd been in hiding, too." He had known he would have to bear this or something like it, but was obliged to pay the price; and at long last she said: "I will see to it that their lips are sealed; their cunning chops shut up."

"But are you sure you can?"

"I think I know how to manage my own children. See how obedient you yourself have grown. I cross my heart they shall not breathe a word of it in front of Natalie."

He thanked her coldly and walked away. In spite of his gratitude, he thought: 'She is so dreadfully chummy and slangy. I wish she wouldn't be. And why say just "Natalie" when there are two girls coming? I think she tries to be "knowing" as well,' he decided.

Two girls were coming. His sister, Katie, was picking sweet-peas for the room these school-friends were to share with her.

"You are supposed to cut those with scissors," Charles said. The ones she couldn't strip off, she was breaking with her teeth. "What time are they coming?"

"In the station-taxi at half-past three."

"Shall I come with you to meet them?"

"No, of course not. Why should you?"

Katie was sixteen and a year younger than Charles. It is a very feminine age and she wanted her friends to herself.

At school they slept in the same bedroom, as they would here. They were used to closing the door upon a bower of secrets and intrigue and diary-writing; knew how to keep their jokes to themselves and their conversations as incomprehensible as possible to other people. When Charles's friends came to stay, Katie did not encroach on them, and now she had no intention of letting him spoil that delightful drive back from the station: she could not imagine what her friends would think of her if she did.

So after luncheon she went down alone in the big, musty-smelling taxi. The platform of the country station was quite deserted: a porter was whistling in the office, keeping out of the hot sun. She walked up and down, reading the notices of Estate Agents posted along the fence and all the advertisements of auction-sales. She imagined the train coming nearer to her with every passing second; yet it seemed unbelievable that it would really soon materialise out of the distance, bringing Frances and Natalie.

They would have the compartment to themselves at this time of the day on the branch line and she felt a little wistful thinking that they were together and having fun and she was all alone, waiting for them. They would be trying out dance-steps, swaying and staggering as the train rocked; dropping at last, weak with laughter, full-length on the seats. Then, having been here to stay with Katie on other occasions, as they came near to the end of their journey they would begin to point out landmarks and haul down their luggage from the rack—carefully, because in the suitcases were the dresses for this evening's dance.

The signal fell with a sharp clatter making Katie jump. 'Now where shall I be standing when the train stops?' she wondered, feeling self-conscious suddenly and full of responsibility. 'Not here, right on top of the Gents' lavatory of all places. Perhaps by the entrance.' Nonchalantly, she strolled away.

The porter came out of the office, still whistling, and stared up the line. Smoke, bowing and nodding like a plume on a horse's head, came, round a bend in the distance and Katie, watching it, felt sick and anxious. 'They won't enjoy themselves at all,' she thought. 'I wish I hadn't asked them. They will find it dreadfully dull at home and the dance is bound to be a failure. It will be babyish with awful things like "The Dashing White Sergeant" and "The Gay Gordons". They will think Charles is a bore and the twins a bloody nuisance.'

But the moment they stepped out of the train all her constraint vanished. They caught her up into the midst of their laughter. "You can't think what happened," they said. "You'll never believe what happened at Paddington." The ridiculous story never did quite come clear, they were so incoherent with giggling. Katie smiled in a grown-up way. She was just out of it for the moment, but would soon be in the swim again.

As they drove up the station-slope towards the village, they were full of anticipation and excitement. "And where is Charles?" asked Natalie, smoothing her dark hair.

*   *   *

Tea was such great fun, their mother, Myra Pollard, told herself: though one moment she felt rejuvenated; the next minute, as old as the world. She had a habit of talking to herself, as to another person who was deeply interested in all her reactions: and the gist of these conversations was often apparent on her face.

'They keep one young oneself—all these young people,' she thought as she was pouring out the tea. Yet the next second, her cheek resting on her hand as she watched them putting away great swags and wadges and gobbets of starch, she sighed; for she had not felt as they all felt, eager and full of nonsense, for years and years. To them, though they

were polite, she was of no account, the tea pourer-out, the
starch-provider, simply. It was people of her own generation
who said that Charles and she were like brother and sister—
not those of Charles's generation, to whom the idea would
have seemed absurd.

Frances and Natalie were as considerate as could be and
even strove to be a little woman-to-womanly with her.
"Did you ever find your bracelet, Mrs Pollard? Do you
remember you'd lost it when we were here last time? At
a . . . a dance, wasn't it?" Natalie faltered. Of course,
Katie's mother went to dances, too. Indeed, why not?
Grotesque though they must be. She was glad that her own
parents were more sedate and did not try to ape the young.

"I wish *we* could go to a ball," said Lucy, one of the
twins.

"Your time will come," their mother said. She laid her
hand to the side of the silver tea-pot as if to warm and
comfort herself.

"Oh, do you remember that boy, Sandy, in the elimina-
tion dance?" Katie suddenly exploded.

Frances, who was all beaky and spectacly, Mrs Pollard
thought, exploded with her.

"The one who was wearing a kilt?" Natalie asked, with
more composure. She wondered if Charles was thinking
that she must be older than the other girls and indeed she
was, by two and a half months.

"Will Mrs Frensham-Bowater be there?" Lucy asked.

Her sly glance, with eyelids half-lowered, was for
Caroline's—her twin's—benefit.

"Of course, Mrs Frensham-Bowater always organises the
dance," their mother said briskly, and changed the subject.

Charles was grateful to her for keeping her promise; but
all the same he had had an irritating afternoon. The twins,
baulked in one direction, found other ways of exasperating
him. When he came out of the house with his gun under

his arm, they had clapped their hands over their ears and fled shrieking to the house. "Charles is pointing his gun at us," they shouted. "Don't be bloody silly," he shouted back. "Charles swore," they cried.

'What an unholy gap between Katie and me and those little perishers,' he thought. 'Whatever did mother and father imagine they were up to? What can the neighbours have thought of them—at their time of life?' He shied away from the idea of sexual love between the middle-aged; though it was ludicrous, evidence of it was constantly to be seen.

"Did you shoot anything?" his mother asked him.

"There wasn't anything to shoot." He had known there wouldn't be and had only walked about in the woods with his gun for something to do until the taxi came.

"And the girl next door?" Frances asked. "I have forgotten her name. Will she be going to the dance tonight?"

"Oh, Deirdre," said Caroline to Lucy.

"Yes, Deirdre," Lucy said, staring across the table at Charles.

"No, she has gone to school in Switzerland," said Katie.

"Poor Charles!" the twins said softly.

"Why not try to be your age?" he asked them in a voice which would, he hoped, sound intimidating to them, but nonchalant to everybody else.

"Have you had nice holidays?" Mrs Pollard asked, looking from Frances to Natalie, then thinking that she was being far too hostessy and middle-aged, she said without waiting for their answer; "I do adore your sweater, Natalie."

"Jesus bids us shine, with a pure, clear light," Caroline began to sing, as she spread honey on her bread.

"Not at the table," said her mother.

*   *   *

"What shall we do now?" Katie asked after tea. She was beginning to feel her responsibility again. There was no doubt that everything was very different from school; there were Frances and Natalie drawn very close together from sharing the same situation; and she, apart, in the predicament of hostess. It was now that she began to see her home through their eyes—the purple brick house looked heavy and ugly now that the sun had gone behind a cloud; the south wall was covered by a magnolia tree; there were one or two big, cream flowers among the dark leaves: doves were walking about on the slate roof; some of the windows reflected the blue sky and moving clouds. To Katie, it was like being shown a photograph which she did not immediately recognise—unevocative, as were the photographs of their mothers in the dormitory at school—they seldom glanced at them from the beginning of term to the end.

They sat down on the grass at the edge of the orchard and began to search for four-léaf clovers. Their conversation consisted mostly of derogatory remarks about themselves— they were hopeless at dancing, each one said; could never think what to say to their partners; and they had all washed their hair that morning and now could do simply nothing with it.

"So lucky having red hair, Katie. How I envy you."

"But it's horrible. I hate it."

"It's so striking. Isn't it, Frances?"

"Well, yours is, too, in a different way. It's this awful mousiness of mine I can't abide."

"You can't call it mousy: it's chestnut."

It was just a game they played and when they had finished with their hair they began on the shape of their hands. There was never any unkindness in anything they said. They were exploring themselves more than each other.

The twins wandered about the garden, shaking milk in jars to make butter: every few minutes they stopped to compare the curd they had collected. They had been doing this tirelessly for days, but were near the time when that game would seem dull and done with and they would never play it again. This evening, they marched about the lawn, chanting a meaningless song.

The older girls were discussing whether they would rather be deaf or blind. Frances lay on her stomach watching the children and wondering if they were not lucky to be so free of care and without the great ordeal of the dance ahead of them.

"Deaf any day," said Katie.

"Oh, no!" said Natalie. "Only think how cut off you'd be from other people; and no one is ever as nice to the deaf or has much patience with them. Everyone is kinder to the blind."

"But imagine never seeing any of this ever again," said Frances. Tears came up painfully in Katie's eyes. "This garden, that lovely magnolia tree, sunsets. Never to be able to read 'Jane Eyre' again."

"You could read it in Braille," Katie said.

"It wouldn't be the same. You know it wouldn't be. Oh, it would be appalling . . . I can't contemplate it . . . I really can't."

Anyone who reminded them that the choice might not arise would have been deeply resented.

"I suppose we had better go in and iron our frocks," Katie said. No one had found a four-leaf clover.

"Where is Charles?" Natalie asked.

"The Lord knows," said Katie.

Frances was silent as they went towards the house. She could feel the dance coming nearer to her.

*   *   *

"The house is full of girls," Charles told his father. George Pollard left the car in the drive and went indoors. "And steam," he said.

Natalie, Frances and Katie had been in the bathroom for nearly an hour and could hardly see one another across the room. Bath-salts, hoarded from Christmas, scented the steam and now, still wearing their shower-caps, they were standing on damp towels and shaking their Christmas talcum powder over their stomachs and shoulders.

"Will you do my back and under my arms?" asked Katie, handing to Frances the tin of Rose Geranium. "And then I will do yours."

"What a lovely smell. It's so much nicer than mine," said Frances, dredging Katie as thoroughly as if she were a fillet of fish being prepared for the frying-pan.

"Don't be too long, girls!" Mrs Pollard called, tapping at the door. She tried to make her voice sound gay and indulgent. "The twins are waiting to come in and it's rather past their bedtime." She wondered crossly if Katie's friends were allowed to monopolise bathrooms like that in their own homes. Katie was plainly showing off and would have to be taken aside and told so.

"Just coming," they shouted.

At last they opened the door and thundered along the passage to their bedroom where they began to make the kind of untidiness they had left behind them in the bathroom.

Yvette, the French mother's-help, whose unenviable task it now was to supervise the twins' going to bed, flung open the bathroom window and kicked all the wet towels to one side. 'They will be clean, certainly,' she was thinking. 'But they will not be chic.' She had seen before the net frocks, the strings of coral, the shining faces.

She rinsed the dregs of mauve crystals from the bath and called out to the twins. The worst part of her day was about to begin.

*   *   *

"This is the best part of the day," George said. He shut the bedroom door and took his drink over to the window. Myra was sitting at her dressing-table. She had taken off her ear-rings to give her ears a little rest and was gently massaging the reddened lobes. She said: "It doesn't seem a year since that other dance, when we quarrelled about letting Katie go to it."

"She was too young. And still is."

"There were girls of thirteen there."

"Well, that's no affair of mine, thank God."

"I wonder if Ronnie what's-his-name will be sober. For the M.C. of a young people's dance I consider he was pretty high last time. He always has drunk unmercifully."

"What the devil's this?" George asked. He had gone into his dressing-room and now came back with his safety-razor in his hand.

"Oh, the girls must have borrowed it."

"Very hospitable guests they are, to be sure. They manage to make me feel quite at home."

"Don't fuss. You were young yourself once."

She dotted lipstick over her cheekbones and he watched her through the looking-glass, arrested by the strange sight. The incredulous expression made her smile, eyebrows raised, she was ready to tease. He tilted her face back towards him and kissed her quickly on the mouth.

"You look absurd," he said.

As soon as she was released, she leant to the mirror again and began to smooth the dots of colour over her cheeks until they were merged into the most delicate flush. "A clever girl," he said, finishing his drink.

*   *   *

The girls were still not dressed when a boy called Benedict Nightingale arrived in his father's car—and dinner-jacket, George decided. 'Katie's first beau,' he told himself, 'come calling for her.' He felt quite irritable as he took the boy into the drawing-room.

"They won't be long," he said, without conviction.

"Don't be too long, girls," Myra called again in her low, controlled and unexasperated voice. She stopped to tap on their bedroom door before she went downstairs; then, knowing that Charles would be having trouble with his tie, she went in to his rescue.

"What about a drink?" George asked Benedict reluctantly.

"No thank you, sir."

"Cigarette?"

"No thank you, sir."

"I don't know what they can be doing all this time. Now what the hell's happening up there?"

The twins were trying to get into Katie's bedroom to pry into adolescent secrets, and the girls, still in their petticoats, held the door against them. From the other side of it Lucy and Caroline banged with their fists and kicked until dragged away at last by Yvette.

"Now we shall be late," said Katie.

They lifted their frocks and dropped them over their heads, their talcumed armpits showed white as they raised their elbows to hook themselves at the back. Frances tied Natalie's sash, Natalie fastened Katie's bracelet.

"Is this all right? Does it hang down? You're sure? Am I done up?" they asked.

"Oh, yes, yes, yes, I mean no," they all answered at once, not one of them attending.

"*This* is what *I'm* allowed," said Katie, smudging on lipstick, stretching her mouth as she had seen her mother do. "So pale, I'm wasting my time."

Natalie twisted her bracelet, shook back her hair: she hummed; did a glissade across the clothes-strewn floor, her skirts floating about her. She was away, gone, in Charles's arms already. She held her scented arm to her face and breathed deeply and smiled.

Frances stood uncertainly in the middle of the room. 'I am the one who will be asked to dance last of all,' she thought, cold with the certainty of her failure. 'Katie and Natalie will go flying away and I shall be left there on my own, knowing nobody. The time will go slowly and I shall wish that I were dead.' She turned to the long looking-glass and smoothed her frock. "I hate my bosoms," she suddenly said. "They are too wide apart."

"Nonsense, that's how they're supposed to be," Katie said, as brisk as any Nannie.

*   *   *

"Give those girls a shout, Charles," George said and helped himself to another drink.

But they were coming downstairs. They had left the room with its beds covered with clothes, its floor strewn with tissue-paper. They descended; the rose, the mauve, the white. Like a bunch of sweet-peas they looked, George thought.

"What a pretty frock, Frances," Myra said, beginning with the worst. 'Poor pet,' she thought, and Frances guessed the thought, smiling primly and saying thank you.

"And such a lovely colour, Natalie," Myra went on.

"But is it, though?" Natalie asked anxiously. "And don't my shoes clash terribly?" "I think I look quite bleak in it, and it is last year's, really."

Myra had scarcely wanted to go into all that. "Now, Katie," she began to say, as soon as she could. "I don't think your friends know Benedict. And when you have introduced them we must be on our way. Your father and I have to go out to dinner after we've taken you to the dance. So who's to go with whom?"

That was what Frances had wondered. The worst part of

being a guest was not being told enough about arrangements. One was left in a shifting haze of conjecture.

Benedict had come to attention as the girls came in and now he stepped forward and said with admirable firmness: "I will take Katie in my car." Then he was forced to add: "I would have room for someone else in the back."

'That's me,' thought Frances.

"Good! Now don't crush your dresses, girls," said Myra. "Gather them up—so—from the back of the skirt. Have you got everything?"

"Of course, mother," said Katie. 'We aren't children,' she thought.

*   *   *

Four hours later, Charles let go of Natalie's hand and took a pace forward from the circle of 'Auld Lang Syne'. "Three Cheers for Mrs Frensham-Bowater," he shouted. "Hip, hip, hooray!"

Myra, standing in the entrance hall with the other parents, tried to look unconcerned. She knew that Charles had been nervous all along of doing that little duty and she was thankful that it was safely over. And that meant that the dance was over, too.

With the first bars of "God Save The Queen", they all became rigid, pained-looking, arms to their sides and heads erect; but the moment it was over, the laughter and excitement enlived their faces again. They began to drift reluctantly towards the hall.

"How pretty the girls are," the mothers said to one another. "Goodness, how they grow up. That isn't Madge's girl, surely, in the yellow organza? They change from day to day at this age."

"Was it lovely?" Myra asked Katie.

"So lovely! Oh and someone spilt fruit-cup all down poor Natalie's front."

"Oh, no!" said Myra.

"She doesn't care though."

"But her mother. . . . I feel so responsible."

"Oh, her mother's awfully understanding. She won't give a damn." ('Unlike you,' Katie's voice seemed to imply.) "It was last year's, anyway."

Benedict was hovering at Katie's shoulder.

"Charles had torn the hem already, anyway," Katie said.

"But how on earth?"

"They won a prize in the River Dance."

Myra had not the faintest idea what a River Dance was and said so.

"The boys have to run across some chalk lines carrying their partners and he tore her skirt when he picked her up. She's no light weight, I can assure you."

"I hope it hasn't been rowdy," Myra said, but this remark was far too silly to receive an answer.

Frances had attached herself to Charles and Natalie, so that she would not seem to leave the floor alone; but she knew that Mrs Pollard had seen her standing there by the door, without a partner, and for the last waltz of all things. To be seen by her hostess in such a predicament underlined her failure.

"Did you enjoy it, Frances?" Myra asked. And wasn't that the only way to put her question, Frances thought, the one she was so very anxious to know—"Did you dance much?"

"We had better go back as we came," Myra said. "Have you all got everything? Well then, you go on, Benedict dear, with Frances and Katie, and we will follow."

'I wish she wouldn't say "dear" to boys,' Katie thought. 'And she doesn't trust us, I suppose, to come on after. I hope that Benedict hasn't noticed that she doesn't trust him: he will think it is his driving, or worse, that she is thoroughly evil-minded. Goodness knows what she got up to in her young days to have such dreadful ideas in her head.'

*   *   *

The untidy room was waiting for them. Five hours earlier, they had not looked beyond the dance or imagined a time after it.

"Well, I don't think that poor boy, Roland, will thank you much for asking him in your party," Frances said. "He was wondering how he would ever get away from me."

She thought, as many grown-up women think, that by saying a thing herself she prevented people from thinking it. She had also read a great many nostalgic novels about girls of long ago spending hours in the cloakroom at dances and in her usual spirit of defiance she had refused to go there at all, had stuck the humiliation out and even when she might have taken her chance with the others in the Paul Jones had stuck that out, too.

"He told me he thought you danced very well," Katie said.

This made matters worse for Frances. So it wasn't just the dancing, but something very much more important— her personality, or lack of it; her plainness—what she was burdened with for the rest of her life, in fact.

Natalie seemed loth to take off her frock, stained and torn though it now was. She floated about the room, spreading the skirt about her as she hummed and swayed and shook her hair. She would not be back on earth again until morning.

"Here is your safety-pin, Katie," said Frances.

"And here, with many thanks, your necklace safe and sound."

The trinkets they had borrowed from one another were handed back; they unhooked one-another; examined their stockings for ladders. Katie took a pair of socks out of her brassière.

One by one, they got into bed. Natalie sat up writing her diary and Katie thought hers could wait till morning. Benedict's amusing sayings would be quite safe till then and by tomorrow the cloud that had been over the evening might have dispersed. The next day, when they were swimming in the lake, or cleaning out the rabbits or making walnut-fudge, surely Frances would be re-established among them, not cut off by her lack of success as she now was, taking the edge off Benedict's remembered wit, making Katie's heart ache just when it was beginning to behave as she had always believed a heart should.

Turning in Benedict's arms as they danced she had sometimes caught Frances's eyes as she stood there alone or with some other forlorn and unclaimed girl. Katie had felt treachery in the smile she had been bound to give—the most difficult of smiles, for it had to contain so much, the assurance that the dance was only a dance and nothing very much to miss, a suggestion of regret at her—Katie's—foolishness in taking part in it and surprise that she of all people had been chosen. 'It is soon over,' she tried to signal to Frances. 'You are yourself. I love you. I will soon come back.'

And Frances had received the smiles and nodded. 'There are other things in the world,' she tried to believe.

"Shall we have a picnic tomorrow?" Katie asked. She snuggled down into bed and stared up at the ceiling.

"Let's have one day at a time," said Natalie. She had filled in the space in her diary and now locked the book up with a little key that hung on a chain round her neck.

"Do put out the light before the moths come in," said Frances.

They could hear Katie's parents talking quietly in the next room. Frances thought; 'I expect she is saying, "Poor Frances." I'm afraid she didn't get many dances; but I am sure that Katie did what she could for her. It would really

have been kinder not to have invited her.' The unbroken
murmuring continued on the other side of the wall and
Frances longed for it to stop. She thought: 'She is for ever
working things out in her mind, and cruelly lets people
guess what they are. It would be no worse if she said them
out loud.' She had prayed that before Myra came to fetch
them from the dance it would all be over; "God Save The
Queen safely" sung and her own shame at last behind her.
As the last waltz began, she had longed for someone to claim
her—any spotty, clammy-handed boy would do. Benedict
and Katie had hovered by her, Benedict impatient to be
away, but Katie reluctant to leave her friend alone at such
a crucial moment. "Please go," Frances had told them and
just as they danced away, Myra had appeared in the doorway, looking tired but watchful, her eyes everywhere—
Katie accounted for, Charles, Natalie, then a little encouraging smile and nod to Frances herself, trying to shrink out of
sight on the perimeter of the gaiety. 'As I expected,' her
eyes said.

Gradually, the murmurings from the other room petered
out and the house became silent. Then, in Charles's room
across the landing, Natalie heard a shoe drop with a thud
on the floor and presently another. 'Sitting on the edge of
the bed, dreaming,' she thought. She lay awake, smiling in
the darkness and stroking her smooth arms long after the
other two had fallen asleep.

Summer Schools

SITTING outside on the sill, the cat watched Melanie through the window. The shallow arc between the tips of his ears, his baleful stare, and his hunched-up body blown feathery by the wind, gave him the look of a barn-owl. Sometimes, a strong gust nearly knocked him off balance and bent his whiskers crooked. Catching Melanie's eye, he opened his mouth wide in his furious, striped face, showed his fangs and let out a piteous mew instead of a roar.

Melanie put a finger in her book and padded across the room in her stockinged feet. When she opened the french windows, the gale swept into the room and the fire began to smoke. Now that he was allowed to come in, the cat began a show caprice; half in, he arched his back and rubbed against the step, purring loudly. Some leaves blew across the floor.

"Either in or out, you fool," Melanie said impatiently. Still holding the door, she put her foot under the cat's belly and half-pushed, half-lifted him into the room.

The french windows had warped, like all the other wooden parts of the house. There were altogether too many causes for irritation, Melanie thought. When she had managed to slam the door shut, she stood there for a moment, looking out at the garden, until she had felt the full abhorrence of the scene. Her revulsion was so complete as to be almost unbelievable; the sensation became ecstatic.

On the veranda, a piece of newspaper had wrapped itself,

quivering frenziedly, round a post. A macrocarpa hedge tossed about in the wind; the giant hydrangea by the gate was full of bus-tickets, for here was the terminus, the very end of the esplanade. The butt and end, Melanie thought, of all the long-drawn-out tedium of the English holiday resort. Across the road a broken bank covered with spiky grass hid most of the sands, but she could imagine them clearly, brown and ribbed, littered with bits of cuttle-fish and mussel-shells. The sea—far out—was staved with white.

Melanie waited as a bowed-over, mufflered man, exercising a dog, then a duffel-coated woman with a brace of poodles on leads completed the scene. Satisfied, she turned back to the fire. It was all as bad as could be and on a bright day it was hardly better, for the hard glitter of the sun seemed unable to lift the spirits. It was usually windy.

The creaking sound of the rain, its fitful and exasperated drumming on the window, she listened to carefully. In one place at the end of the veranda, it dropped more heavily and steadily: she could hear it as if the noise were in her own breast. The cat—Ursula's—rubbed its cold fur against her legs and she pushed him away crossly, but he always returned.

"A day for indoors," Ursula said gaily. She carried in the tea-tray, and set down a covered dish on the hearth with the smug triumph of one giving a great treat.

I am to be won over with buttered scones, Melanie thought sulkily. The sulky expression was one that her face, with its heavy brows and full mouth, fell into easily. "One of Miss Rogers's nasty looks," her pupils called it, finding it not alarming, but depressing. Ursula, two years younger, was plumper, brighter, more alert. Neither was beautiful.

"Oh, sod that cat of yours," Melanie said. He was now mewing at the french windows to be let out. Melanie's swearing was something new since their father had died—an act of desperation, such as a child might make. Father would turn in his grave, Ursula often said. Let him turn, said Melanie. "Who will look after him while you're away?" she asked, nodding at the cat. Ursula put him outside again and came back to pour out the tea. "How do you mean, look after him? Surely you don't mind. I'll order the fish. You'll only have to cook it and give it to him."

"I shan't be here."

The idea had suddenly occurred, born of vindictiveness and envy. For Pamela had no right to invite Ursula to stay there on her own. Melanie was only two years their senior; they had all been at the same school. Apart from all that, the two sisters always spent their holidays together; in fact, had never been separated. To Melanie, the invitation seemed staggering insolent, and Ursula's decision to accept it could hardly be believed. She had read out the letter at breakfast one morning and Melanie, on her way out of the room to fetch more milk, had simply said, "How extraordinary," her light, scornful voice dismissing the subject. Only a sense of time passing and middle-age approaching had given Ursula the courage (or effrontery) to renew the subject. For the first time that either she or Melanie could remember, her energy and enthusiasm overcame the smothering effect of her sister's lethargy.

She means to go, Melanie told herself. Her sensation of impotence was poison to her. She had a bitter taste in her mouth, and chafed her hands as if they were frozen. If Ursula were truly going, though, Melanie determined that the departure should be made as difficult as possible. Long before she could set out for the station she should be worn out with the obstacles she had had to overcome.

"You can't expect me to stay here on my own just in order to look after your cat."

And lest Ursula should ask where she was going before she had had time to make her plans, she got up quickly and went upstairs.

*　　　*　　　*

The cat was to stay in kennels and Ursula grieved about it. Her grief Melanie brushed aside as absurd, although she was at the same time inclined to allow Ursula a sense of guilt. "A dog one can at least take with one," she told her. She had decided that the cat reflected something of Ursula's own nature—too feminine (although it was a tom); it might be driven, though not led, and the refusal to co-operate mixed, as it was, with cowardice resulted in slyness.

The weather had not improved. They could remember the holidays beginning in this way so often, with everything —rain, flowers, bushes—aslant in the wind. It will be pretty miserable at Pamela's, Melanie thought. She could imagine that house and its surroundings—a parade of new shops nearby, a tennis club, enormous suburban pubs at the corners of roads. She was for ever adding something derogatory to the list. "Dentists' houses always depress me," she said. "I don't think I could stay in one—with all that going on under the same roof."

What awaited herself was much vaguer.

"It will be like being at school—though having to run to the bell instead of ringing it," Ursula said, when she had picked up the prospectus for the Summer Lecture Course. "A pity you can't just go to the discussions and not stay there. Breakfast 8.15," she read. "Oh, Lord. The Victorian Novel. Trollope. 9.30."

Melanie, in silence, held out her hand for the prospectus and Ursula gave it to her. She did not see it again.

"Will you want Mother's fur?" she asked, when she began to pack. "I just thought . . . evenings, you know, it might be useful . . ."

"I shall have evenings, too," Melanie reminded her.

Their mother could not have guessed what a matter of contention her ermine wrap would turn out to be when she was dead.

*　　　*　　　*

"How is Melanie?" Pamela asked.

"Oh, she's well. She's gone on a little holiday, too."

"I'm so glad. I should have liked to have asked her to come with you," Pamela lied. "But there's only this single bed."

Ursula went over to the window. The spare room was at the back of the house and looked across some recreation grounds—a wooden pavilion, a bowling-green; and tennis courts—just as Melanie had said there would be.

That evening, there was the pub.

All afternoon the front-door bell had rung, and Pamela and Ursula, sitting in the drawing-room upstairs could hear the crackle of Miss Potter's starched overall as she crossed the hall to answer it. Patients murmured nervously when they entered, but shouted cheerful good-byes as they left, going full tilt down the gravelled drive and slamming the gate after them.

"I'm sorry about the bell," Pamela said. "At first, I thought it would send me out of my mind, but now it's no worse than a clock striking."

Ursula thought it extraordinary that she had changed so much since their schooldays. It was difficult to find anything to talk about. The books they had once so passionately discussed were at the very bottom of the glass-fronted case, beneath text-books on dentistry and Book Club editions, and Ursula, finding Katherine Mansfield's Journal covered with dust, felt estranged. Perhaps Pamela had become a good cook instead, she thought, for there were plenty of books on that.

Melanie would have scorned the room, with its radiogram and cocktail cabinet and the matching sofa and chairs. The ash-trays were painted with bright sayings in foreign languages; there were piles of fashion magazines that later —much later, Ursula guessed—would be put in the waiting-room downstairs. The parchment lamp-shades were stuck over with wine labels and the lamps were made out of chianti bottles. The motif of drinking was prevalent, from a rueful yet humorous viewpoint. When Pamela opened the cigarette-box it played "The More we are Together", and Ursula wondered if the clock would call "Prosit" when it struck six.

"That's the last patient," Pamela said. "Mike will come up panting for a drink."

Her full-skirt, printed with a jumble of luggage-labels, flew out wide as she made a dash to the cocktail cabinet. She was as eager to be ready with everything as if she were opening a pub.

Panic now mingled with the feeling of estrangement, as Ursula listened to the footsteps on the stairs. "Hello, there, Ursula," said Mike as he threw open the door. "And how are you? Long time, no see, indeed."

"Not since our wedding," Pamela reminded him.

"Well, what will you be after taking?" Mike asked. He slapped his hands together, ready for action, took up a bottle and held it to the light.

'I suppose he feels uneasy because I am a school-mistress,' Ursula thought; 'And perhaps also—lest I shall think Pam married beneath her.'

Pamela put out the glasses and some amusing bottle-openers and corkscrews. Ursula remembered staying with her as a girl, had a clear picture of the gloomy dining-room: a dusty, cut-glass decanter, containing the dregs of some dark, unidentified liquid had stood in the centre of the great sideboard, its position never shifting an inch to the right or left. From that imprisoning house and those oppressive parents, Mike had rescued his betrothed and, though she had shed Katherine Mansfield somewhere on the way, she seemed as gay as could be that she had escaped.

Now she kissed her husband, took her drink and went

downstairs—to turn the waiting-room back into a dining-room, she said. Mike's uneasiness increased. He was clearly longing for her to return.

"You must be a brave man," Ursula said suddenly. "I remember Pam's mother and father and how nervous I was when I stayed there. Even when we were quite well on in our teens, we were made to lie down after luncheon, in a darkened room for ages and ages. 'And no reading, dears,' her mother always said as we went upstairs. At home, we never rested—or only when we were little children, but I pretended that we did, in case Pam's mother should think badly of mine. They seemed so very stern. To snatch away their only daughter must have needed courage."

For the first time, he looked directly at her. In his eyes was a timid expression. He may have been conscious of this and anxious to hide it, for almost immediately he glanced away.

"I girded on my armour," he said, "and rode up to the portcullis and demanded her. That was all there was to it."

She smiled, thinking, 'So this room is the end of a fairy tale.'

"Astonishing good health, my dear," Mike said, lifting his glass.

*   *   *

Melanie took her coffee and, summoning all her courage, went to sit down beside Mrs Rybeck, who gave her a staving-off smile, a slight shake of her head as she knitted, her lips moving silently. When she came to the end of the row, she apologised, and jotted down on her knitting-pattern, what-ever it was she had been counting.

"What a stimulating evening," Melanie said.

"Have you not heard George Barnes lecture before?" Mrs Rybeck was obviously going to be condescending again, but

Melanie was determined to endure it. Then—what she had hoped—Professor Rybeck came in. She felt breathless and self-conscious as he approached.

"Darling!" he murmured, touching his wife's hair, then bowed to Melanie.

"Miss Rogers," his wife reminded him quickly. "At Saint Winifred's, you know, where Ethel's girls were."

"Yes, of course I know Miss Rogers," he said.

His dark hair receded from a forehead that seemed always moist, as were his dark and mournful eyes. As soon as they heard his voice—low, catarrhal and with such gentle inflections—some of the women, who had been sitting in a group by the window, got up and came over to him.

"Professor Rybeck," one said. "We are beside ourselves with excitement about your lecture tomorrow."

"Miss Rogers was just saying that she thought highly of George's talk this evening," said Mrs Rybeck.

"Ah, George!" her husband said softly. "I think George likes to think he has us all by the ears. Young men do. But we mustn't let him sharpen his wits on us till we ourselves are blunt. None the less, he knows his Thackeray."

Melanie considered herself less esteemed for having mentioned him.

"How I love 'Middlemarch'," some woman said. "I think it is my favourite novel."

"Then I only hope I do it justice tomorrow," Professor Rybeck said. Although he seemed full of confidence, he smiled humbly. Nothing was too much trouble.

*   *   *

Pamela had insisted that the three of them should squeeze into the front of the car and Ursula, squashed up in the middle, sat with rounded shoulders and her legs tucked to one side. She was worried about the creases in her skirt. The wireless was on very loud and both Pamela and Mike joined

in the Prize Song from Die Meistersinger. Ursula was glad
when they reached The Swan.

The car-park was full. This pub was where everybody
went, Pamela explained; "at the moment," she added. In
the garden, the striped umbrellas above the tables had been
furled; the baskets of geraniums over the porch were
swinging in the wind.

"Astonishingly horrid evening," Mike said, when some
of his acquaintances greeted him. "This is Pam's friend,
Ursula. Ursie, this is Jock"—or Jean or Eve or Bill. Ursula
lost track. They all knew one another and Mike and Pam
seemed popular. "Don't look now, the worst has happened," someone had said in a loud voice when Mike opened
the door of the Saloon Bar.

Ursula was made much of. From time to time, most of
them were obliged to bring out some dull relation or duty-
guest. ("Not really one of us"), and it was a mark of
friendliness to do one's best to help with other people's
problems—even the most tiresome of old crones would be
attended to; and Ursula, although plump and prematurely
grey, was only too ready to smile and join in the fun.

"You're one of us, I can see," someone complimented her.

"Cheers!" said Ursula before she drank. Melanie would
have shivered with distaste.

"We are all going on to Hilly's," Pam called to Mike
across the bar at closing-time.

This moving-on was the occasion for a little change round
of passengers and, instead of being squeezed in between
Pamela and Mike, Ursula was taken across the car-park by a
man called Guy.

"Daddy will give you a scarf for your head," he promised,
opening the door of his open car. The scarf tucked inside his
shirt was yellow, patterned with horses and when he took it
off and tied it round Ursula's head, the silk was warm to her
cheeks.

They drove very fast along the darkening roads and were the first to arrive.

"Poor frozen girl," said Guy when he had swung the car round on the gravelled sweep in front of the house and brought it up within an inch of the grass verge. With the driving off his mind, he could turn his attention to Ursula and he took one of her goosefleshy arms between his hands and began to chafe it. "What we need is a drink," he said. "Where the hell have they all got to?"

She guessed that to drive fast and to arrive first was something he had to do and, for his sake and to help on the amiability of the evening, she was glad that he had managed it.

"You're sure it's the right house?" she asked.

"Dead sure, my darling."

She had never been called 'darling' by a man and, however meaningless the endearment, it added something to her self-esteem, as their arriving first had added something to his.

She untied the scarf and gave it back to him. He had flicked on his cigarette lighter and was looking for something in the dash-pocket. For a moment, while the small glow lasted, she could study his face. It was like a ventriloquist's dummy's—small, alert, yet blank; the features gave the appearance of having been neatly painted.

He found the packet of cigarettes; then he put the scarf round his neck and tied it carefully. "Someone's coming," he said. "They must have double-crossed us and had one somewhere on the way."

"You drove fastest, that's all," she said, playing her part in the game.

"Sorry if it alarmed you, sweetheart." He leaned over and kissed her quickly, just before the first of the cars came round the curve of the drive.

* * *

'That's the first evening gone,' Ursula thought, when later, she lay in bed, rather muzzily going over what had happened. She could remember the drawing-room at Hilly's. She had sat on a cushion on the floor and music from a gramophone above her had spilled over her head, so that she had seen people's mouths opening and shutting but had not been able to hear the matching conversations. In many ways the room—though it was larger—had seemed like Pamela's, with pub-signs instead of bottle-labels on the lampshades. Her sense of time had soon left her and her sense of place grew vaguer, but some details irritated her because she could not evade them—particularly a warming-pan hanging by the fireplace in which she confronted her distorted reflection.

There had seemed no reason why the evening should ever end and no way of setting going all the complications of departure. Although she was tired, she had neither wanted to leave or to stay. She was living a tiny life within herself, sitting there on the cushion; sipping and smiling and glancing about her. Mike had come across the room to her. She turned to tilt back her head to look up into his face but at once felt giddy and had to be content with staring at his knees, at the pin stripes curving baggily, a thin stripe, then a wider, more feathery one. She began to count them, but Mike had come to take her home to bye-byes he said, stretching out a hand. If I can only do this, I can do anything, Ursula thought, trying to rise and keep her balance. I was silly to sit so low down in the first place, she decided. "I think my foot has gone to sleep," she explained and smiled confidingly at his knees. His grip on her arm was strong; although appearing to be extending a hand in gallantry, he was really taking her weight and steadying her, too. She had realised this, even at the time and later, lying safe in bed at last, she felt wonderfully grateful for his kindness, and did not at all mind sharing such a secret with him.

E

Pamela had put a large jug of water by her bed. An hour earlier, it had seemed unnecessary, but now water was all she wanted in the world. She sat up and drank, with a steady, relentless rhythm, as animals drink. Then she slid back into the warm bedclothes and tried to reconstruct in her mind that drive with Guy and became, in doing so, two people, the story teller and the listener; belittling his endearments, only to reassure herself about them. The sports car, the young man (he was not very old, she told herself), the summer darkness, in spite of its being so windy, were all things that other young girls she had known had taken for granted, at Oxford and elsewhere, and she herself had been denied. They seemed all the more miraculous for having been done without for so long.

Of recent years she had often tried to escape the memory of two maiden-ladies who had lived near her home when she and Melanie were girls. So sharp-tongued and cross-looking, they had seemed then as old as could be, yet may have been no more than in their fifties, she now thought. Frumpish and eccentric, at war with one another as well as all their neighbours, they were to be seen tramping the lanes, single-file and in silence, with their dogs. To the girls, they were the most appalling and unenviable creatures, smelling of vinegar, Melanie had said. The recollection of them so long after they were dead disturbed Ursula and depressed her, for she could see how she and Melanie had taken a turning in their direction, yet scarcely anything as definite as this, for there had been no action, no decision; simply, the road they had been on had always, it seemed, been bending in that direction. In no time at all, would they not be copies of those other old ladies? The Misses Rogers, the neighbours would think of them, feeling pity and nervousness. The elder Miss Rogers would be alarmingly abrupt, with her sarcastic voice and old-fashioned swear-words. They won't be afraid of me, Ursula decided; but had

no comfort from the thought. People would think her
bullied and would be sorry. She, the plumper one, with her
cat and timid smiles, would give biscuits to children when
Melanie's back was turned. Inseparable, yet alien to one
another, they would become. Forewarned as she was, she
felt herself drifting towards that fate and was afraid when
she woke at night and thought of it.

Her first drowsiness had worn off and her thirst kept her
wakeful. She lay and wondered about the details of
Pamela's escape from her parents' sad house and all that
had threatened her there—watchfulness, suspicion, envy
and capricious humours; much of the kind of thing she
herself suffered from Melanie. Pamela's life now was bright
and silly, and perhaps she had run away from the best part
of herself; but there was nothing in the future to menace
her as Ursula was menaced by her own picture of the
elderly Misses Rogers.

*   *   *

"But *surely*," insisted the strained and domineering
voice. The woman gripped the back of the chair in front of
her and stared up at Professor Rybeck on the platform.

At the end of his lecture, he had asked for questions or
discussions. To begin with, everyone had seemed too
stunned with admiration to make an effort; there were
flutterings and murmurings, but for some time no one stood
up. Calmly, he waited, sitting there smiling, eyes half-
closed and his head cocked a little as if he were listening
to secret music, or applause. His arms were crossed over his
chest and his legs were crossed too, and one foot swayed
back and forth rhythmically.

The minute Mr Brundle stood up, other people wanted to.
He was an elderly, earnest man, who had been doggedly on
the track of culture since his youth. His vanity hid from him
the half-stifled yawns he evoked, the glassy look of those

who, though caught, refused to listen and also his way of melting away to one victim any group of people he approached. Even Professor Rybeck looked restless, as Mr Brundle began now to pound away at his theory. Then others, in disagreement or exasperation, began to jump to their feet, or made sharp comments, interrupting; even shot their arms into the air, like schoolchildren. World Peace they might have been arguing about, not George Eliot's Dorothea Casaubon.

"Please, please," said Professor Rybeck, in his melodious protesting voice. "Now, Mrs Thomas, let us hear you."

"But *surely*," Mrs Thomas said again.

"Wouldn't it be time to say?" asked Mrs Wetherby— She sounded diffident and had blushed; she had never spoken in the presence of so many people before, but wanted badly to make her mark on the Professor. She was too shy to stand upright and leaned forward, lifting her bottom a couple of inches from the chair. Doing so, she dropped her notebook and pencil, her stole slipped off and when she bent down to pick it up she also snatched at some large, tortoise-shell pins that had fallen out of her hair. By the time she had done all this, her chance was gone and she had made her mark in the wrong way. The one and only clergyman in the room had sprung to his feet and, knowing all the tricks needed to command, had snatched off his spectacles and held them high in the air while, for some reason no one was clear about, he denounced Samuel Butler.

"I think, Comrade . . . Professor, I should say," Mr Brundle interrupted. "If we might return but briefly to the subject. . . ."

Melanie closed her eyes and thought how insufferable people became about what has cost them too much to possess —education, money, or even good health.

Lightly come or not at all, is what I like, she told herself crossly and, when she opened her eyes, glanced up at

Professor Rybeck, who smiled with such placid condescension as the ding-dong argument went on between clergyman and atheist (for literature—Victorian or otherwise—had been discarded) and then she looked for Mrs Rybeck and found her sitting at the end of the second row, still knitting. She gave, somehow, an impression of not being one of the audience, seemed apart from them, preoccupied with her own thoughts, lending her presence only, like a baby-sitter or the invigilator at an examination—well accustomed to the admiration her husband had from other women of her own age, she made it clear that she was one with him in all he did and thought; their agreement, she implied, had come about many years ago and needed no more discussion, and if the women cared to ask her any of the questions he had no time to answer, then she could give the authorised replies. With all this settled, her placidity, like his, was almost startling to other people, their smiling lips (not eyes), their capacity for waiting for others to finish speaking (and it was far removed from the act of listening), is often to be found in the mothers of large families. Yet she was childless. She had only the Professor, and the socks she knitted were for him. She is more goddessy than motherly, Melanie thought.

"We are summoned to the banqueting-hall," said the Professor, raising his hand in the air, as a bell began to ring. This was the warning that lunch would be ready in ten minutes, the Secretary had told them all when they arrived, and "warning" was a word she had chosen well. The smell of minced beef and cabbage came along passages towards them. To Melanie it was unnoticeable, part of daily life, like other tedious affairs; one disposed of the food, as of any other small annoyance, there were jugs of water to wash it down and slices of bread cut hours before that one could crumble as one listened to one's neighbour.

One of Melanie's neighbours was an elementary school-teacher to whom she tried not to be patronising. On her other side was a Belgian woman whose vivacity was intolerable. She was like a bad caricature of a foreigner, primly sporty and full of gay phrases. "Mon Dieu, we have had it, chums," she said, lifting the water-jug and finding it empty. The machine-gun rattle of consonants vibrated in Melanie's head long after she was alone. "Oh, là, là!" the woman sometimes cried, as if she were a cheeky French maid in an old-fashioned farce.

"You think 'Meedlemahtch' is a good book," she asked Melanie. They all discussed novels at mealtimes too; for they were what they had in common. Melanie was startled, for Professor Rybeck had spent most of the morning explaining its greatness. "It is one of the great English novels," she said.

"As great as Charles Morgan, you think? In the same class?"

Melanie looked suspicious and would not answer.

"It is such a funny book. I read it last night and laughed so much."

"And will read 'War and Peace' between tea and dinner, I suppose," the elementary school-teacher murmured. "Oh dear, how disgusting!" She pushed a very pale, boiled caterpillar to the side of her plate. "If that happened to one of our little darlings at school dinner, the mother would write at once to her M.P."

At Melanie's school, the girls would have hidden the creature under a fork in order not to spoil anyone else's appetite, but she did not say so.

"A *funny* book?" she repeated, turning back to the Belgian woman.

"Yes, I like it so much when she thinks that the really delightful marriage must be that where your husband was a sort of father, and could teach you Hebrew if you wished it. Oh, là, là! For heaven's sake."

"Then she did read a page or two," said the women on Melanie's other side.

A dreadful sadness and sense of loss had settled over Melanie when she herself had read those words. They had not seemed absurd to her; she had felt tears pressing at the back of her eyes. So often, she had longed for protection and compassion, to be instructed and concentrated upon; as if she were a girl again, yet with a new excitement in the air.

As they made their way towards the door, when lunch was over, she could see Professor Rybeck standing there talking to one or two of his admirers. Long before she drew near to him, Melanie found another direction to glance in. What she intended for unconcern, he took for deliberate hostility and wondered at what point of his lecture he had managed to offend her so.

In a purposeless way, she wandered into the garden, The Georgian house—a boys' preparatory-school in the term-time—stood amongst dark rhododendron bushes and silver birches. Paths led in many directions through the shrub-beries, yet all converged upon the lake—a depressing stretch of water, as bleary as an old looking-glass, shadowed by trees and broken by clumps of reeds.

The pain of loneliness was a worse burden to her here than it had ever been at home and she knew—her behaviour as she was leaving the dining-room had reminded her—that the fault was in herself.

"Don't think that I will make excuses to speak to you," she had wanted to imply. "I am not so easily dazzled as these other women." But I wanted him to speak to me, she thought, and perhaps I only feared that he would not.

She sat down on the bank above the water and thought about the Professor. She could even imagine his lustrous eyes turned upon her, as he listened.

"I give false impressions," she struggled to explain to him. "In my heart . . . I am . . ."

"I know what you are," he said gently. "I knew at once."

The relief would be enormous. She was sure of that. She could live the rest of her life on the memory of that moment.

"But he is a fraud," the other, destructive voice in her insisted, the voice that had ruined so much for her. "He is not a fraud," she said firmly; her lips moved; she needed to be so definite with herself. "Perhaps he cannot find the balance between integrity and priggishness."

"Is that all?" asked the other voice.

The dialogue faded out and she sighed, thinking: I wish I hadn't come. I feel so much worse here than I do at home.

Coming round the lake's edge towards her was the atrocious little Mr Brundle. She pretended not to have seen him and got to her feet and went off in the other direction.

By the afternoon post came a letter from Ursula, saying how dull she was and that Melanie had been so right about it all—and that comforted her a little.

*   *   *

Ursula was polishing a glass on a cloth printed with a chart of vintage years for champagne. Although she was drunk, she wondered at the usefulness of this as a reference. It would be strange to go home again to a black telephone, white sheets and drying-up cloths on which there was nothing at all to read, not a recipe for a cocktail or a cheerful slogan.

On the draining-board two white tablets fizzed, as they rose and fell in a glass of water. The noise seemed very loud to her and she was glad when the tablets dissolved and there was silence.

"There you are," Guy said, handing the glass to her. The water still spat and sparkled and she drank it slowly, gasping between sips.

"Pamela will wonder where I am," she said. She put

the glass on the draining-board and sat down with a bump on one of the kitchen chairs. She had insisted on washing the two glasses before she went home, and had devoted herself to doing so with single-mindedness; but Guy had been right, and she gave in. Everything she had to do had become difficult—going home, climbing the stairs, undressing. I shall just have to sit on this chair and let time pass, she decided. It will pass, she promised herself, and it mends all in the end.

"Where did we go after that Club?" she suddenly asked frowning.

"Nowhere," said Guy. "On our way back to Pamela's we stopped here for a drink. That's all."

"Ah, yes!"

She remembered the outside of this bungalow and a wooden gate with the name Hereiam. It had been quite dark when they walked up the stony path to the front door. Now, it seemed the middle of the night. "I think you gave me too much whisky," she said, with a faint, reproachful smile.

"As a matter of fact, I gave you none. It was ginger-ale you were drinking."

She considered this and then lifted her eyes to look at him and asked anxiously: "Then had I had . . . was I . . .?"

"You were very sweet."

She accepted this gravely. He put his hands under her arms and brought her to her feet and she rested the side of her face against his waistcoat and stayed very still, as if she were counting his heart-beats. These, like the fizzing drink, also sounded much too loud.

"I didn't wash the other glass," she said.

"Mrs Lamb can do it in the morning."

She went from one tremulous attempt at defence to another, wanting to blow her nose, or light a cigarette or put something tidy. In the sitting-room, earlier, when he had sat down beside her on the sofa, she had sprung up and gone rapidly across the room to look for an ash-tray. "Who is this?" she had asked, picking up a framed photograph and holding it at arm's length, as if to ward him off. "Girl friend," he said briefly, drinking his whisky and watching her manœuvres with amusement.

"Haven't you ever wanted to get married?" she had asked.

"Sometimes. Have you?"

"Oh, sometimes . . . I daresay," she answered vaguely.

Now, in the kitchen, he had caught her at last, she was clasped in his arms and feeling odd, she told him.

"I know. There's some coffee nearly ready in the other room. That will do untold good."

What a dreadful man he is, really, in spite of his tenderness, she thought. So hollow and vulgar that I don't know what Melanie would say.

She was startled for a moment, wondering if she had murmured this aloud; for, suddenly, his heartbeat had become noisier—from anger, she was afraid.

"You are very kind," she said appeasingly. "I am not really used to drinking as much as people do here—not used to drinking at all."

"What *are* you used to?"

"Just being rather dull, you know—my sister and I."

His way of lifting her chin up and kissing her was too accomplished and she was reminded of the way in which he drove the car. She was sure that there was something here she should resent. Perhaps he was patronising her; for the kiss had come too soon after her remark about the dullness of her life. I can bring *some* excitement into it, he may have thought.

Without releasing her, he managed to stretch an arm and put out the light. "I can't bear to see you frowning," he explained. "Why frown anyway?"

"That coffee . . . but then I mustn't stay for it, after all.
Pamela will be wondering . . ."

"Pam will understand."

"Oh, I hope not."

She frowned more than ever and shut her eyes tightly
although the room was completely dark.

*   *   *

Melanie sat on the edge of the bed, coughing. She was
wondering if she had suddenly got T.B. and kept looking
anxiously at her handkerchief.

The sun was shining, though not into her room. From the
window, she could see Professor Rybeck sitting underneath
the Wellingtonia with an assortment of his worshippers.
From his gestures, Melanie could tell that it was he who was
talking, and talking continuously. The hand rose and fell
and made languid spirals as he unfolded his theme, or else
cut the air decisively into slices. Mrs Rybeck was, of course,
knitting. By her very presence, sitting a little apart from her
husband, like a woman minding a stall on a fairground, she
attracted passers-by. Melanie watched the Belgian woman
now approaching, to say her few words about the knitting,
then having paid her fee, to pass on to listen to the Professor.

Desperately, Melanie wished to be down there listening,
too; but she had no knowledge of how to join them.
Crossing the grass, she would attract too much attention.
Ah, *she* cannot keep away, people would think, turning to
watch her. She must be in love with the Professor after all,
like the other women; but perhaps more secretly, more
devouringly.

She had stopped coughing and forgotten tuberculosis for
the moment, as she tried to work out some more casual way
than crossing the lawn. She might emerge less noticeably
from the shrubbery behind the Wellingtonia, if only she
could be there in the first place.

She took a clean handkerchief from a drawer and smoothed her hair before the looking-glass; and then a bell rang for tea and, when she went back to the window, the group under the tree was breaking up. Mrs Rybeck was rolling up her knitting and they were all laughing.

I shall see him at tea, Melanie thought. She could picture him bowing to her, coldly, and with the suggestion that it was she who disliked him rather than he who disliked her. I could never put things right now, she decided.

She wondered what Ursula would be doing at this minute. Perhaps sitting in Pamela's little back garden having tea, while, at the front of the house, the patients came and went. She had said that she would be glad to be at home again, for Pamela had changed and they had nothing left in common. And coming here hasn't been a success, either, Melanie thought, as she went downstairs to tea. She blamed Ursula very much for having made things so dull for them both. There must be ways of showing her how mistaken she had been, ways of preventing anything of the kind happening again.

"Miss Rogers," said the Professor with unusual gaiety. They had almost collided at the drawing-room door. "Have you been out enjoying the sun?"

She blushed and was so angry that she should that she said quite curtly, "No, I was writing letters in my room."

He stood quickly aside to let her pass and she did so without a glance at him.

*   *   *

Their holiday was over. On her way back from the station, Ursula called at the kennels for the cat and Melanie, watching her come up the garden path, could see the creature clawing frantically at her shoulder, trying to hoist himself out of her grasp. The taxi-driver followed with the suitcase.

Melanie had intended to be the last home and had even caught a later train than was convenient, in order not to have to be waiting there for her sister. After all her planning, she was angry to have found the house empty.

"Have you been home long?" Ursula asked rather breathlessly. She put the cat down and looked round. Obviously Melanie had not, for her suitcase still stood in the hall and not a letter had been opened.

"Only a minute or two," said Melanie.

"That cat's in a huff with me. Trying to punish me for going away, I suppose. He's quite plump though. He looks well, doesn't he? Oh, it's so lovely to be home."

She went to the hall-table and shuffled the letters, then threw them on one side. Melanie had said nothing.

"Aren't *you* glad to be home?" Ursula asked her.

"No, I don't think so."

"Well I'm glad you had a good time. It was a change for you."

"Yes."

"And now let's have some tea."

She went into the kitchen and, still wearing her hat, began to get out the cups and saucers. "They didn't leave any bread," she called out. "Oh, yes, it's all right, I've found it." She began to sing, then stopped to chatter to the cat, then sang again.

Melanie had been in the house over an hour and had done nothing.

"I'm so glad you had a good time," Ursula said again, when they were having tea.

"I'm sorry you didn't."

"It was a mistake going there, trying to renew an old friendship. You'd have hated the house."

"You'd have liked *mine*. Grey stone, Georgian, trees and a lake."

"Romantic," Ursula said and did not notice that

Melanie locked her hands together in rather a theatrical gesture.

"Pam seems complacent. She's scored over me, having a husband. Perhaps that's why she invited me."

"What did you do all the time?"

"Just nothing. Shopped in the morning—every morning—the housewife's round—butcher, baker, candlestick maker. 'I'm afraid the piece of skirt was rather gristly, Mr Bones.' That sort of thing. She would fetch half a pound of butter one day and go back for another half-pound the next morning—just for the fun of it. One day, she said, 'I think we'll have some hock for supper.' I thought she was talking about wine, but it turned out to be some bacon—not very nice. Not very nice of me to talk like this, either."

However dull it had been, she seemed quite excited as she described it; her cheeks were bright and her hands restless.

"We went to the cinema once, to see a Western," she added. "Mike is very fond of Westerns."

"How dreadful for you."

Ursula nodded.

"Well, that's their life," she said, "I was glad all the time that you were not there. Darling puss, so now you've forgiven me."

To show his forgiveness, the cat jumped on to her lap and began dough-punching, his extended claws catching the threads of her skirt.

"Tell me about *you*," Ursula said. She poured out some more tea to sip while Melanie had her turn; but to her surprise Melanie frowned and looked away.

"Is something the matter?"

"I can't talk about it yet, or get used to not being there. This still seems unreal to me. You must give me time."

She got up, knocked over the cream jug and went out of the room. Ursula mopped up the milk with her napkin and then leant back and closed her eyes. Her moment's consternation at Melanie's behaviour had passed; she even forgot it. The cat relaxed, too, and, curled up against her, slept.

Melanie was a long time unpacking and did nothing towards getting supper. She went for a walk along the sea road and watched the sunset on the water. The tide was out and the wet sands were covered with a pink light. She dramatised her solitary walk and was in a worse turmoil when she reached home.

"Your cough is bad," Ursula said when they had finished supper.

"Is it?" Melanie said absent-mindedly.

"Something has happened, hasn't it?" Ursula asked her, and then looked down quickly, as if she were confused.

"The end of the world," said Melanie.

"You've fallen in love?" Ursula lifted her head and stared at her.

"To have to go back to school next week and face those bloody children—and go on facing them, for ever and for ever—or other ones exactly like them . . . the idea suddenly appals me."

Her bitterness was so true, and Ursula could hear her own doom in her sister's words. She had never allowed herself to have thoughts of that kind.

"But can't you . . . can't he?" she began.

"We can't meet again. We never shall. So it *is* the end of the world, you see," said Melanie. The scene gave her both relief and anguish. Her true parting with Professor Rybeck (he had looked up from *The Times* and nodded as she crossed the hall) was obliterated for ever. She could more easily bear the agonised account she now gave to Ursula and she would bear it—their noble resolve, their last illicit embrace.

"He's married, you mean?" Ursula asked bluntly.

"Yes, married."

Mrs Rybeck, insensitively knitting at the execution of

their hopes, appeared as an evil creature, tenacious and sinister.

"But to say good-bye for ever . . ." Ursula protested. "We only have one life . . . would it be wicked, after all?"

"What could there be . . . clandestine meetings and sordid arrangements?"

Ursula looked ashamed.

"I should ruin his career," said Melanie.

"Yes, I see. You could write to one another, though."

"Write!" Melanie repeated in a voice as light as air. "I think I will go to bed now. I feel exhausted."

"Yes, do, and I will bring you a hot drink." As Melanie began to go upstairs, Ursula said, "I am very sorry, you know."

While she was waiting for the milk to rise in the pan, she tried to rearrange her thoughts, especially to exclude (now that there was so much nobility in the house) her own squalid—though hazily recollected—escapade. Hers was a more optimistic nature than Melanie's and she was confident of soon putting such memories out of her mind.

When she took the hot milk upstairs, her sister was sitting up in bed reading a volume of Keats' letters. "He gave it to me as I came away," she explained, laying the book on the bedside table, where it was always to remain.

We have got this to live with now, Ursula thought, and it will be with us for ever, I can see—the reason and the excuse for everything. It will even grow; there will be more and more of it, as time goes on. When we are those two elderly Miss Rogers we are growing into it will still be there. "Miss Melanie, who has such a sharp tongue," people will say. "Poor thing . . . a tragic love-affair a long way back." I shall forget there was a time when we did not have it with us.

Melanie drank her milk and put out the light; then she lay down calmly and closed her eyes and prepared herself for her dreams. Until they came, she imagined walking by the lake, as she had done, that afternoon, only a few days ago; but instead of Mr Brundle coming into the scene, Professor Rybeck appeared. He walked towards her swiftly, as if by assignation. Then they sat down and looked at the tarnished water—and she added a few swans for them to watch. After a long delicious silence, she began to speak. Yet words were not really necessary. She had hardly begun the attempt; her lips shaped the beginning of a sentence— "I am . . ." and then he took her hand and held it to his cheek. "I know what you are," he said. "I knew at the very beginning."

Although they had parted for ever, she realised that she was now at peace—She felt ennobled and enriched, and saw herself thus, reflected from her sister's eyes, and she was conscious of Ursula's solemn wonder and assured by it.

Perhaps a Family Failing

OF course, Mrs Cotterell cried. Watery-eyed, on the arm of the bridegroom's father, she smiled in a bewildered way to left and right, coming down the aisle. Outside, on the church steps, she quickly dashed the tears away as she faced the camera, still arm-in-arm with Mr Midwinter, a man she detested.

He turned towards her and gave a great meaningless laugh just as the camera clicked and Mrs Cotterell had his ginny breath blown full in her face. Even in church he had to smell like that, she thought, and the grim words, "Like father, like son", disturbed her mind once more.

Below them, at the kerb's edge, Geoff was already helping his bride into the car. The solemnity of the service had not touched him. In the vestry, he had been as jaunty as ever, made his wife blush and was hushed by his mother, a frail, pensive creature, who had much, Mrs Cotterell thought, to be frail and pensive about.

It was Saturday morning and the bridal car moved off slowly amongst the other traffic. Mrs Cotterell watched until the white-ribboned motor disappeared.

The bridesmaids, one pink, one apple-green, were getting into the next car. Lissport was a busy place on Saturdays and to many of the women it was part of the morning's shopping-outing to be able to stand for a minute or two to watch a bride coming out of the church. Feeling nervous and self-conscious, Mrs Cotterell, who had often herself stood and watched and criticised, crossed the pavement to the car. She was anxious to be home and wondered if everything was all right there. She had come away in a flurry of confused directions, leaving two of her neighbours slicing beetroot and sticking blanched almonds into the trifles. She was relieved that the reception was her own affair, that she could be sure that there would be no drunkenness, no rowdy behaviour and suggestive speeches, as there had been at Geoff's sister's wedding last year. One glass of port to drink a toast to the bride and bridegroom she had agreed to. For the rest she hoped that by now her kindly neighbours had mixed the orange cordial.

* * *

Mrs Cotterell cried again, much harder, when Beryl came downstairs in her going-away suit, and kissed her and thanked her (as if her mother were a hostess, not her own flesh and blood, Mrs Cotterell thought sorrowfully) and with composure got into Geoff's little car, to which Mr Midwinter had tied an empty sardine-tin.

Then everyone else turned to Mrs Cotterell and thanked her and praised the food and Beryl's looks and dress. It had all gone off all right, they said, making a great hazard of it. "You'll miss her," the women told her. "I know what it's like," some added.

The bridesmaids took off their flower wreaths and put on their coats. Geoff's brothers, Les and Ron, were taking them out for the evening. "Not long till opening-time," they said.

Mrs Cotterell went back into the house, to survey the wedding-presents, and the broken wedding-cake, with the trellis work icing she had done so lovingly, crumbled all over the table. Beryl's bouquet was stuck in a vase, waiting to be taken tomorrow to poor Grandma in hospital.

In the kitchen, the faithful neighbours were still hard at work, washing up the piles of plates stained with beetroot and mustard and tomato sauce.

"She's gone," Mrs Cotterell whispered into her crumpled handkerchief as her husband came in and put his arm round her.

*   *   *

"Soon be opening-time," Geoff said, driving along the busy road to Seaferry. He had long ago stopped the car, taken the sardine-tin off the back axle and thrown it over a hedge. "Silly old fool, Dad," he had said fondly. "Won't ever act his age."

Beryl thought so, too, but decided not to reopen that old discussion at such a time. For weeks, she had thought and talked and dreamt of the wedding, studied the advice to brides in women's magazines, on make-up, etiquette and Geoff's marital rights—which he must, she learnt, not be allowed to anticipate. "Stop it, Geoff!" she had often said firmly. "I happen to want you to respect me, thank you very much." Unfortunately for her, Geoff was not the respectful kind, although, in his easy-going way he consented to the celibacy—one of her girlish whims—and had even allowed the gratifying of his desires to be postponed from Easter until early summer, because she had suddenly decided she wanted sweet peas in the bridesmaids' bouquets.

To the women's magazines Beryl now felt she owed everything; she had had faith in their advice and seen it justified. I expect Geoff's getting excited, she thought. She was really quite excited herself.

"Now where are you going?" she asked, as he swerved suddenly off the road. It was perfectly plain that he was going into a public house, whose front door he had seen flung open just as he was about to pass it by.

"Well, here it is," he said. "The White Horse. The very first pub to have the privilege of serving a drink to Mr and Mrs Geoffrey Midwinter."

This pleased her, although she wanted to get to the hotel as quickly as she could, to unpack her trousseau, before it creased too badly.

It was a dull little bar, smelling frowsty. The landlord was glumly watchful, as if they might suddenly get out of hand, or steal one of his cracked ashtrays.

Geoff, however, was in high spirits, and raised his pint pot and winked at his wife. "Well, here's in anticipation," he said. She looked demurely at her gin and orange, but she smiled. She loved him dearly. She was quite convinced of this, for she had filled in a questionnaire on the subject of love in one of her magazines, and had scored eighteen out of twenty, with a rating of "You and Cleopatra share the honours." Only his obsession with public houses worried her, but she was sure that—once she had him away from the influence of his father and brothers—she would be able to break the habit.

* * *

At six o'clock Mr Midwinter took his thirst and his derogatory opinions about the wedding down to the saloon bar of The Starter's Orders. His rueful face, as he described the jugs of orangeade, convulsed his friends. "Poor Geoff, what's he thinking of, marrying into a lot like that?" asked the barmaid.

"Won't make no difference to Geoff," said his father. "Geoff's like his Dad. Not given to asking anybody's by-your-leave when he feels like a pint."

Mrs Midwinter had stayed at home alone. It had not occurred to her husband that she might be feeling flat after the day's excitement. She would not have remarked on it herself, knowing the problem was insoluble. He could not have taken her to a cinema, because Saturday evening was sacred to drinking, and although she would have liked to go with him for a glass of stout, she knew why she could not. He always drank in the Men Only bar at The Starter's Orders. "Well, you don't want me drinking with a lot of prostitutes, do you?" he often asked, and left her no choice, as was his habit.

*   *   *

Beryl had never stayed in an hotel before, and she was full of admiration at the commanding tone Geoff adopted as they entered the hall of The Seaferry Arms.

"Just one before we go up?" he inquired, looking towards the bar.

"Later, dear," she said firmly. "Let's unpack and tidy ourselves first; then we can have a drink before dinner." The word "dinner" depressed him. It threatened to waste a great deal of Saturday evening drinking time.

From their bedroom window they could see a bleak stretch of promenade, grey and gritty. The few people down there either fought their way against the gale, with their heads bowed and coats clutched to their breasts, or seemed tumbled along with the wind at their heels. The sun, having shone on the bride, had long ago gone in and it seemed inconceivable that it would ever come out again.

"No strolling along the prom tonight," said Geoff.

"Isn't it a shame? It's the only thing that's gone wrong."

Beryl began to hang up and spread about the filmy, lacy, ribboned lingerie with which she had for long planned to tease and entice her husband.

"The time you take," he said. He had soon tipped everything out of his own case into a drawer. "What's this?" he asked, picking up something of mauve chiffon.

"My nightgown," she said primly.

"What ever for?"

"Don't be common." She always affected disapproval when he teased her.

"What about a little anticipation here and now?" he suggested.

"Oh, don't be so silly. It's broad daylight."

"Right. Well, I'm just going to spy out the lie of the land. Back in a minute," he said.

She was quite content to potter about the bedroom, laying traps for his seduction; but when she was ready at last, she realised that he had been away a long time. She stood by the window, wondering what to do, knowing that it was time for them to go in to dinner. After a while, she decided that she would have to find him and, feeling nervous and self-conscious, she went along the quiet landing and down the stairs. Her common sense took her towards the sound of voices and laughter and, as soon as she opened the door of the bar, she was given a wonderful welcome from all the new friends Geoff had suddenly made.

*   *   *

"It seems ever so flat, doesn't it?" Mrs Cotterell said. All of the washing-up was done, but she was too tired to make a start on packing up the presents.

"It's the reaction," her husband said solemnly.

Voices from a play on the wireless mingled with their own, but were ignored. Mrs Cotterell had her feet in a bowl of hot water. New shoes had given her agony. Beryl, better informed, had practised wearing hers about the house for days before.

"Haven't done my corns any good," Mrs Cotterell mourned. Her feet ached and throbbed, and so did her heart.

"It all went off well, though, didn't it?" she asked, as she had asked him a dozen times before.

"Thanks to you," he said dutifully. He was clearing out

the budgerigar's cage and the bird was sitting on his bald head, blinking and chattering.

Mrs Cotterell stared at her husband. She suddenly saw him as a completely absurd figure, and she trembled with anger and self-pity. Something ought to have been done for her on such an evening, she thought, some effort should have been made to console and reward her. Instead, she was left to soak her feet and listen to a lot of North Country accents on the radio. She stretched out her hand and switched them off.

"What ever's wrong, Mother?"

"I can't stand any more of that 'By goom' and 'Nowt' and 'Eee, lad'. It reminds me of that nasty cousin Rose of yours."

"But we always listen to the play on a Saturday."

"This Saturday isn't like other Saturdays." She snatched her handkerchief out of her cuff and dabbed her eyes.

Mr Cotterell leaned forward and patted her knee and the budgerigar flew from his head and perched on her shoulder.

"That's right, Joey, You go to Mother. She wants a bit of cheering-up."

"I'm not his mother, if you don't mind, and I don't want cheering-up from a bird."

"One thing I know is you're overtired. I've seen it coming. You wouldn't care to put on your coat and stroll down to the Public for a glass of port, would you?"

"Don't be ridiculous," she said.

* * *

After dinner, they drank their coffee, all alone in the dreary lounge of The Seaferry Arms, and then Beryl went to bed. She had secret things to do to her hair and her face. "I'll just pour you out another cup," she said. "Then, when you've drunk it, you can come up."

"Right," he said solemnly, nodding his head.

"Don't be long, darling."

When she had gone, he sat and stared at the cupful of black coffee and then got up and made his way back to the bar.

All of his before-dinner cronies had left and a completely different set of people stood round the bar. He ordered some beer and looked about him.

"Turned chilly," said the man next to him.

"Yes. Disappointing," he agreed. To make friends was the easiest thing in the world. In no time, he was at the heart of it all again.

*   *   *

At ten o'clock, Beryl, provocative in chiffon, as the magazines would have described her, burst into tears of rage. She could hear the laughter—so much louder now, towards closing-time—downstairs in the bar and knew that the sound of it had drawn Geoff back. She was powerless—so transparently tricked out to tempt him—to do anything but lie and wait until, at bar's emptying, he should remember her and stumble upstairs to bed.

*   *   *

It was not the first happy evening Geoff had spent in the bar of The Seaferry Arms. He had called there with the team, after cricket-matches in the nearby villages. Seaferry was only twenty miles from home. Those summer evenings had all merged into one another, as drinking evenings should—and this one was merging with them. 'I'm glad I came,' he thought, rocking slightly as he stood by the bar with two of his new friends. He couldn't remember having met nicer people. They were a very gay married couple. The wife had a miniature poodle who had already wetted three times on the carpet. "She can't help it, can you, Angel?" her mistress protested. "She's quite neurotic; aren't you, precious thing?"

Doris—as Geoff had been told to call her—was a heavy jolly woman. The bones of her stays showed through her frock, her necklace of jet beads was powdered with cigarette ash. She clutched a large, shiny handbag and had snatched from it a pound note, which she began to wave in the air, trying to catch the barmaid's eye. "I say, Miss! What's her name, Ted? Oh, yes. I say, Maisie! Same again, there's a dear girl."

It was nearly closing-time, and a frenzied reordering was going on. The street door was pushed open and a man and woman with a murderous-looking bull terrier came in. "You stay there," the man said to the woman and the dog, and he left them and began to force his way towards the bar.

"Miss! Maisie!" Doris called frantically. Her poodle, venturing between people's legs, made another puddle under a table and approached the bull terrier.

"I say, Doris, call Zoë back," said her husband. "And put that money away. I told you I'll get these."

"I insist. They're on me."

"Could you call your dog back?" the owner of the bull terrier asked them. "We don't want any trouble."

"Come, Zoë, pet!" Doris called. "He wouldn't hurt her, though. She's a bitch. Maisie! Oh, there's a dear. Same again, love. Large ones."

Suddenly, a dreadful commotion broke out. Doris was nearly knocked off her stool as Zoë came flying back to her for protection, with the bull terrier at her throat. She screamed and knocked over somebody's gin.

Geoff, who had been standing by the bar in a pleasurable haze, watching the barmaid, was, in spite of his feeling of unreality, the first to spring to life and pounce upon the bull terrier and grab his collar. The dog bit his hand, but he was too drunk to feel much pain. Before anyone could snatch Zoë out of danger, the barmaid lifted the jug of water and meaning to pour it over the bull terrier, flung it instead over Geoff. The shock made him loosen his grip and the fight began again. A second time he grabbed at the collar and had his hand bitten once more; but now—belatedly, everyone else thought—the two dog-owners came to his help. Zoë, with every likelihood of being even more neurotic in the future, was put, shivering, in her mistress's arms, the bull terrier was secured to his lead in disgrace, and Maisie called Time.

After some recriminations between themselves, the dog-owners thanked and congratulated Geoff. "Couldn't get near them," they said. "The bar was so crowded. Couldn't make head or tail of what was going on."

"Sorry you got so wet," said Doris.

The bull terrier's owner felt rather ashamed of himself when he saw how pale Geoff was. "You all right?" he asked. "You look a bit shaken up."

Geoff examined his hand. There was very little blood, but he was beginning to be aware of the pain and felt giddy. He shook his head, but could not answer. Something dripped from his hair onto his forehead, and when he dabbed it with his handkerchief, he was astonished to see water and not blood.

"You got far to go?" the man asked him. "Where's your home?"

"Lissport."

"That's our way, too, if you want a lift." Whether Geoff had a car or not, the man thought he was in no condition to drive it; although, whether from shock or alcohol or both, it was difficult to decide.

"I'd *like* a lift," Geoff murmured drowsily. "Many thanks."

"No, any thanks are due to *you*."

* * *

"Doesn't it seem strange without Geoff?" Mrs Midwinter asked her husband. He was back from The Starter's Orders, had taken off his collar and tie and was staring gloomily at the dying fire.

"Les and Ron home yet?" he asked.

"No, they won't be till half-past twelve. They've gone to the dance at the Town Hall."

"Half-past twelve! It's scandalous the way they carry on. Drinking themselves silly, I've no doubt at all. Getting decent girls into trouble."

"It's only a dance, Dad."

"*And* their last one. I'm not having it. Coming home drunk on a Sunday morning and lying in bed till all hours to get over it. When was either of them last at Chapel? Will you tell me that?"

Mrs Midwinter sighed and folded up her knitting.

"I can't picture why Geoff turned from Chapel like that." Mr Midwinter seemed utterly depressed about his sons, as he often was at this time on a Saturday night.

"Well, he was courting . . ."

"First time I've been in a church was today, and I was not impressed."

"I thought it was lovely, and you looked your part just as if you did it every day."

"I wasn't worried about *my* part. Sort of thing like that makes no demands on *me*. What I didn't like was the service, to which I took exception, and that namby-pamby parson's voice. To me, the whole thing was—insincere."

Mrs Midwinter held up her hand to silence him. "There's a car stopping outside. It can't be the boys yet."

From the street, they both heard Geoff's voice shouting good-bye, then a car door was slammed, and the iron gate opened with a whining sound.

"Dad, it's Geoff!" Mrs Midwinter whispered. "There must have been an accident. Something's happened to Beryl."

"Well, he sounded cheerful enough about it."

They could hear Goeff coming unsteadily up the garden-path. When Mrs Midwinter threw open the door, he stood blinking at the sudden light, and swaying.

"Geoff! What ever's wrong?"

"I've got wet, Mum, and I've hurt my hand," Geoff said.

Good-Bye, Good-Bye

ON his last evening in England he broke two promises—one, that he would dine with his brother, and another, older promise made to a woman whom he loved. When he and Catherine had tried, years before, to put an end to this impermissible love for one another the best they could decide was to give it no nourishment and let it wither if it would. "No messages," she had said when they parted, "no letters." His letters had always incapacitated her: on days when she received them, she moved slowly at her work, possessed by his words, deaf to any others, from husband or children or friends. "I don't want to know how you are getting on," she told him, "or to think of you in any particular place. You might die: you might marry. I never want to know. I want you to stop, here, for ever." (*Then, there*, an autumn night, a railway station.) As his train moved off he saw that her face had a look of utter perplexity, as if the meaning of her future were beyond her comprehension. The look had stayed in his mind and was in his imagination this evening as he walked from the bus stop in the village and out on the sea-road towards the house.

This house, which she rented each summer for the children's holidays, was where they had sometimes been together. The recklessness, the deceit which, in London, they suppressed, they had indulged here, as if a different sort of behaviour were allowed at the seaside. Returning to her husband, who had no part in those holidays, she would at once feel so mortified and so uneasily ashamed, that their few meetings were humiliating to them both and full of recriminations and despair; and it was after such a summer that they had parted—for ever, both had believed.

The road under the sea-wall was sheltered. Inland, sheep cropped the salt-marshes where he and Catherine had walked in the evening when the children were in bed. When it was dark, they would kiss and say good-bye, then kiss again. He would walk back to the village along this sea-road and she would tiptoe into the house, so that the children's nurse would not be wakened or discover how late she had stayed out.

Memories agitated him as he walked along the road. The landscape seemed to have awaited him, to have kept itself unchanged to pain him now with a great sense of strangeness. He had no hopes for this visit, no vestige of confidence in it, knew that it was mistakenly made and fraught with all perils—her anger, her grief, her embarrassment. In him, love could not be reawakened, for it had not slept. He did not know what risk faced her; how she had dealt with her sadness, or laid him away in his absence. He was compelled to find out, to discover if he were quick or dead in her mind, and to see if the look—the perplexed expression—had hardened on her face, or vanished. But as he came round a bend in the road and saw the chimneys of the house and the beginning of the garden, he was so appalled by his venture that he walked more slowly and longed to turn back. He thought: 'She will be changed, look different, wear new clothes I have never seen, the children will be older, and, oh God,' he prayed, his heart swerving at the sudden idea, 'let there be no more! Let her not have had more children! Let her not have filled her life that way!'

He stopped in the road and listened for children's voices in the garden but in the still evening the bleating of sheep was the only sound. High up on the orchard trees red apples

shone in the sun. An old net sagged across the tennis-lawn.
The gabled, hideous house with its verandas and balconies
came into view. At the open windows, faded curtains flapped
over the newly-cleaned tennis-shoes bleaching on sills and
sandy swim-suits and towels hung out to dry. The house,
which looked as if it had been burst asunder, and left with
all its doors ajar, had a vacant—though only lately vacant—
appearance.

In the conservatory-porch a tabby cat was sleeping on a
shelf among flower-pots and tennis racquets. A book lying
open had all its pages arched up in the sun and a bunch of
wild flowers were dying on a ledge. He pressed the bell and
away at the back of the house heard it ringing. The heat
under the dusty panes made him feel faint and he stepped
back from it, away from the door. As he did so, a girl leaned
from an upstairs window and called down to him. "Do you
want mother?"

Hit by the irony of the words, the shock of seeing
Catherine's eyes looking down at him, he could not answer
her at once. Her daughter did not wait for his reply. "She's
on the beach. They're all there. I'm just going, too. One
moment!" She moved from sight, he heard her running
downstairs, then she came to the door.

"You are Sarah?" he said.

"Yes."

'Oh, Catherine's eyes, those eyes!' he thought. 'The
miracle, but the enormity, that they should come again;
clearer, more beautiful'—he would not think it. "You
don't remember me. I am Peter Lord."

"I remember the name. I remember *you* now. I had only
forgotten. You came here once and helped us with a picnic
on the beach; lit a fire, do you remember that? It's what
they are all doing at this moment. I was waiting for a
friend." She hesitated, looked towards the gate. "But they
didn't come."

F

' "They" because she will not say "he",' Peter thought. 'The embarrassments of the English language!' She was bright with some disappointment.

"Shall we go down together and find them?" she asked; then, in the patronising tone young people use when they try to carry on conversations with their elders on equal terms, she asked: "Let me see, you went abroad, didn't you? Wasn't it South America?"

"South Africa."

"I always get those two muddled. And now you have come back home again?"

"For a short time. I am off in the morning."

"Oh, what a pity; but mother *will* be pleased that you came to say good-bye."

They crossed the road and climbed the bank to the top of the sea-wall. There they paused. The tide was out and the wet sand far down the beach reflected a pink light from the sun, which was going down in an explosive, Turneresque brilliance above the sand-hillocks. Farther along, they could see figures busily bringing driftwood to a fire and two children at the sea's edge were digging in the sand.

Seeing Peter and Sarah on the skyline, one of the group waved, then turned away again.

"He thinks you are my friend," Sarah said. She wore Catherine's anxious look. "That's Chris. Do you remember Chris? He is fifteen—nearly two years younger than me."

"Yes, I remember him." Peter was feeling tired now, rather puffed by keeping up with her across a stretch of hot white sand in which his feet sank at every step. This sand, seldom washed by the sea, was full of dried seaweed and bits of old newspapers. Clumps of spiky reed grew in it and sea-poppies and thistles.

"Who are all those other children?" he asked. He stopped and took off his shoes and socks, rolled his trousers above his ankles. 'A fine sight,' he thought crossly. 'Completely ridiculous.'

"Our friends," said Sarah, turning and waiting for him.

He could see Catherine. She was apart from the others and was bending over a picnic-basket. When Sarah called to her, she turned and, still kneeling in the sand, looked up towards them, her arm shading her eyes. The incredulous look was on her face as if it had never left it and at the sight of the agitation she could not hide from her children and their friends, he realised the full cruelty of his treachery. She took his hand, and recovered enough to hide shock beneath a show of superficial surprise, glossing over the grotesque situation with an hostessy condescension.

"Are you on leave?" Her voice indicated his rôle of old friend of the family.

"No, my father died. I had to come over in a hurry."

"I am sorry. Graham will be sad when he hears that."

'So I am to be her husband's comrade, too!' he thought.

As if she were in her drawing-room she invited him to sit down, but before he could do so, the younger children had run up from the sea and stood on either side of their mother, staring in curiosity at him and awaiting an explanation.

They were all variations of her, her four sons and daughters and these two, a boy and a girl, with their unguarded, childish gaze, were more like her than the other two whose defined features were brightly masked to preserve the secrets of adolescence.

"Lucy, this is Mr Lord. He gave you your Fairy-Tale book that you love so much."

"Yes, I do."

"And this is Ricky."

"What did you give *me*?" the boy asked.

"I'm sure I don't know. Perhaps you were to share the book."

"No, it is only mine," Lucy said certainly.

"He gave you lots of things," said Catherine.

"More than me?"

"No, Lucy, I am sure not."

"I think *I* only had the book."

"This isn't a nice conversation. You should think of other things than what you are given. Go and help Chris to find some firewood. You can't enjoy the fire and the supper if you do nothing to help."

The children wandered off, but back to the edge of the sea. They left a vacuum. She had tried to fill it with what he disliked and had always thought of as 'fussing with the children'—the children whom he had half-loved, for having her likeness, and half-resented, for not being his, for taking her attention from him and forbidding their life together.

"They've grown," he said.

"Yes, of course."

She put her hand deep in the sand, burying it in coolness. He watched her, remembering how once long ago she had done that and he had made a tunnel with his own hand and clasped hers and they had sat in silence, their fingers entwined beneath the sand. Such far-off lovers' games seemed utterly sad now, utterly forlorn, dead, their meaning brushed away like dust.

"Why did you come?" she whispered, her eyes fixed on the young ones building their fire; but fearing his answer, she caught her breath and called to her son. "Chris, darling, bring the others over to meet Mr Lord."

They came over, polite and estranged, willing to be kind. Chris hadn't remembered, but now he did. He introduced his friends, the same bright, polite boys and girls as himself. The boys called him "Sir," the girls smiled warmly and encouragingly. 'You are quite welcome, don't feel out of it—the fun, the lovely evening—just because you are old,' their smiles said.

They diminished Catherine. They were all taller. She seemed to Peter now to be set apart as 'mother', their voices were protective to her, undemanding. (Once they had clamoured for her attention, claimed every second. "Look at me, mummy! Look at me!") They had set her firmly in her present rôle and, instinctively, they made her part quite clear to Peter.

They returned to the fire. Chris was peeling sticks and sharpening the ends so that they could hold sausages over the fire to cook.

"What about the children?" Sarah asked. "How long are you staying, Mother?"

This was Catherine's dilemma which she had been pondering as she sat there with her hand buried in the sand.

"They can stay up," she said. "We will all stay. It will be a special treat for the little ones and they can sleep late in the morning. You others shall have a party on your own another night."

She looked away from Sarah and her voice was gentle, for she knew that *this* could not be Sarah's special night, that the girl was desperate with disappointment. 'This evening is nothing,' Catherine tried to imply. 'There will be so many others for you.'

"We always like it better if you are here," Sarah said. "I was wondering about the children." She dreaded that her mother should feel old or left out, and she often was alone on these long holidays. Peter's presence lightened the load of responsibility she felt towards her. For an hour or two, Catherine had someone of her own and Sarah could let go of her, could turn back to her own secrets, aloof, in love.

'Has she a confidante among the other girls?' Catherine wondered. Remembering her own girlhood she did not hope to be confided in herself; the very last, she knew—even if first to know, before Sarah sometimes, yet still the last of all to be told.

If she had taken Lucy and Ricky home to bed, Peter would have gone with her. Then they would be alone and nothing could prevent him from talking to her. To stay where she was not much wanted and to endure an evening of social exchanges before the children—painful though it must be—would be less menacing than that.

She turned to the picnic-basket, put a loaf of bread on a board and began to cut it into slices. "You haven't changed much," she said. "Are you happy in South Africa and is the work interesting? How is your brother?"

"I had no intention of coming here, but suddenly, this morning, it seemed so unreasonable, so falsely dramatic— our promise."

"No, sensible."

"I'm sorry I gave no warning."

"You could have telephoned," she said lightly, her back turned to him.

"You would have said 'No'."

She wrapped the slices of bread in a napkin and put them back in the hamper. 'Being needlessly busy,' he thought. 'Fussing with the children, anything to exclude me.'

"You *would* have said 'No', wouldn't you?"

"Yes, of course."

"You haven't changed either," he said at last, dutifully.

She was smoothing her hair, thinking, 'I don't know what I look like.' She wished that she could glance in a mirror, or that she had done so before she had left the house.

In her brown hair, some strands, coarser than the others, were silver. Fine lines crossed her forehead, and deeper ones curved from the corners of her eyes.

"Graham all right?" he asked.

"Yes, very well. Very busy. He gets tired."

'And bloody cross, I bet,' Peter thought. He imagined the tetchy, pompous little man, returning from the city, brief-case full of documents and stomach full of bile.

"And is he as rich as ever?" he asked.

"I've noticed no difference," Catherine said angrily. "Have *you* prospered? You always had such money-troubles."

"Father's dying should help."

He had always refused to see Graham as anything but a monstrous begetter of money and children, and showed himself up in contrast—the bachelor beyond the gates, without home or family, whose schemes came to nothing as his love-making came to nothing, neither bearing fruit. His insistence on her wealth was partly from a feeling that she had shared too much with her husband and he could not bear her to share any more, not even anxieties about money.

"They are nice children," he said, looking on the sunnier side of her marriage. "A great credit to you."

"Thank you." Her eyes filled with tears and at that moment Sarah, standing by the fire, turned and looked curiously at her, then at Peter.

The fire was burning high and the young people moved about it continually as if performing some ceremony. As the sun went down, shadows fell across the beach from the sea-wall, cooling the sand quickly. Catherine spread out a rug for Peter to sit on and then sat down herself on a corner of it, as far from him as she could.

"Come by the fire," Chris shouted to her.

"It is too smoky for her," said Sarah.

"Not on the other side."

"It blows about."

Catherine had not asked her the one question she had dreaded—"He didn't come then?"—and so in turn she would protect her mother. She, Sarah, no longer prayed for him to come, for her thoughts of him were angry now. Absorbed in this anger, she asked only that no one should speak of him. Waiting for him and the gradual loss of hope had been destructive, and a corrosive indignation worked on her love; it became non-love, then nothing.

"Is that Ronnie coming?" Chris asked, mopping his eyes with a handkerchief, waving away smoke.

A figure in the dusk appeared on the sea-wall, then a dog followed and flew down through the sand, crashed over the stretch of loose shingle to the wet, runnelled sands where the children worked, murmuring and intent, over their digging. Lucy cried out as the dog bounded towards her and a man's voice—nothing like Ronnie's—called the dog back.

Sarah was glad that she had not moved forward to wave or made any mistake. Standing quite still by the fire, she had kept her patience; but all the carefully-tended hatred had vanished in those few seconds, love had come hurrying back with hope and forgiving. 'It is worse for her now,' Catherine thought, and she felt hostility towards men. 'As it is worse for me.'

The man and the dog disappeared. Lucy and Ricky, disturbed into realisation of the darkness falling, began to trail up from the sea. The water between the hard ribs of sand felt cold to their bare feet and they came up to the bonfire and stood watching it, at the fringe of their elders and betters who laughed and danced and waved their speared sausages in the air to cool.

"Let them cook their own," said Catherine, and Chris handed the little ones two sticks and fixed on the sausages for them. They stood by the fire holding the sticks waveringly over the flames. Once, Ricky's nervousness broke into a laugh, his serious expression disintegrated into excited pleasure. "It will never cook like that," Chris said. "Keep it to the hot part of the fire." He sighed affectedly and murmured, "Pesky kids" to one of the girls, who said haughtily: "*I* think they're sweet."

"They're all yours, then," said lordly Chris.

"I never had anything like this when I was young."
Peter said. "I didn't even know any girls."

The children had their feast and Catherine and Peter
sat and watched them; even, Catherine thought, in Peter's
case, sat in judgment on them—'as if he were their father
and jealous of their youth, saying "*I* didn't have this or do
that when *I* was a boy; but was made to do such and such,
and go without etcetera, and be grateful for nothing. And
look at me. . . ." If he were their father, that is how he
would be, if he had not come back to me this evening, I
should never have thought such a thing of him. How I loved
you, my darling, darling. The passion of tears, the groping
bewilderment of being without you, the rhythm of long
boredom and abrupt grief, that I endured because of you;
then my prayers, my prayers especially that Sarah shall
have a happier time, and a more fortunate love.'

The children brought them sausages wrapped in bread.
The young girls were attentive to Catherine. "I *adore* your
jersey," one said, and Catherine would not conceal her
pleasure. "But it's so old. It's Chris's, really."

"Then you shouldn't let him have it back," the girl said.
"*He* couldn't look so nice in it."

"All right!" said Chris. "You may cook your own
sausages now. Didn't you know that the whole family wear
my old cast-offs?"

"Not I," said Sarah.

"Not I," said Lucy.

Peter had glanced at the jersey in annoyance. He was
beginning, Catherine knew, to harden against Chris,
identifying him with his father, comparing himself and his
own lost opportunitites with the boy and the life lying
before him. When Chris brought sausages, said "For you,
sir," he refused to eat.

"Then coffee," Catherine suggested, beginning to un-
screw a flask.

"Oh, dear, it is so cold," Lucy cried, and she flung herself against Catherine's thighs, burrowing under her arm.

"Steady, my love, I can't pour out," Catherine said, and she held the flask and the cup high out of reach and for the first time looked truly at Peter and laughed.

"Come to me, then," he said, and he lifted Lucy away and held her to him. She lolled against him, her salty, sticky hair touching his cheek. "That isn't good for you," he said, taking the half-eaten sausage, which was pink inside, uncooked, and throwing it away across the sand.

"Fishes will eat it," Ricky said. "When the tide comes up."

"Coffee!" Catherine called out and they came over to fetch it, then went back to gather round the dying fire. The girls began to sing, one of their school songs, which the boys did not know and Chris said: "What a filthy row."

"Did you read that fairy book to me when I was in bed?" Lucy asked Peter drowsily.

"I don't know."

"Yes, you did,"

"Do you remember then?"

"No, Mummy told me."

Then Catherine had talked of him! He had often wanted to talk to someone about *her*, to say her name. In Africa, he had nicknamed a little native girl—his servant's child—'Catherine', for the sake of saying the name occasionally. "Good morning, Catherine" or "What a pretty frock, Catherine!" The child could not understand English. He might, he had sometimes thought, have said anything, out loud, bold and clear. "I cannot forget you, Catherine, and my life is useless without you."

Lucy had crawled inside his jacket for warmth, he rubbed her cold, sandy legs, held her bare feet, and once kissed her forehead. Catherine sipped her coffee, looking away from this display of tenderness, thinking: 'A barren evening.

Nothing said; nothing felt, but pain. The wheel starting to creak again, starting to revolve in agony.'

"If any . . . regrets . . . have arisen from my visit," Peter said, trying to speak obscurely, above Lucy's head in two senses, "I couldn't blame myself more or detest my own egotism."

"There is no need to say anything," she said hurriedly. "No need at all. I would rather you didn't."

"Are you . . . ?"

"No," she interrupted him, afraid of what Lucy might hear. 'Am I what?' she wondered. 'I am in love with you still. In love, certainly. And there isn't a way out and never will be now.'

Her eyes might say this without Lucy knowing, and she turned to him so that before he went away he could be a witness to her constancy; but their situation was changed now; the observant eyes of the children were on them, Sarah's, the other girls, and Chris, brusque and guarded, goodness knew what thoughts *he* had about her.

"I shall soon have to go," Peter said and as he glanced at his watch, Lucy pushed herself closer to him, almost asleep.

Singing together now, the girls and boys were beginning to pack up—one of the girls turned cartwheels, and Sarah suddenly spun round, her bell-like skirt flying out.

"Are you staying at the pub?" Catherine asked.

"No, I am catching the last bus, then the last train."

"The last train," Lucy murmured cosily, as if there were no such thing save in a story he was telling her.

Catherine shivered.

"Are you sure you won't write to me?" Peter asked her, as quietly as he could. "Or let me write to you?"

"Quite sure."

"She will," said Lucy. "She writes to Sarah and Chris every day when they are at school."

"Then there wouldn't be time for me," said Peter.

Catherine packed the basket wishing that she might pack up the evening, too, and all that it had brought to the light, but it lay untidily about them. The children ran to and fro, clearing up, exhilarated by the darkness and the sound of the sea, the tide coming up across the sands, one wave unrolling under the spray of the next. The boys took the baskets and the girls looked the beach over, as if it were a room in some home of their own which they wished to leave tidy until they returned.

'Who will remember the evening?' Catherine wondered. 'Perhaps only he and I, and Sarah.' Little Ricky had attached himself to the others as they left the beach. He walked beside Sarah, clinging to her skirt. Peter had Lucy on his back, his shoes dangling by their laces round his neck as he walked unsteadily on the cold, loose sand.

"We live only once," he said.

"Of course," said Lucy, awake now and laughing. She wriggled her sandy feet, trying to force them into the pockets of his jacket.

"Lucy, sit still or walk," her mother said sharply.

A little surprised, she sat still for a bit and then, when she could see the house, the lights going on as the others went indoors, she slipped down and ran away from Peter, down the bank and across the lane.

Catherine and Peter sat down just below the sea-wall and put on their shoes.

"Will you forgive me?" he asked.

"I might have done the same."

"There is far too much to say for us to begin talking."

"And no time," she said. She fastened her sandals, then looked up at the sky, as if she were scanning it anxiously for some weather-sign, but he knew that she was waiting for tears to recede, her head high, breath held. If he kissed her, she would fail, would break, weep, betray herself to the children. 'To have thought of her so long, imagined,

dreamed, called that child "Catherine" for her sake,
started at the sight of her name printed in a book, pretended
her voice to myself, called her in my sleep, and now sit close
to her and it is almost over.' He stood up and took her hand,
helping her to her feet.

In the lane the children were trying one another's
bicycles, the lamp light swung over the road and hedges.
Lucy was crying and Sarah attempted to comfort her, but
impatiently. "The same old story," she told her mother.
"Stayed up too late."

"Yes, she did."

"I didn't undo my sand-castle," Lucy roared.

"Hush, dear. It doesn't matter."

"I like to undo it. You know I like to undo it and now the
sea will get it."

"It doesn't matter."

"Don't *say* it doesn't matter."

"Peter, do borrow Chris's bicycle. You can leave it at the
pub and he can fetch it tomorrow."

"I like the walk."

'I am not leaving her like that,' he thought, 'not
bicycling off up the road with a mob of adolescents.'

"Good-bye, and thank you for the picnic," the children
began to say, coming one after another to shake hands with
Catherine.

"You should have *reminded* me," shrieked Lucy, at the
end of her tether.

"Oh, Christ . . ." said Chris.

"Chris, I won't have that," said Catherine.

"Good-bye, and thank you so much."

"I hope you will come again."

"Good-bye, good-bye," Chris shouted.

They swung on to their bicycles and began to ride away,
turning often to wave.

"Good-bye, Fanny! Good-bye, Sue!" Chris shouted.

The voices came back, as the lights bobbed along the lane. "Good-bye, Sarah! Good-bye, Chris!"

Sarah called once, then she shook hands with Peter and turned towards the house, gathering up Ricky, who was swinging on the gate as if hypnotised, too tired to make the next step.

"Good-bye, Catherine, or I shall miss the bus."

"Yes. Good-bye, Peter."

"Take care of yourself. And *you* take care of her," he said to Chris with bright jocularity, as he began to walk away down the road.

"What, my dear old mum?" Chris said, and flung his arm across her shoulder so that she staggered slightly. Then, hearing a faint cry in the distance he rushed from her into the middle of the road and shouted again, his hands cupped to his mouth. "Good-bye, Good-bye."

Poor Girl

MISS CHASTY'S first pupil was a flirtatious little boy. At seven years, he was alarmingly precocious, and sometimes she thought that he despised his childhood, regarding it as a waiting time which he used only as a rehearsal for adult life. He was already more sophisticated than his young governess and disturbed her with his air of dalliance, the mockery with which he set about his lessons, the preposterous conversations he led her into, guiding her skilfully away from work, confusing her with bizarre conjectures and irreverent ideas, so that she would clasp her hands tightly under the plush table-cloth and pray that his father would not choose such a moment to observe her teaching, coming in abruptly as he sometimes did and signalling to her to continue the lesson.

At those times, his son's eyes were especially lively, fixed cruelly upon his governess as he listened, smiling faintly, to her faltering voice, measuring her timidity. He would answer her questions correctly, but significantly, as if he knew that by his aptitude he rescued her from dismissal. There were many governesses waiting employment, he implied—and this was so at the beginning of the century. He underlined her good fortune at having a pupil who could so easily learn, could display the results of her teaching to such an advantage for the benefit of the rather sombre, pompous figure seated at the window. When his father, apparently satisfied, had left them without a word, the boy's manner changed. He seemed fatigued and too absent-minded to reply to any more questions.

"Hilary!" she would say sharply. "Are you attending to me?" Her sharpness and her foolishness amused him, coming as he knew they did from the tension of the last ten minutes.

"Why, my dear girl, of course."

"You must address me by my name."

"Certainly, dear Florence."

"Miss Chasty."

His lips might shape the words, which he was too weary to say.

Sometimes, when she was correcting his sums, he would come round the table to stand beside her, leaning against her heavily, looking closely at her face, not at his book, breathing steadily down his nose so that tendrils of hair wavered on her neck and against her cheeks. His stillness, his concentration on her and his too heavy leaning, worried her. She felt something experimental in his attitude, as if he were not leaning against her at all, but against someone in the future. "He is only a baby," she reminded herself, but she would try to shift from him, feeling a vague distaste. She would blush, as if he were a grown man, and her heart could be heard beating quickly. He was aware of this and would take up the corrected book and move back to his place.

Once he proposed to her and she had the feeling that it was a proposal-rehearsal and that he was making use of her, as an actor might ask her to hear his lines.

"You must go on with your work" she said.

"I can shade in a map and talk as well."

"Then talk sensibly."

"You think I am too young, I daresay; but you could wait for me to grow up, I can do that quickly enough."

"You are far from grown-up at the moment."

"You only say these things because you think that governesses ought to. I suppose you don't know how governesses go on, because you have never been one until now, and you were too poor to have one of your own when you were young."

"That is impertinent, Hilary."

"You once told me your father couldn't afford one."

"Which is a different way of putting it."

"I shouldn't have thought they cost much." He had a way of just making a remark, of breathing it so gently that it was scarcely said, and might conveniently be ignored.

He was a dandified boy. His smooth hair was like a silk cap, combed straight from the crown to a level line above his topaz eyes. His sailor-suits were spotless. The usual boldness changed to an agonised fussiness if his serge sleeve brushed against chalk or if he should slip on the grassy terrace and stain his clothes with green. On their afternoon walks he took no risks and Florence, who had younger brothers, urged him in vain to climb a tree or jump across puddles. At first, she thought him intimidated by his mother or nurse; but soon she realised that his mother entirely indulged him and the nurse had her thoughts all bent upon the new baby; his fussiness was just another part of his grown-upness come too soon.

The house was comfortable, although to Florence rather too sealed-up and overheated after her own damp and draughty home. Her work was not hard and her loneliness only what she had expected. Cut off from the kitchen by her education, she lacked the feuds and camaraderie, gossip and cups of tea, which make life more interesting for the domestic staff. None of the maids—coming to light the lamp at dusk or laying the schoolroom-table for tea—ever presumed beyond a remark or two about the weather.

One late afternoon, she and Hilary returned from their walk and found the lamps already lit. Florence went to her room to tidy herself before tea. When she came down to the schoolroom, Hilary was already there, sitting on the window-seat and staring out over the park as his father did. The room was bright and warm and a maid had put a white cloth over the plush one and was beginning to lay the table.

The air was full of a heavy scent, dry and musky. To Florence, it smelt quite unlike the eau de cologne she sometimes sprinkled on her handkerchief, when she had a headache, and she disapproved so much that she returned the maid's greeting coldly and bade Hilary open the window.

"Open the window, dear girl?" he said. "We shall catch our very deaths."

"You will do as I ask and remember in future how to address me."

She was angry with the maid—who now seemed to her an immoral creature—and angry to be humiliated before her.

"But why?" asked Hilary.

"I don't approve of my schoolroom being turned into a scented bower." She kept her back to the room and was trembling, for she had never rebuked a servant before.

"I approve of it," Hilary said, sniffing loudly.

"I think it's lovely," the maid said. "I noticed it as soon as I opened the door."

"Is this some joke, Hilary?" Florence asked when the girl had gone.

"No. What?"

"This smell in the room?"

"No. You smell of it most, anyhow." He put his nose to her sleeve and breathed deeply.

It seemed to Florence that this was so, that her clothes had caught the perfume among the folds. She lifted her palms to her face, then went to the window and leant out into the air as far as she could.

"Shall I pour out the tea, dear girl?"

"Yes, please."

She took her place at the table abstractedly, and as she drank her tea she stared about the room, frowning. When Hilary's mother looked in, as she often did at this time, Florence stood up in a startled way.

"Good-evening, Mrs Wilson. Hilary, put a chair for your mamma."

"Don't let me disturb you."

Mrs Wilson sank into the rocking-chair by the fire and gently tipped to and fro.

"Have you finished your tea, darling boy?" she asked. "Are you going to read me a story from your book? Oh, there is Lady scratching at the door. Let her in for mamma."

Hilary opened the door and a bald old pug-dog with bloodshot eyes waddled in.

"Come, Lady! Beautiful one. Come to mistress! What is wrong with her, poor pet lamb?"

The bitch had stepped just inside the room and lifted her head and howled. "What has frightened her, then? Come, beauty! Coax her with a sponge-cake, Hilary."

She reached forward to the table to take the dish and doing so noticed Florence's empty tea-cup. On the rim was a crimson smear, like the imprint of a lip. She gave a sponge-finger to Hilary, who tried to quieten the pug, then she leaned back in her chair and studied Florence again as she had studied her when she engaged her a few weeks earlier. The girl's looks were appropriate enough, appropriate to a clergyman's daughter and a governess. Her square chin looked resolute, her green eyes innocent, her dress was modest and unbecoming. Yet Mrs Wilson could detect an excitability, even feverishness, which she had not noticed before and she wondered if she had mistaken guardedness for innocence and deceit for modesty.

She was reaching this conclusion—rocking back and forth —when she saw Florence's hand stretch out and turn the cup round in its saucer so that the red stain was out of sight.

"What is wrong with Lady?" Hilary asked, for the dog would not be pacified with sponge-fingers, but kept making barking advances farther into the room, then growling in retreat.

"Perhaps she is crying at the new moon," said Florence and she went to the window and drew back the curtain. As she moved, her skirts rustled. 'If she has silk underwear as well!' Mrs Wilson thought. She had clearly heard the sound of taffetas, and she imagined the drab, shiny alpaca dress concealing frivolity and wantonness.

"Open the door, Hilary," she said. "I will take Lady away. Vernon shall give her a run in the park. I think a quiet read for Hilary and then an early bed-time, Miss Chasty. He looks pale this evening."

"Yes, Mrs Wilson." Florence stood respectfully by the table, hiding the cup.

'The hypocrisy!' Mrs Wilson thought and she trembled as she crossed the landing and went downstairs.

She hesitated to tell her husband of her uneasiness, knowing his susceptibilities to the kind of women whom his conscience taught him to deplore. Hidden below the apparent urbanity of their married life were old un-happinesses—little acts of treachery and disloyalty which pained her to remember, bruises upon her peace of mind and her pride: letters found, a pretty maid dismissed, an actress who had blackmailed him. As he read the Lesson in church, looking so perfectly upright and honourable a man, she sometimes thought of his escapades; but not with bitterness or cynicism, only with pain at her memories and a whisper of fear about the future. For some time she had been spared those whispers and had hoped that their marriage had at last achieved its calm. To speak of Florence as she must might both arouse his curiosity and revive the past.

Nevertheless, she had her duty to her son to fulfil and her own anger to appease and she opened the library door very determinedly.

"Oliver, I am sorry to interrupt your work, but I must speak to you."

He put down the *Strand Magazine* quite happily, aware that she was not a sarcastic woman.

Oliver and his son were extraordinarily alike. "As soon as Hilary has grown a moustache we shall not know them apart," Mrs Wilson often said, and her husband liked this little joke which made him feel more youthful. He did not know that she added a silent prayer—"O God, please do not let him *be* like him, though."

"You seem troubled, Louise." His voice was rich and authoritative. He enjoyed setting to rights her little domestic flurries and waited indulgently to hear of some tradesman's misdemeanour or servant's laziness.

"Yes, I am troubled about Miss Chasty."

"Little Miss Mouse? I was rather troubled myself. I noticed two spelling faults in Hilary's botany essay, which she claimed to have corrected. I said nothing before the boy, but I shall acquaint her with it when the opportunity arises."

"Do you often go to the schoolroom, then?"

"From time to time. I like to be sure that our choice was wise."

"It was not. It was misguided and unwise."

"All young people seem slip-shod nowadays."

"She is more than slip-shod. I believe she should go. I think she is quite brazen. Oh, yes, I should have laughed at that myself if it had been said to me an hour ago, but I have just come from the schoolroom and it occurs to me that now she has settled down and feels more secure—since you pass over her mistakes—she is beginning to take advantage of your leniency and to show herself in her true colours. I felt a sinister atmosphere up there, and I am quite upset and exhausted by it. I went up to hear Hilary's reading. They were finishing tea and the room was full of the most over-powering scent, *her* scent. It was disgusting.''

"Unpleasant?''

"No, not at all. But upsetting.''

"Disturbing?''

She would not look at him or reply, hearing no more indulgence or condescension in his voice, but the quality of warming interest.

"And then I saw her teacup and there was a mark on it— a red smear where her lips had touched it. She did not know I saw it and as soon as she noticed it herself she turned it round, away from me. She is an immoral woman and she has come into our house to teach our son.''

"I have never noticed a trace of artificiality in her looks. It seemed to me that she was rather colourless.''

"She has been sly. This evening she looked quite different, quite flushed and excitable. I know that she had rouged her lips or painted them or whatever those women do.'' Her eyes filled with tears.

"I shall observe her for a day or two,'' Oliver said, trying to keep anticipation from his voice.

"I should like her to go at once.''

"Never act rashly. She is entitled to a quarter's notice unless there is definite blame. We should make ourselves very foolish if you have been mistaken. Oh, I know that you are sure; but it has been known for you to misjudge others. I shall take stock of her and decide if she is unsuitable. She is still Miss Mouse to me and I cannot think otherwise until I see the evidence with my own eyes.''

"There was something else as well,'' Mrs Wilson said wretchedly.

"And what was that?''

"I would rather not say.'' She had changed her mind

about further accusations. Silk underwear would prove, she guessed, too inflammatory.

"I shall go up ostensibly to mention Hilary's spelling faults." He could not go fast enough and stood up at once.

"But Hilary is in bed."

"I could not mention the spelling faults if he were not."

"Shall I come with you?"

"My dear Louise, why should you? It would look very strange—a deputation about two spelling faults."

"Then don't be long, will you? I hope you won't be long."

He went to the schoolroom, but there was no one there. Hilary's story-book lay closed upon the table and Miss Chasty's sewing was folded neatly. As he was standing there looking about him and sniffing hard, a maid came in with a tray of crockery.

"Has Master Hilary gone to bed?" he asked, feeling rather foolish and confused.

The only scent in the air was a distinct smell—even a haze—of cigarette smoke.

"Yes, sir."

"And Miss Chasty—where is she?"

"She went to bed, too, sir."

"Is she unwell?"

"She spoke of a chronic head, sir."

The maid stacked the cups and saucers in the cupboard and went out. Nothing was wrong with the room apart from the smell of smoke and Mr Wilson went downstairs. His wife was waiting in the hall. She looked up expectantly, in some relief at seeing him so soon.

"Nothing," he said dramatically. "She has gone to bed with a headache. No wonder she looked feverish."

"You noticed the scent."

"There was none," he said. "No trace. Nothing. Just imagination, dear Louise. I thought that it must be so."

He went to the library and took up his magazine again, but he was too disturbed to read and thought with impatience of the following day.

Florence could not sleep. She had gone to her room, not with a headache but to escape conversations until she had faced the predicament alone. This she was doing, lying on the honeycomb quilt which, since maids do not wait on governesses, had not been turned down.

The schoolroom this evening seemed to have been wreathed about with a strange miasma; the innocent nature of the place polluted in a way that she could not understand or have explained. Something new, it seemed, had entered the room—the scent had clung about her clothes; the stained cup was her own cup, and her handkerchief with which she had rubbed it clean was still reddened; and finally, as she stared in the mirror, trying to re-establish her personality, the affected little laugh which startled her had come from herself. It had driven her from the room.

'I cannot explain the inexplicable,' she thought wearily and began to prepare herself for bed. Home-sickness hit her like a blow on the head. 'Whatever they do to me, I have always my home,' she promised herself. But she could not think who 'They' might be; for no one in this house had threatened her. Mrs Wilson had done no more than irritate her with her commonplace fussing over Hilary and her dog, and Florence was prepared to overcome much more than irritation. Mr Wilson's pomposity, his constant watch on her works, intimidated her, but she knew that all who must earn their living must have fears lest their work should not seem worth the wages. Hilary was easy to manage; she had quickly seen that she could always deflect him from rebelliousness by opening a new subject for conversation; any idea would be a counter-attraction to naughtiness; he wanted her to sharpen his wits upon. 'And is that all that teaching is, or should be?' she had wondered. The servants had been good to her, realising that she would demand nothing of them. She had suffered great loneliness, but had foreseen it as part of her position. Now she felt fear nudging it away. 'I am not lonely any more,' she thought. 'I am not alone any more. And I have lost something.' She said her prayers; then, sitting up in bed, kept the candle alight while she brushed her hair and read the Bible.

'Perhaps I have lost my reason,' she suddenly thought, resting her finger on her place in the Psalms. She lifted her head and saw her shadow stretch up the powdery, rose-sprinkled wall. 'How can I keep that secret?' she wondered. 'When there is no one to help me do it? Only those who are watching to see it happen.'

She was not afraid in her bedroom as she had been in the schoolroom, but her perplexed mind found no replies to its questions. She blew out the candle and tried to fall asleep, but lay and cried for a long time, and yearned to be at home again and comforted in her mother's arms.

In the morning she met kind enquiries. Nurse was so full of solicitude that Florence felt guilty. "I came up with a warm drink and put my head round the door but you were in the land of Nod so I drank it myself. I should take a grey powder; or I could mix you a gargle. There are a lot of throats about."

"I am quite better this morning," said Florence and she felt calmer as she sat down at the schoolroom-table with Hilary. 'Yet, it was all true,' her reason whispered. 'The morning hasn't altered that.'

"You have been crying," said Hilary. "Your eyes are red."

"Sometimes people's eyes are red from other causes—headaches and colds." She smiled brightly.

"And sometimes from crying, as I said. I should think usually from crying."

"Page fifty-one," she said, locking her hands together in her lap.

"Very well." He opened the book, pressed down the pages and lowered his nose to them, breathing the smell of print. 'He is utterly sensuous,' she thought. 'He extracts every pleasure, every sensation, down to the most trivial.'

They seemed imprisoned in the schoolroom, by the silence of the rest of the house and by the rain outside. Her calm began to break up into frustration and she put her hands behind her chair and pressed them against the hot mesh of the fireguard to steady herself. As she did so, she felt a curious derangement of both mind and body; of desire unsettling her once sluggish peaceful nature, desire horribly defined, though without direction.

"I have soon finished those," said Hilary, bringing his sums and placing them before her. She glanced at her palms which were criss-crossed deep with crimson where she had pressed them against the fireguard, then she took up her pen and dipped it into the red ink.

"Don't lean against me, Hilary," she said.

"I love the scent so much."

It had returned, musky, enveloping, varying as she moved.

She ticked the sums quickly, thinking that she would set Hilary more work and escape for a moment to calm herself —change her clothes or cleanse herself in the rain. Hearing Mr Wilson's footsteps along the passage, she knew that her escape was cut off and raised wild-looking eyes as he came in. He mistook panic for passion, thought that by opening the door suddenly he had caught her out and laid bare her secret, her pathetic adoration.

"Good morning," he said musically and made his way to the window-seat. "Don't let me disturb you." He said this without irony, although he thought: 'So it is that way the

wind blows! Poor creature!' He had never found it difficult
to imagine women were in love with him.

'I will hear your verbs,' Florence told Hilary, and
opened the French Grammar as if she did not know them
herself. Her eyes—from so much crying—were a pale and
brilliant green, and as the scent drifted in Oliver's direction
and he turned to her, she looked fully at him.

'Ah, the still waters!' he thought and stood up suddenly.
"Ils vont," he corrected Hilary and touched his shoulder
as he passed. "Are you attending to Miss Chasty?"

"Is she attending to me?" Hilary murmured. The risk
was worth taking, for neither heard. His father appeared to
be sleep-walking and Florence deliberately closed her eyes,
as if looking down were not enough to blur the outlines
of her desire.

"I find it difficult," Oliver said to his wife, "to reconcile
your remarks about Miss Chasty with the young woman
herself. I have just come from the schoolroom and she was
engaged in nothing more immoral than teaching French
verbs—that not very well incidentally."

"But can you explain what I have told you?"

"I can't do that," he said gaily. For who can explain a
jealous woman's fancies? he implied.

He began to spend more time in the schoolroom; from
surveillance, he said. Miss Chasty, though not outwardly of
an amorous nature, was still not what he had at first
supposed. A suppressed wantonness hovered beneath her
primness. She was the ideal governess in his eye—
irreproachable, yet not unapproachable. As she was so conveniently installed, he could take his time in divining the
extent of her willingness; especially as he was growing
older and the game was beginning to be worth more than
the triumph of winning it. To his wife, he upheld Florence,
saw nothing wrong save in her scholarship, which needed to
be looked into—this, the explanation for his more frequent

visits to the schoolroom. He laughed teasingly at Louise's fancies.

The schoolroom indeed became a focal point of the house —the stronghold of Mr Wilson's desire and his wife's jealousy.

"We are never alone," said Hilary. "Either Papa or Mamma is here. Perhaps they wonder if you are good enough for me."

"Hilary!" His father had heard the last sentence as he opened the door and the first as he hovered outside listening. "I doubt if my ears deceived me. You will go to your room while you think of a suitable apology and I think of an ample punishment."

"Shall I take my history book with me or shall I just waste time?"

"I have indicated how to spend your time."

"That won't take long enough," said Hilary beneath his breath as he closed the door.

"Meanwhile, I apologise for him," said his father. He did not go to his customary place by the window, but came to the hearth-rug where Florence stood behind her chair. "We have indulged him too much and he has been too much with adults. Have there been other occasions?"

"No, indeed, sir."

"You find him tractable?"

"Oh, yes."

"And are you happy in your position?"

"Yes."

As the dreaded, the now so familiar scent began to wreath about the room, she stepped back from him and began to speak rapidly, as urgently as if she were dying and must make some explanation while she could. "Perhaps, after all, Hilary is right and you do wonder about my competence—and if I can give him all he should have. Perhaps a man would teach him more. . . ."

She began to feel a curious infraction of the room and of her personality, seemed to lose the true Florence, and the room lightened as if the season had been changed.

"You are mistaken," he was saying. "Have I ever given you any hint that we were not satisfied?"

Her timidity had quite dissolved and he was shocked by the sudden boldness of her glance.

"I should rather give you a hint of how well pleased I am."

"Then why don't you?" she asked.

She leaned back against the chimney-piece and looped about her fingers a long necklace of glittering green beads. "Where did these come from?" she wondered. She could not remember ever having seen them before, but she could not pursue her bewilderment, for the necklace felt familiar to her hands, much more familiar than the rest of the room.

"When shall I?" he was insisting. "This evening, perhaps, when Hilary is in bed?"

'Then who is *he*, if Hilary is to be in bed?' she wondered. She glanced at him and smiled again. "You are extraordinarily alike," she said. "You and Hilary." 'But Hilary is a little boy,' she reminded herself. 'It is silly to confuse the two.'

"We must discuss Hilary's progress," he said, his voice so burdened with meaning that she began to laugh at him.

"Indeed we must," she agreed.

"Your necklace is the colour of your eyes." He took it from her fingers and leaned forward, as if to kiss her. Hearing footsteps in the passage she moved sharply aside, the necklace broke and the beads scattered over the floor.

"Why is Hilary in the garden at this hour?" Mrs Wilson asked. Her husband and the governess were on their knees, gathering up the beads.

"Miss Chasty's necklace broke," her husband said. She

had heard that submissive tone before: his voice lacked authority only when he was caught out in some infidelity.

"I was asking about Hilary. I have just seen him running in the shrubbery without a coat."

"He was sent to his room for being impertinent to Miss Chasty."

"Please fetch him at once," Mrs Wilson told Florence. Her voice always gained in authority what her husband's lacked.

Florence hurried from the room, still holding a handful of beads. She felt badly shaken—as if she had been brought to the edge of some experience which had then retreated beyond her grasp.

"He was told to stay in his room," Mr Wilson said feebly.

"Why did her beads break?"

"She was fidgeting with them. I think she was nervous. I was making it rather apparent to her that I regarded Hilary's insubordination as proof of too much leniency on her part."

"I didn't know that she had such a necklace. It is the showiest trash I have ever seen."

"We cannot blame her for the cheapness of her trinkets. It is rather pathetic."

"There is nothing pathetic about her. We will continue this in the morning-room and they can continue their lessons, which are, after all, her reason for being here."

*   *   *

"Oh, they are gone," said Hilary. His cheeks were pink from the cold outside.

"Why did you not stay in your bedroom as you were told?"

"I had nothing to do. I thought of my apology before I got there. It was: 'I am sorry, dear girl, that I spoke too near the point'."

"You could have spent longer and thought of a real apology."

"Look how long Papa spent and he did not even think of a punishment, which is a much easier thing."

Several times during the evening Mr Wilson said: "But you cannot dismiss a girl because her beads break."

"There have been other things and will be more," his wife replied.

So that there should not be more that evening, he did not move from the drawing-room where he sat watching her doing her wool-work. For the same reason, Florence left the schoolroom early. She went out and walked rather nervously in the park, feeling remorseful, astonished and upset.

"Did you mend your necklace?" Hilary asked her in the morning.

"I lost the beads."

"But my poor girl, they must be somewhere."

She thought: 'There is no reason to suppose that I shall get back what I never had in the first place.'

"Have you got a headache?"

"Yes. Go on with your work, Hilary."

"Is it from losing the beads?"

"No."

"Have you a great deal of jewellery I have not seen yet?"

She did not answer and he went on: "You still have your brooch with your grandmother's plaited hair in it. Was it cut off her head when she was dead."

"Your work, Hilary."

"I shudder to think of chopping it off a corpse. You could have some of my hair, now, while I am living." He fingered it with admiration, regarded a sum aloofly and jotted down his answer. "Could I cut some of yours?" he asked, bringing his book to be corrected. He whistled softly, close to her, and the tendrils of hair round her ears were gently blown about.

"It is ungentlemanly to whistle," she said.

"My sums are always right. It shows how I can chatter and subtract at the same time. Any governess would be annoyed by that. I suppose your brothers never whistle."

"Never."

"Are they to be clergymen like your father?"

"It is what we hope for one of them."

"I am to be a famous judge. When you read about me, will you say: 'And to think I might have been his wife if I had not been so self-willed'?"

"No, but I hope that I shall feel proud that once I taught you."

"You sound doubtful."

He took his book back to the table. "We are having a quiet morning," he remarked. "No one has visited us. Poor Miss Chasty, it is a pity about the necklace," he murmured, as he took up his pencil again.

Evenings were dangerous to her. 'He said he would come,' she told herself, 'and I allowed him to say so. On what compulsion did I?"

Fearfully, she spent her lonely hours out in the dark garden or in her cold and candle-lit bedroom. He was under his wife's vigilance and Florence did not know that he dared not leave the drawing-room. But the vigilance relaxed, as it does; his carelessness returned and steady rain and bitter cold drove Florence to warm her chilblains at the schoolroom fire.

Her relationship with Mrs Wilson had changed. A wary hostility took the place of meekness, and when Mrs Wilson came to the schoolroom at tea-times, Florence stood up defiantly and cast a look round the room as if to say: 'Find what you can. There is nothing here.' Mrs Wilson's suspicious ways increased her rebelliousness. 'I have done nothing wrong,' she told herself. But in her bedroom at night: '*I* have done nothing wrong,' she would think.

"They have quite deserted us," Hilary said from time to time. "They have realised you are worth your weight in gold, dear girl; or perhaps I made it clear to my father that in this room he is an interloper."

"Hilary!"

"You want to put yourself in the right in case that door opens suddenly as it has been doing lately. There, you see! Good-evening, Mamma. I was just saying that I had scarcely seen you all day." He drew forward her chair and held the cushion behind her until she leaned back.

"I have been resting."

"Are you ill, Mamma?"

"I have a headache."

"I will stroke it for you, dear lady."

He stood behind her chair and began to smooth her forehead. "Or shall I read to you?" he asked, soon tiring of his task, "Or play the musical-box?"

"No, nothing more, thank you."

Mrs Wilson looked about her, at the tea-cups, then at Florence. Sometimes it seemed to her that her husband was right and that she was growing fanciful. The innocent appearance of the room lulled her and she closed her eyes for a while, rocking gently in her chair.

*   *   *

"I dozed off," she said when she awoke. The table was cleared and Florence and Hilary sat playing chess, whispering so that they should not disturb her.

"It made a domestic scene for us," said Hilary. "Often Miss Chasty and I feel that we are left too much in solitary bliss."

The two women smiled and Mrs Wilson shook her head. "You have too old a head on your shoulders," she said. "What will they say of you when you go to school?"

"What shall I say of *them*?" he asked bravely, but he lowered his eyes and kept them lowered. When his mother had gone, he asked Florence: "Did you go to school?"

"Yes."

"Were you unhappy there?"

"No, I was homesick at first."

"If I don't like it, there will be no point in my staying," he said hurriedly. "I can learn anywhere and I don't particularly want the corners knocked off, as my father once spoke of it. I shouldn't like to play cricket and all those childish games. Only to do boxing and draw blood," he added, with sudden bravado. He laughed excitedly and clenched his fists.

"You would never be good at boxing if you lost your temper."

"I suppose your brothers told you that. They don't sound very manly to me. They would be afraid of a good fight and the sight of blood, I daresay."

"Yes, I daresay. It is bedtime."

He was whipped up by the excitement he had created from his fears.

"Chess is a woman's game," he said and upset the board. He took the cushion from the rocking-chair and kicked it inexpertly across the room. "I should have thought the door would have opened then," he said. "But as my father doesn't appear to send me to my room, I will go there of my own accord. It wouldn't have been a punishment at bedtime in any case. When I am a judge I shall be better at punishments than he is."

When he had gone, Florence picked up the cushion and the chess-board. 'I am no good at punishments either,' she thought. She tidied the room, made up the fire, then sat down in the rocking-chair, thinking of all the lonely schoolroom evenings of her future. She bent her head over her needlework—the beaded sachet for her mother's birthday present. When she looked up she thought the lamp was smoking and she went to the table and turned down the wick. Then she noticed that the smoke was wreathing upwards from near the fireplace, forming rings which drifted towards the ceiling and were lost in a haze. She could hear a woman's voice humming softly and the floorboards creaked as if someone were treading up and down the room impatiently.

She felt in herself a sense of burning impatience and anticipation and watching the door opening found herself thinking: 'If it is not he, I cannot bear it.'

He closed the door quietly. "She has gone to bed," he said in a lowered voice. "For days I dared not come. She has watched me every moment. At last, this evening, she gave way to a headache. Were you expecting me?"

"Yes."

"And once I called you Miss Mouse! And you are still Miss Mouse when I see you about the garden, or at luncheon."

"In this room I can be by myself. It belongs to us."

"And not to Hilary as well—ever?" he asked her in amusement.

She gave him a quick and puzzled glance.

"Let no one intrude," he said hastily. "It is our room, just as you say."

She had turned the lamp too low and it began to splutter. "Firelight is good enough for us," he said, putting the light out altogether.

When he kissed her, she felt an enormous sense of disappointment, almost as if he were the wrong person embracing her in the dark. His arch masterfulness merely bored her. 'A long wait for so little,' she thought.

He, however, found her entirely seductive. She responded

with a sensuous languor, unruffled and at ease like the most
perfect hostess.

"Where did you practise this, Miss Mouse?" he asked
her. But he did not wait for the reply, fancying that he
heard a step on the landing. When his wife opened the door,
he was trying desperately to light a taper at the fire. His
hand was trembling, and when at last, in the terribly silent
room, the flame crept up the spill it simply served to show up
Florence's disarray, which, like a sleep-walker, she had not
noticed or put right.

*   *   *

She did not see Hilary again, except as a blurred little
figure at the schoolroom window—blurred because of her
tear-swollen eyes.

She was driven away in the carriage, although Mr Wilson
had suggested the station-fly. "Let us keep her disgrace and
her tearfulness to ourselves," he begged, although he was
exhausted by the repetitious burden of his wife's grief.

"*Her* disgrace!"

"My mistake, I have said, was in not taking your
accusations about her seriously. I see now that I was in
some way bewitched—yes, bewitched, is what it was—
acting against my judgment; nay, my very nature. I am
astonished that anyone so seemingly meek could have cast
such a spell upon me."

*   *   *

Poor Florence turned her head aside as Williams, the
coachman, came to fetch her little trunk and the basket-
work holdall. Then she put on her cloak and prepared herself to go downstairs, fearful lest she should meet anyone
on the way. Yet her thoughts were even more on her
journey's end; for what, she wondered, could she tell her
father and how expect him to understand what she could
not understand herself?

Her head was bent as she crossed the landing and she hurried past the schoolroom door. At the turn of the staircase she pressed back against the wall to allow someone to pass. She heard laughter and then up the stairs came a young woman and a little girl. The child was clinging to the woman's arm and coaxing her, as sometimes Hilary had tried to coax Florence. "After lessons," the woman said firmly, but gaily. She looked ahead, smiling to herself. Her clothes were unlike anything that Florence had ever seen. Later, when she tried to describe them to her mother, she could only remember the shortness of a tunic which scarcely covered the knees, a hat like a helmet drawn down over eyes intensely green and matching a long necklace of glass beads which swung on her flat bosom. As she came up the stairs and drew near to Florence, she was humming softly against the child's pleading: silk rustled against her silken legs and all of the staircase, as Florence quickly descended, was full of fragrance.

In the darkness of the hall a man was watching the two go round the bend of the stairs. The woman must have looked back, for Florence saw him lift his hand in a secretive gesture of understanding.

'It is Hilary, not his father!' she thought. But the figure turned before she could be sure and went into the library.

Outside on the drive Williams was waiting with her luggage stowed away in the carriage. When she had settled herself, she looked up at the schoolroom window and saw Hilary standing there rather forlornly and she could almost imagine him saying: 'My poor dear girl; so you were not good enough for me, after all?'

"When does the new governess arrive?" she asked Williams in a casual voice, that strove to conceal both pride and grief.

"There's nothing fixed as far as I have heard," he said.

They drove out into the lane.

'When will it be *her* time?' Florence wondered. 'I am glad that I saw her before I left.'

"We are sorry to see you going, Miss." He had heard that the maids were sorry, for she had given them no trouble.

"Thank you, Williams."

As they went on towards the station, she leaned back and looked at the familiar places where she had walked with Hilary. 'I know what I shall tell my father now,' she thought, and she felt peaceful and meek as though beginning to be convalescent after a long illness.

Hare Park

AT an early hour, the pale deer moved down from the high slopes of the park towards the lakes. Sunlight gilded the stone deer on the piers of the main gates, where the steward stopped his horse and shouted to the lodge-keeper to take in a line of washing. As he rode on up the great avenue he could not see a twig that was out of place; on either side, stretches of water—one harp-shaped, one heart-shaped—glinted as if they had been polished. The landscape might have been submerged all night and now risen, cleansed and dazzling, as new as the beginning of the world, this April morning.

Along the avenue, the clear shadow of the man and horse slanted across the gravel. To the steward this was a wonderful hour of the day. His master, the Duke, slept late, shut away in the great house, and until the moment when he rose and came out on to the terrace, his steward claimed his possessions for himself, watched *his* pheasants fly up in a flurry disturbed by the horse, as he passed, *his* hare leaping through the grass. When he met any of the estate men, he lifted his crop as affably as the Duke himself.

Farther up the hill, the road forked. The avenue with its lime-trees continued up towards the stables, and the second road, treeless, austere, led over the Palladian bridge which spanned the narrow end of the harp lake; and there the house came into view.

The steward took this road, and, looking up at the great

building, felt his sense of ownership lessening. The stained, brown sandstone was crowned with a vast green dome. In some weathers it could look frightening; but this morning the sun mellowed it.

The grassland swept right up to the terrace. There were no flowers, no shrubs to spoil the formality. Even the runs along the terrace were empty. Stuck rakishly among the hundreds of chimneys were three television aerials. Holland blinds made blanks of rows of windows, but at one window on the second storey the curtains were parted and a young boy, still in his pyjamas, was looking out.

* * *

Arthur was watching his father's steward riding along before the house. The horse dancing like a race-horse seemed to be trying to shake off his own shadow. There was a tremendous certainty about the weather, unlike the apprehensions which had gathered about the day itself. The sun went up in triumph and drenched the park-land with gold. Arthur had a feeling that he was looking down upon an empty stage, awaiting the development of a drama which he wondered if he would ever understand. He imagined, later in the day, cars coming up the drive; the invasion, as his mother named it, beginning—the great house, Hare Park, thrown open to the enemy at half-a-crown a ticket, exposed for the first time in its history to shuffling sightseers, sullied, cheapened. So the Duchess protested. Her husband was robust enough to laugh at her charges and she could not goad him with the sharpness of her tongue. Upon all his money-raising schemes she had poured her scorn. "You could let them be photographed in our bed at twopence a time," she cried. "Or I could pose stark naked on a plinth in the Orangery. I should be no more exposed than I shall be."

"What would your Mamma have said to that?" he asked gravely.

"What would Mamma have said?" had been her theme for months. Once upon a time, Mamma and her friends had supposed that she had married well. Yorkshire had thought it a staggering match. She had gone from the manor house near Harrogate to the great ducal seat in the south; had gone, as now was shown, from gentility and decency, to vulgarity, publicity and flamboyance. Mamma was dead, though, and spared knowledge of such an indecorous trapesing about her daughter's home, of pryings and pokings, ribald comments, names scribbled, souvenirs stolen, germs breathed out.

All the preparations were made. Red ropes made passageways through the rooms, heirlooms were brought out and personal possessions put away. The dogs and their baskets were moved from the library to the gun room. A stall for picture postcards and ice-cream was built in the courtyard, and upon two of the doors hung notices printed 'Ladies' and 'Gentlemen.'

"Ladies! Gentlemen!" said the Duchess. "What lady or gentleman would wish to spy upon us just because we are poor?" She could hear all the tea-cups of Harrogate tinkling as the cries of pity passed above them, eager and energetic as cries of pity are. "How dreadful for her! Imagine one's own feelings!" And the coronet and the seat in the Abbey would be forgiven.

Arthur had felt the air about him riven with expectation and dissent. The staff had split apart, as his parents had. The steward, the wood ranger—but not the gardeners—stood close to the Duke. Footmen and housemaids were excited; the butler saddened, but understanding. The housekeeper was in a frenzy of indignation and the Duchess's maid aligned herself fully with Harrogate and almost outdid the Duchess herself in sensibility and distaste. Arthur's tutor, who had begun to see his present employment coming to an end as talk of Eton grew more frequent, was wondering if he might not make himself indispensable in other ways: his attachment to the house, and the knowledge of its history he had come by, fitted him beautifully for the task of Guide or Lecturer. Perhaps Guide and Librarian would be a pleasant combination and might keep him settled for the rest of his life. He became as eager as the Duke to bring in the half-crowns and to have the ice-creams sold. He had written a little guide-book and Arthur's lessons were neglected while he polished up his commentary.

"When they are about the place, you are to keep to the schoolroom or play in the walled garden," the Duchess had told her son. As for herself, her pianoforte, her painting materials, her tapestry canvas with enough wools to last five years or more, were carried to her sitting-room. She gathered her possessions about her, as if to withstand a long siege.

With feelings totally curious and expectations muddled, Arthur had awaited the day. He sensed surveillance lifting from him, authority rising away from him, as indifferent as the sun going up in the sky. He was sure that neither schoolroom nor walled garden should play any part in his day.

His father now came out on the terrace below. He stood looking across the lakes, his hand resting on the winged foot of a stone Mercury, whose shadow mingled with his own. All along the front of the house the sun was bleaching the statues. Rain-pitted, damp from the dew-fall, with mossy drapery and eye-sockets, they held out their shells and grapes and cornucopias to dry.

* * *

"Nothing gives me more pleasure than the notion that

every little helps," the Duke had told the steward. This feeling had led him to what his wife called 'excesses of vulgarity' and which had even slightly estranged those who were sympathetic to him. The steward was obliged to turn his eyes from the litter of paddle-boats on the harp-shaped lake.

The first cars to drive in when the gates were opened came very slowly and looked purposeful and menacing to Arthur—like a funeral procession—but soon the atmosphere became jollier; the car-park filled up; the crowds spread about the terrace, invading the house from all sides, like an army of ants, penetrating in no time the stables and court-yard and lining up for the house itself. The tutor, Mr Gilliat, soon collected his first batch of sightseers and fluently and facetiously began his description of pictures and cabinets and carvings.

Arthur had wandered round into the courtyard. Helpers from the village, selling postcards and refreshments, might have recognised him and he dared not buy an ice-cream and so risk being identified and imprisoned in the walled garden for the afternoon. When the steward came through the courtyard, people looked at him respectfully. A boy beside Arthur nudged him and whispered: "That's the Duke."

"No, it isn't," Arthur said.

"How do you know? He's got a badge on with the coat of arms."

The boy was running his tongue over his ice-cream cornet, long, slow licks which Arthur watched with increasing irritation. They leant against the warm stone wall. The sun in this enclosed place made them feel drowsy.

"I've shaken my lot off. Gave Dad the slip," the boy said. He was about Arthur's age. He wore a school blazer with a row of fountain-pens clipped to the pocket. His lapels were covered with little enamel badges. Ice-cream, melting fast, dripped on to his trousers, and he spat on his handkerchief and wiped it off.

"I gave mine the slip, too," Arthur said.

"They get my goat," said the boy.

"And mine."

"Once they're safely inside we might get on a boat. What say?"

The afternoon now seemed to Arthur to have expanded with brilliant promise.

They moved on together as if by a silent arrangement and came to the Orangery which was apart from the house. Crowds shuffled through it, looking at the rows of statues and busts, and nymphs and goddesses and broken-nosed emperors.

"Might as well have a look round as it's free," said the boy. "What's your name?"

"Arthur Blanchflower."

"You're kidding."

"No I'm not."

"Well, rather you than me. I bet it takes some living down at school. My name's Derek Beale," he added with simple pride.

The Orangery smelt of damp stone and a chalky dust filtered down through the sunlight over all the mutilated and dismembered sculpture.

"What a lot of rubbish," said Derek, and in fact this was so. The statues had become a burden and problem, accumulating through the centuries, breaking and flaking; crumbling, but never quite away. Until today, no one had glanced at them for years. Now they were the object of derision and ribaldry. Laughter echoed round as the crowds drifted through the building.

"Look at this one! He's had his knocked off," said Derek.

Arthur felt vexed. He had begun to toady to Derek, who had taken the initiative from the start, but he wondered if he was prepared to toady to the extent of disloyalty towards his home.

"Some of the best statues have bits knocked off," he said. "Everyone knows that."

But Derek only went eagerly ahead and now was testing the strength of the armature upholding a disintegrating torso of Aphrodite.

"You're not supposed to touch them," Arthur said nervously.

"I should bloody care," said Derek.

*　　　*　　　*

Difficulties arose all the afternoon. On the lake, taking turns to manage the little boat, Arthur felt exposed to view from the house.

"What will happen when your father finds you?" he asked Derek.

"I shall tell him where he gets off."

"Won't he mind that?"

"What he minds or doesn't mind's up to him, isn't it?"

"Yes, I suppose it is."

"Let's go and chase those deer," said Derek, when they got out of the boat.

Arthur could see the deer-keeper riding up the avenue. "There's . . . a man's watching." He sat down on the grass with his face turned away.

"He can't do anything to you."

"Yes, he can. He did once before," Arthur said truthfully.

"What, for chasing the deer?"

"Yes."

"What did he do?"

"He told my father."

"What of it? I thought you meant he had used that whip on you."

Arthur's wits were exhausted with all the day's evasions and the risks he had run. A girl from a nearby riding-stables was walking his pony round at the edge of the lake, giving sixpenny rides to the children—since every little helped, His Grace had said.

"Want a ride?" Derek asked.

"Not much."

"I'm going to. I've only ever been on a donkey. I shall tell her where she gets off, if she thinks she's going to walk round with me, though. You go first."

"I don't want to go at all."

"She'll hold you if you're afraid."

He was forced to go up and pay his sixpence and the pony recognised him if the girl did not. She insisted on walking beside him.

"They're my orders," she said. "I'm responsible. You can take it or leave it."

He was led round the lake's edge in humiliation. His face burning with embarrassment, he dismounted and threw himself on to the grass while Derek had his turn. Yet, despite the anxieties and indignities, he clung greedily to this casual encounter, his first meeting with another boy, free of the incidence of hovering adults. He tried to make the most of the opportunity to discover a great deal that he needed to know, and doggedly asked his questions and listened with respect to Derek's terse replies.

"You swear a lot, don't you?"

"Yep."

"Do you like school?" (He could not ask, "What is school like?")

"No."

"Do the bigger boys bully you?"

"They better not try it on."

Derek's father, mother, and auntie were now seen coming away from the house. The boys hid behind a tree until they had disappeared into a tunnel of wistaria which led to a grotto.

"Now they've come out, we can go in," said Derek. "You don't have to pay extra so we might as well take a quick butcher's."

A 'quick butcher's' sounded vaguely brutal to Arthur but he would not demean himself by asking for translations of slang.

"I'll stay out here," he said. "It's too hot to go inside. I'm not interested in houses. My father might be in there."

"If he is, he'll have gone to the front by now. We can hang about at the back so no one sees us."

"I'd rather not."

"Are you afraid of your father?"

"No."

"Well then . . ."

He went towards the house as if hypnotised by the older boy. Waiting wretchedly for the appalling moment when he would meet his tutor's eye, and to delay his discovery and disgrace, he stood behind two fat women and tried to merge with their swarm of children.

Mr Gilliat had become rather tangled up and confused with the queue and most people were simply drifting through at their own pace, not listening to him. The group which he had gathered about him stayed only from courtesy and listened with a sense of rebellion, eyeing with envy and reproach those who had escaped. Too slowly they were taken down the long gallery, past one Duchess after another, by Romney, by Gainsborough, by Sargent.

"The mistress of the Third Duke, by Lely," said Mr Gilliat, standing coyly before the portrait.

"That means they weren't married," Derek whispered. "She was breaking the law all right. What a mug, I ask you! She looks like a bloody horse."

"Lady Constance Considine, the present Duchess, before

her marriage," said Mr Gilliat. They all gazed up at Arthur's mother. "Lovely gold tints in her hair," one fat woman said. "The lace is quite life-like." "She looks half asleep," said someone else, and Arthur bowed his head.

Mr Gilliat drew them on. He was almost hysterical with fatigue and with the failure of all his little jokes. Like cows they herded together, his unworthy audience, gazing blankly, mute and stupid. He felt like taking a stick and whacking their rumps. His domed and nearly bald head glistened with sweat, his hands flapped and gesticulated and he smiled until his face was stiff.

"Proper pansy," one young woman murmured to another.

All the time Arthur managed to conceal himself behind the fat women; but Mr Gilliat was no longer looking at the crowd, could meet the bovine stares no more.

The Haunted Bedroom with its legend of scandal and tragedy interested only Arthur from whom such frightening stories had been kept. The others stared dully at the worn brocade hangings and at the priedieu where some wanton forebear had been strangled while she was praying—presumably for the forgiveness of her sins. A burden of vice and terror was descending upon poor Arthur. The best that any of his ancestors had done was to be arrogant in battle. They were painted against backgrounds of carnage, standing, with curls blowing and armour shining, among contorted and dying horses.

Mr Gilliat now brought them to the partition chambers. Here, he explained, was an ancient, creaking apparatus which could lift one wall in its entirety so that eighteenth-century house-parties might be diverted by having a curtain as it were, raised without warning to disclose their friends' discomfiture and deshabille. Arthur felt shame to hear of such behaviour and he did not wonder that these rooms were usually locked. Scenes of cruel embarrassment he could imagine, obscene hordes of mockers in night-caps and ruffled wraps jeering at sudden exposure, invading the privacy of their fellows' undressing or praying or making love.

This last possibility Mr Gilliat did not suggest. He merely dwelt laughingly upon the picture of an imaginary lady discovered without her wig—bad enough, thought Arthur.

Derek moved closer to him and murmured: "Yes, and people might be . . . you know."

"Rather childish," someone said. "They might have had something better to do with their time."

Arthur felt stifled and frightened.

"My feet!" a woman complained.

They were nearly at the end, had wound through the core of the house and now were to descend the other side of the horse-shoe staircase.

"Fancy keeping it clean," one of the fat women said. She stopped to run a finger along the carved banister and Arthur drew up close behind her.

"Very tiring," they said, coming out into the fresh air again.

"Where the dickens have you been?" shouted Derek's father, pushing into the crowd. "Wasting our time; worrying your mother? Don't answer me back, my lad, or you'll get a taste of my hand."

Disillusioned, Arthur watched the boy pushed on ahead, nagged and ranted at. He took it in silence. He did not tell his father where to get off, but kept his eyes averted. "Where have you been?" cried his mother, "we've been beside ourselves." He straightened the row of fountain-pens in his pocket, looked nervous and meek, did not glance back at Arthur, who could not bear to witness this sudden change in him and turned away in the opposite direction.

*   *   *

The Duchess went to her bath as the last visitors departed. Although she had kept to her room, she felt bruised and buffeted and contaminated. "The noise!" she said, pressing her fingers to her temples and thrusting back her beautiful golden hair. "I tried to be brave," she told her maid.

The Duke was exhilarated as he walked in the grounds with his steward. "A good day," he said. "A nice crowd and no litter."

The steward picked up an empty cigarette packet.

"I wonder what they all think and why they come, and do they resent my having such a place as this, I wonder?"

The steward could not say: "No, your Grace, they pity you, and go back to their own homes in relief."

*   *   *

As the last cars went down the drive, Arthur, watching from the schoolroom window, felt a sense of isolation coming over him. In the new silence a cuckoo called. Two other birds in a bush below him carried on a boring exchange. He was loth to explore his own loneliness. It was distasteful to him, and the day had done too much.

He did not turn from the window, when Mr Gilliat came in.

"What a day!" fussed the tutor. "Oh, dear, my head! The hoi polloi! One despairs. Have you done your Latin?"

"I couldn't find the book."

"But"—his voice rose hysterically—"you should have asked me for it."

"I couldn't find you either."

"Someone could have done so. I was not entirely inaccessible. So you have idled your day away? It is too vexing for words. You will have to put your back into it tomorrow to make up. Yes, you really will. To take advantage at a time like this when we all have so much to cope with! More than enough on our hands. All of us tired and trying to do our best, and this is to be our reward, is it? You have fallen short of all your Papa would expect of you."

Arthur stood quite still, watching the deer moving across the park, up towards the wooded slopes for the night. "I should bloody care," he said.

You'll Enjoy It When You Get There

"SHYNESS is *common*," Rhoda's mother insisted. "I was never *allowed* to be shy when I was a girl. Your grandparents would soon have put a stop to *that*."

The stressed words sounded so peevish. Between each sentence she refreshed herself with a sip of invalid's drink, touched her lips with her handkerchief, and then continued.

"Self-consciousness it was always called when I was young, and that is what it is. To imagine that it shows a sense of modesty is absurd. *Modesty*. Why, I have never known a *truly* modest person to be the least bit shy."

The jaundice, which had discoloured her face and her eyes, seemed as well to wash all her words in poison.

"It's all right for you, mother," Rhoda said. "You can drink. Then anyone can talk."

Mrs Hobart did not like to be reminded that she drank at all: that she drank immoderately, no one—she herself least of all—would ever have dared to remind her.

Rhoda, who was sitting by the window, nursing her cat, stared down at the gardens in the square and waited huffily for an indignant rebuke. Instead, her mother said wearily:

"Well, you will have a drink, too, before the banquet, and no nonsense. A 'girl of eighteen'."

"I hate the taste."

207

"I, I, I. I hate this; I loathe that. What do you think would have happened if *I* had considered what *I* liked through all these years. Or the Queen," she added. "The poor girl! The rubbish she's been forced to eat and drink in foreign countries. And never jibbed."

"You and the Queen are different kettles of fish from me," Rhoda said calmly. Then she threw up the window from the bottom and leant out and waved to her father, who was crossing the road below.

"Please shut that window," Mrs Hobart said. "Leaning out and waving, like a housemaid. I despair." She put the glass of barley-water on one side and said again: "I despair."

"There is no need. I will do my best," said Rhoda. "Though no one likes to be frightened in quite such a boring way."

* * *

She sat in the train opposite her father and wedged in by business-men. In books and films, she thought, people who go on train journeys always get a corner seat.

In a corner, she could have withdrawn into her day-dreaming so much more completely; but she was cramped by the fat men on either side, whose thighs moved against hers when they uncrossed and recrossed their legs, whose newspapers distracted her with their puzzling headlines—for instance 'Bishop Exorcises £5,000 Ghost,' she read. Her father, with his arms folded neatly across his chest, dozed and nodded, and sometimes his lips moved as if he were rehearsing his speech for that evening. They seemed to have been in the train for a long time, and the phlegmy fog, which had pressed to the windows as they left London, was darkening quickly. The dreadful moment of going into dinner was coming nearer. Her father suddenly woke up and lifted his head. He yawned and winked a watery eye at her, and yawned and yawned again. She sensed that to be taking his daughter instead of his wife to what her mother called the Trade Banquet made it seem rather a spree to him and she wished that she could share his light-hearted-ness.

Like sleepwalkers, the other people in the compartment, still silent and drowsy, began now to fold their newspapers, look for their tickets, lift down their luggage from the racks. The train's rhythm changed and the lights of the station came running past the windows. All that Rhoda was to see of this Midlands town was the dark, windy space between the station entrance and the great station hotel as they followed a porter across the greasy paving-stones and later, a glimpse from her bedroom window of a timber-yard beside a canal.

When she was alone in the hotel bedroom, she felt more uncertain than ever, oppressed by the null effect of raspberry-coloured damask, the large intolerable pieces of furniture and the silence, which only sounds of far-away plumbing broke, or of distant lifts rising and falling.

She shook out her frock and was hanging it in a cavernous wardrobe when somebody in the corridor outside tapped on the door. "Is that you, Father?" she called out anxiously. A waiter came in, carrying a tray high in the air. He swirled it round on his fingers and put down a glass of sherry. "The gentleman in number forty-five ordered it," he explained. "Thank you," Rhoda said timidly, peeping at him round the wardrobe-door, "very much," she added effusively.

The waiter said "Thank *you*, madam," in a quelling voice, and went away.

Rhoda sniffed at the sherry, and then tipped it into the wash-basin. 'I suppose Father's so used to Mamma,' she thought. She knew the bedroom imbibing that went on, as her mother moved heavily about, getting dressed: every time she came back to her mirror, she would take a drink from the glass beside it.

The hotel room was a vacuum in which even time had no reality to Rhoda. With no watch to tell her, she began to wonder if she had been there alone for ten minutes or an hour and in sudden alarm she ran to the bathroom and turned on taps and hurriedly unpacked.

She put on a little confidence with her pretty frock; but, practising radiant smiles in the looking-glass, she was sure that they were only grimaces. She smoothed on her long white gloves and took up her satin bag, then heard a distant clock, somewhere across the roofs of high buildings, strike the half-hour and knew that she must wait all through the next, matching half-hour for her father to come to fetch her.

As she waited, shivering as she paced about the room, growing more and more goose-fleshed, she saw the reasonableness in her father's thought about the sherry and wished that she had not wasted it and, even more, that she had lain twenty minutes longer in her warm bath.

He came as the clock struck out the hours and, when she ran and opened the door to him said: "Heavens, ma'am, how exquisite you look!"

They descended the stairs.

In the reception-room, another waiter circled with a tray of filled glasses. Four people stood drinking by the fire—two middle-aged men, one wearing a mayoral chain, the other a bosomful of medals; and two middle-aged women, stiffly corseted, their hair set in tight curls and ridges. Diamonds shone on their freckled chests and pink carnations slanted heads downwards across their bodices. They look as if they know the ropes, thought Rhoda, paralysed with shyness. They received her kindly, but in surprise. "Why, where is Ethel?" they asked her father, and they murmured in concern over the jaundice and said how dreary it must be to be on the waggon. 'Especially for her', the tone of their voices seemed to Rhoda to suggest.

A bouquet was taken from a little side table and handed to Rhoda, who held it stiffly at her waist where it contended fiercely with the colour of her dress.

The six of them were, in their importance, shut off from a crowded bar where other guests were drinking cocktails: on this side of the door there was an air of confidence and expectation, of being ahead of the swim, Rhoda thought. She wished passionately, trying to sip away her sherry, that she might spend the entire evening shut away from the hordes of strangers in the bigger room but, only too soon, a huge toast-master, fussing with his white gloves, brought the three couples into line and then threw wide the doors; inclining his head patronisingly to guest after guest, he bawled out some semblance of the names they proffered. As the first ones came reluctantly forward from the gaiety of the bar, Mr Hobart leaned towards Rhoda and took the glass from her hand and put it on the tray with the others. "How do you do," she whispered, shaking hands with an old gentleman, who was surprised to see that her eyes were filled with tears. "You are deputising for your dear mother?" he asked. "And very charmingly you do it, my dear," he added, and passed on quickly, so that she could brush her wet lashes with her gloved hand.

"Good-evening, Rhoda," The bracing mockery of this new voice jolted her, the voice of Digby Lycett Senior, as she always called him in her mind—the mind which for months had been conquered and occupied by Digby Lycett Junior. This unexpected appearance was disastrous to her. She felt indignantly that he had no right to be there, so remotely connected was he with the trade the others had in common. "Nice of you to come," her father was now telling him. They were old business friends. It was Digby Lycett who sold her father the machinery for making

Hobart's Home-made Cookies. It was *loathsome* of you to come, Rhoda thought, unhappily.

She took one gloved hand after another, endlessly—it seemed—confronted by pink carnations and strings of pearls. But the procession dwindled at last—the stragglers, who had lingered over their drinks till the last moment, were rounded up by the toast-master and sent resignedly on their way to the banqueting-hall, where an orchestra was playing "Some Enchanted Evening" above the noise of chairs being scraped and voices mounting in volume like a gathering wave.

In the reception-room, the Mayor straightened the chain on his breast. One duty done, he was now prepared to go on to the next. All of his movements were certain and automatic; every evening of his life, they implied, he had a hall full of people waiting for him to take his seat.

As she moved towards the door a sense of vertigo and nausea overcame Rhoda, confronted by the long walk to her place and the ranks of pink faces turned toward her. With bag and bouquet and skirt to manage, she felt that she was bundling along with downcast eyes. Before a great heap of flowers on the table, they stopped. The Mayor was humming very softly to the music. He put on his spectacles, peered at the table and then laid his hand on the back of a gilt chair, indicating that here, next to him, Rhoda was to be privileged to sit.

At the doors, waitresses crowded ready to rush forward with hors-d'œuvres. The music faded. Without raising her eyes, instinctively, wishing to sink out of sight, Rhoda slid round her chair and sat upon it.

Down crashed the toast-master's gavel as the Mayor, in a challenging voice, began to intone Grace. Mr Hobart put his hand under Rhoda's elbow and brought her, lurching, as she could not help doing, to her feet again. The gilt chair tipped, but he saved it from going over, the bouquet shot under the table and Rhoda prayed that she might follow it.

"Please God, let me faint. Let me never have to look up again and meet anybody's glance."

"*Now* you can, young lady," the Mayor said, helping her down again. Then he turned quickly to the woman on his other side and began a conversation. Rhoda's father had done the same. Sitting between them, she swallowed sardines and olives and her bitter, bitter tears. After a time, her isolation made her defiant. She lifted her head and looked boldly and crossly in front of her, and caught the eye of Digby Lycett Senior, just as he raised a fork to his mouth, and smiled at her, sitting not far across the room, at right angles to her table, where he could perfectly observe her humiliation and record it for his son's interest and amusement later. "Poor old Rhoda"—she could hear the words, overlaid with laughter.

She ate quickly, as if she had not touched food for weeks. Once, her father, fingering a wine-glass restlessly, caught and held as he was in conversation by the relentless woman at his side, managed to turn his head for a moment and smile at Rhoda. "All right?" he asked, and nodded his own answer, for it was a great treat for a young girl, he implied—the music, the flowers, the pretty dress, the wine.

Someone *must* talk to me, she thought, for it seemed to her that, through lack of conversation, her expression was growing sullen. She tried to reorganise her features into a look of animation or calm pleasure. She drank a plate of acid-tasting, red soup to its dregs. Chicken followed turbot, as her mother had assured her was inevitable. The Mayor, who went through the same menu nearly every evening, left a great deal on his plate; he scattered it about for a while and then tidied it up: not so Rhoda, who, against a great discomfort of fullness, plodded painstakingly on.

At last, as she was eating some cauliflower, the Mayor turned his moist, purple face towards her. She lifted her eyes to the level of the chain on his breast and agreed with him that she was enjoying herself enormously.

"It is my first visit to Norley," she said gaily, conscious of Digby Lycett Senior's eyes upon her. She hoped that he would think from her expression that some delicious pleasantry was in progress. To keep the Mayor in conversation she was determined. He should not turn away again and Digby Lycett, Senior or Junior, should not have the impression that she sat in silence and disgrace from the beginning to the end.

"But I have a cat who came from here," she added.

The Mayor looked startled.

"A Burmese cat. A man in Norley—a Doctor Fisher—breeds them. Do you know Doctor Fisher?"

"I can't say that I do."

He was plainly unwilling for her to go on. On his other side was feminine flattery and cajolery and he wished to turn back for more, and Rhoda and her cat were of no interest to him.

"Have you ever seen a Burmese cat?" she asked.

He crumbled some bread and looked cross and said that as far as he knew he never had.

"He came to London on the train all by himself in a little basket," Rhoda said. "The cat, I mean, of course. Minkie, I call him. Such a darling, you can't imagine."

She smiled vivaciously for Digby Lycett Senior's benefit; but, try as she might, she could not summon the courage to lift her eyes any higher than the splendid chain on the Mayor's breast, for she shrank from the look of contempt she was afraid he might be wearing.

"They are rather like Siamese cats," she went on. "Though they are brown all over and have golden eyes, not blue."

"Oh?" said the Mayor. He had to lean a little nearer to

her as a waitress put a dish of pistachio ice-cream over his left shoulder.

"But rather the same natures, if you know what I mean," said Rhoda.

"I'm afraid I don't care for cats," said the Mayor, in the voice of simple pride in which this remark is always made.

"On all your many social commitments," the woman on his other side said loudly, rescuing him, "which flavour of ice-cream crops up most often?"

He laughed and turned to her with relief. "Vanilla," he said jovially. "In a ratio of eight to one."

*   *   *

"Enjoying yourself?" Rhoda's father asked her later, as they danced a foxtrot together. "I daresay this is the part of the evening that appeals to you—not all those long-winded speeches."

It appealed to Rhoda because it was nearer to the end, and for no other reason.

"You seemed to be getting on well with the Mayor," Mr Hobart added.

The Mayor had disappeared. Rhoda could see no sign of his glittering chain and she supposed that he disliked dancing as much as he disliked cats. She prayed that Digby Lycett Senior might not ask her to do the Old Fashioned Waltz which followed. She was afraid of his mocking smile and, ostrich-like, opened her bag and looked inside it as he approached.

Another middle-aged man stepped forward first and asked to have the pleasure in a voice which denied the possibility of there being any. Rhoda guessed that what he meant was 'May I get this duty over and done with, pursued as it is as a mark of the esteem in which I hold your father.' And Rhoda smiled as if she were enchanted, and rose and put herself into his arms, as if he were her lover.

He made the waltz more old-fashioned than she had ever known it, dancing stiffly, keeping his stomach well out of her way, humming, but not saying a word to her. She was up against a great silence this evening: to her it was the measure of her failure. Sorting through her mind for something to say, she rejected remarks about the floor and the band and said instead that she had never been to Norley before. The observation should have led somewhere, she thought; but it did not: it was quite ignored.

"But I have a cat who came from here," she added. "A little Burmese cat."

When he did not answer this, either, she thought that he must be deaf and raised her voice. "There is a doctor here who breeds them. Perhaps you have come across him— a Doctor Fisher."

"No, I can't say that I have."

"He sent the kitten to London by train, in a little basket. So pretty and gay. Minkie, I call him. Have you ever seen a Burmese cat?" She could not wait for his answers, lest they never came. "They are not a usual sort of cat at all. Rather like a Siamese in many ways, but brown all over and with golden eyes instead of blue. They are similar in nature though, if you can understand what I mean."

He either could not, or was not prepared to try and at last, mercifully, the music quickened and finally snapped off altogether. Flushed and smiling, she was escorted back to her father who was standing by the bar, looking genial and indulgent.

Her partner's silence seemed precautionary now. He handed her over with a scared look, as if she were some dangerous lunatic. Her father, not noticing this, said: "You are having quite a success with your Mayor, my dear."

"My Mayor?"

She turned quickly and looked after the man who had

just left her. He was talking to a little group of people; they all had their heads together and were laughing.

"He took that chain off then?" she said, feeling sick and dazed. It was all she had had to distinguish him from the rest of the bald-headed and obese middle-aged men.

"You couldn't expect him to dance with that hanging round his neck—not even in your honour," her father said. "And now, I shall fetch you a long, cool drink, for you look as if the dancing has exhausted you."